TRAIL BLAZER

TRAIL BLAZER

My Life as an Ultra-distance Trail Runner

RYAN SANDES
WITH STEVE SMITH

ZEBRA PRESS

Published by Zebra Press
an imprint of Penguin Random House South Africa (Pty) Ltd
Reg. No. 1953/000441/07
The Estuaries No. 4, Oxbow Crescent, Century Avenue, Century City, 7441
PO Box 1144, Cape Town, 8000, South Africa
www.penguinrandomhouse.co.za

Penguin
Random House
South Africa

First published 2016
Reprinted in 2016 (twice) and 2017

5 7 9 10 8 6 4

PUBLISHER: Marlene Fryer
MANAGING EDITOR: Janet Bartlet
EDITOR: Laetitia Sullivan
PROOFREADER: Mark Ronan
COVER AND TEXT DESIGNER: Ryan Africa
TYPESETTER: Monique van den Berg

Set in 11 pt on 15 pt Adobe Garamond

Printed by **novus** print, a Novus Holdings company

MIX
Paper from
responsible sources
FSC
www.fsc.org   FSC® C022948

This book is printed on FSC® certified and controlled sources. FSC (Forest Stewardship Council®)
is an independent, international, non-governmental organization. Its aim is to support environmentally
sustainable, socially and economically responsible global forest management.

ISBN: 978 1 77022 905 1 (print)
ISBN: 978 1 77022 906 8 (ePub)
ISBN: 978 1 77022 907 5 (PDF)

CONTENTS

FOREWORD

However much we might think we know and understand, there are some phenomena which now, and perhaps forever, we will never fully comprehend. We call such happenings 'enigmas'. Or even miracles. Ryan Sandes is one such.

You see, we 'know' what leads to ultimate success as a world-class athlete. First you have to begin young and put in years of training. So you begin by running short distances – a few kilometres at a time – in training. And as you increase your training distances, so that after some months you can run for 30 minutes without stopping, you might consider entering a fun run of, say, five kilometres. If that goes well, and depending on your level of commitment and discipline, you might next consider running even further in training in order to enter a 10-kilometre race. And after many months, perhaps years, of running 10-kilometre races, you may be enticed to take the next big step up by entering a 21-kilometre race. For although a 21-kilometre race is just more than twice the 10-kilometre distance, to complete the added 11 kilometres takes at least three times the effort.

Then, after a year or more of adding 21-kilometre races to your repertoire, you are faced with the final challenge – the one you could never have imagined when you began: the full 42-kilometre marathon – the ultimate running Everest for the great majority of the world's recreational runners.

Only in South Africa is the picture slightly different. For only here is there just one more rung on the ladder. Only here is the ultimate goal of the committed recreational runner an ultra-marathon like the

56-kilometre Two Oceans or the 88-kilometre Comrades Marathon. But even in South Africa, that is where the challenge ends for almost every marathoner – 88 kilometres in a single day. And not one step further.

Having run enough of those races, I have often wondered why, like tens of thousands of other South African ultra-marathoners, I would never for a single moment consider running a race longer than the 88-kilometre Comrades Marathon.

Part of the reason (we must acknowledge) is that most of us are actors and we need an audience to inspire us. So it's easy for us to run the Two Oceans and Comrades secure in the knowledge that millions will be watching our efforts either on the roadside or on national television. We thus see no reason to venture even one kilometre further. So a race of 100 to 160 kilometres? Utter madness.

Then what of a 250-kilometre, seven-day, six-stage race in which, for most of the way, we have only our own company? And, more importantly, only our own thoughts? And did you say the race would be on sand, in desert heat, or in extreme cold, or in the humidity and constant dangers of the Amazon jungle? Or perhaps at an altitude of two to three kilometres? Please – are you crazy?

In this book, Ryan Sandes introduces us to the crazy. And his story raises questions that seriously challenge our comfortable understanding of what determines ultra-endurance performance and how you train to get there. For in his career Ryan has destroyed almost all of our preconceptions of what it takes to become a world-class ultra-distance runner. And if we cannot explain why and how he has achieved what he has, can we scientists really claim to properly understand what we profess as our indisputable truths?

So here are the bare facts that demand our understanding and explanation.

Ryan's dad is a South African ultra-marathon runner, a veteran of the 56-kilometre Two Oceans Marathon. Ryan grows up with little interest in running; in fact, he describes himself as a 'party person'. Then, in June 2006, friends with whom he has shared a few short runs enter a local 21-kilometre half-marathon. Since Ryan's dad is a marathoner, Ryan enters the full marathon. In training he manages a single run of 19 kilometres, during which he is reduced to walking on numerous occasions. Undeterred, he runs the marathon keeping pace with the lead woman for 30 kilometres before fading to finish in 3:28:45. He decides he will break the three-hour barrier in his next marathon, a feat his father never achieved.

Training a bit harder, he runs his next marathon in early 2007, finishing in 3:08. A few months later, he lowers his marathon time to 3:01. He begins to train more regularly and starts to run in trail races, in which he finishes closer to the winners.

In October 2007, he sends off his entry form for the 250-kilometre, seven-day, six-stage Gobi March, to be held in June 2008. More experienced runners point out that this is a 250-kilometre race, that the furthest distance he has ever run in his life is 42 kilometres, and that these races are fully self-supported, meaning that from the start he must carry all he will need for the entire race.

Undeterred, he begins to train intensively with coach Ian Waddell. The first stage of the Gobi March is 40 kilometres. He begins conservatively and has no idea how he is running. With eight kilometres to go, he is informed that he is in second place. He speeds up and wins the stage. He is overcome by emotion. He wins all the next four stages, and the overall race, by 31 minutes. Inspired by his success and realising that he has some ability for this type of event, he enters the 2008 250-kilometre, seven-day, six-stage Sahara Race in Egypt. He again wins all five stages.

In 2009 he places second a few minutes behind the winner in the 250-kilometre, seven-day, six-stage Namibia (Sahara) Desert Race and wins the 2009 242- kilometre, seven-day, six-stage Jungle Marathon in the Amazon. CNN rates this race as the world's toughest endurance race. It includes temperatures of 40 °C, humidity of 98 per cent, a high jungle canopy that admits no direct sunlight, swamps with anacondas, and river crossings with piranhas and caimans 'as companions'.

In 2010 he wins two more 250-kilometre, seven-day, six-stage races in the 4 Deserts Series – the Atacama Challenge in Chile and the Last Desert Race in Antarctica. As a result, by the end of 2010 he is the only competitor to have won every stage of each of the four desert races. In 2011 he wins the 250-kilometre, seven-day, six-stage Racing the Planet in Nepal by more than two-and-a-half hours. The race reaches a peak altitude of 3 200 metres (10 500 feet) and involves total elevation gains of 9 000 metres and descents of 9 700 metres.

Having conquered the seven-day races, he decides to tackle the world's most famous single-day ultra-marathon trail races. In 2011 he wins the Leadville 100 Mile Trail Run at high altitude in the third-fastest time in history. In 2012 he wins the Vibram Hong Kong 100-kilometre ultra in a new record time. He adds the North Face 100-kilometre in Australia and, at his first attempt, finishes second in the second-fastest time in history in perhaps the most famous of all trail races – the Western States 100 Miler USA. He concludes the year by setting a new fastest known time of 6 hours 57 minutes for the Fish River canyon traverse.

In 2013 he wins the 125-kilometre North Face TransGranCanaria race and the 63-kilometre Patagonian International Marathon, becoming the only person to have won an ultra-trail race on every continent.

In 2014, he again wins the 125-kilometre North Face TransGran-Canaria race and the 250-kilometre, seven-day, six-stage Racing the Planet Madagascar, while setting a new record of 41 hours 49 minutes for the 209-kilometre Drakensberg Grand Traverse. He finishes second in the Ultra Trail Mount Fuji race and fifth in the Western States 100 Miler USA. He is rated second overall in the 2014 Ultra Trail World Tour.

These achievements are simply phenomenal. I am unaware of a similar example in the long history of running – of a complete novice becoming a world-leading competitor in extreme ultra-distance racing within a year of taking his first step as a more serious runner. And then becoming as successful at single-day ultra-marathon trail races, which demand a quite different set of skills and abilities … Everything we know about human biology tells us that the rapidity with which Ryan Sandes progressed from utter novice to world-leading athlete in this discipline simply cannot happen. It is a statistical and logical impossibility.

The upshot is that I am often asked what makes Ryan so special. And the truth is, I have no answer – I simply do not know. So I can only speculate.

Usually an athlete who suddenly achieves so much in such a short time will have a massive and obvious physiological advantage. For example, we know that the faster one is at any shorter distance, the quicker that athlete will be at any longer distance. So the fastest 10-kilometre track and cross-country runners will always be the fastest 42-kilometre runners. And the fastest 42-kilometre runners will (usually) be the fastest ultra-marathon runners. But Ryan is not an exceptionally fast 10- or 42-kilometre runner, so this explanation simply doesn't work.

The next option is that Ryan has a unique biology, so that even if he is not the fastest distance racer in the race, he tires less rapidly – that is, he has greater fatigue resistance. But this is merely a statement of the obvious, as this is clearly the reason why he is able to outlast his opposition. But this does not help, since we remain in the dark about the exact biological factors that explain superior fatigue resistance. Is it in the muscles and the heart, for example? Or is it in Ryan's mind?

Or does a unique biology allow Ryan to recover more quickly after each race stage so that he is less fatigued at the start of each subsequent stage and so can again perform better than his competition?

If this is so, to what extent is it a genetic gift or due to more training? I doubt that training can be the factor, as all the athletes whom Ryan races against are among the hardest-training athletes on the planet. You don't out-train those guys. So training is unlikely to be the sole explanation for Ryan's performances.

My bias draws inspiration from what was once written about climbing Mount Everest – the longer the event, the more important is the mind in determining the performance.

When we developed the Central Governor Model of Exercise, we realised that the fatigue we experience during exercise is a mental construct of our own brains, the goal of which is to ensure that we don't overdo the exercise and so damage ourselves. As a result, the discomfort we feel is unique to each of us – only we know exactly how we feel during exercise. We have no reason to believe that the sensations our own brain generates to regulate our exercise performance will be exactly the same as everyone else's. Or, indeed, identical to those of even one other runner on earth.

And therein lies the clue.

Ryan's success requires that the mental strategies he uses to regulate his exercise performance are different from those the rest of us use. In particular, he must have an astonishing ability never to doubt his own ability, even when running by himself in the solitude of his own thoughts in the world's toughest environments for days on end.

To a large extent, his self-belief must be innate, since it was clearly already apparent and very well developed in the first few hours of his first multistage race in the Gobi Desert in June 2008.

This book offers insights on how Ryan came upon the specific mental attitudes that have brought him such success.

If you wish to emulate his performances, you may need to copy them for yourself.

EMERITUS PROFESSOR TIMOTHY NOAKES
CAPE TOWN, SOUTH AFRICA

FOREWORD

The first day I met Ryan Sandes, I had a feeling he was destined for greatness. This wasn't on account of his physical prowess, which turned out to be formidable indeed, but due to his incredible humility and quality of character. He had all the makings of a great champion, though he had yet to win a race.

I must digress, before going on, and confess that I met Ryan during his first race. And this was not just any race, but the 4Deserts Gobi March in the Xinjiang Province of China, taking place in the windiest desert in the world, and one of the most remote and inhospitable places on Earth. This extreme six-day race is self-supported, meaning competitors must carry everything they need in packs on their backs. Not many newbie athletes take on a contest like this, but you don't know Ryan Sandes.

His humble and unassuming demeanour masked an inner fearlessness and an indomitable competitive drive. Not only did he go on to finish the event, he won it! And, in doing so, he defeated an elite field of established international runners, instantly solidifying himself as a force to be reckoned with. The only thing that seemed to be missing was an ego; Ryan didn't appear to have much of one.

Perhaps his victory during the Gobi March was just a fluke. Surely no one new to the sport could be *that* good. I next met Ryan during another 4Deserts race, this one in the sweltering heat and shoe-swallowing sands of the Sahara. If there were any doubts about his talents, they were quickly squashed during the Sahara Race. Ryan once again repeated his performance and took top honours, besting yours truly in the process, who finished runner-up and a long way back.

We talked a lot during the six days of racing across the Sahara, and Ryan confided that he wanted to quit his 'day job' and change careers, becoming a full-time endurance athlete. I was honest with him; it wouldn't be an easy transition. But he was determined to make the switch and applied that same grit and tenacity to remaking his life. The rest, as we say, is history.

Ryan has gone on to establish himself as one of the most recognised and accomplished endurance athletes of our time. He still maintains that same genuine and humble demeanour, which is supremely refreshing in this day of hyped-up, chest-pounding bravado displayed by many mainstream sportsmen. Ryan's results speak for itself, and he's the kind of champion you feel good about seeing on the podium. He's dedicated and hard-working, never taking shortcuts and always going the extra mile, or kilometre, depending on which country he's travelling in.

Ryan's book doesn't just tell the story of this remarkable man's life, but also provides the reader with valuable insights and insider tips garnered through years of racing at the front of the pack. Ryan shares his lessons and advice on training, running technique, race strategy and gear, along with providing recommendations on diet and nutrition for optimal performance. Each chapter takes you through a journey, one that is both inspirational and practical, and is sure to be enjoyable, whether you run great distances, moderate distances, or are just starting out.

DEAN KARNAZES (US ULTRA-MARATHON RUNNER AND AUTHOR)
OCTOBER 2015

1

MY FAMILY –
IT'S COMPLICATED

It came at me out of the shadows. A snake … longer than I was. It looked like a cobra, but this was not the time for a close herpetological study. It was honestly the biggest snake I had ever seen, and I say this having seen plenty of Cape cobras back home.

This place was very different from the familiar mountains and forests of Cape Town, though – it was the Floresta Nacional do Tapajós, a national conservation area in the northern Brazilian state of Pará. The year was 2009 and I was there to run the Jungle Marathon, a legendary 242-kilometre, six-day race through the Amazon jungle. It's a race that ultra-trail runners speak of in hushed tones as one of the gnarliest and most dangerous events you can tackle in a pair of running shorts.

And this was just a training run.

Wanting to acclimatise myself a little a few days before the start, I had asked the race founder, Shirley Thompson, if I could go for a short recce into the jungle to get a feeling of what the terrain was like – you know, just to get a sense of what I was in for. Initially, she wasn't keen but eventually agreed with the condition that I had to take along two armed guards, as it was 'too dangerous'. I was, like, 'Shirley, I'm from Africa. We have wildlife there too. And muggers. I never run with an armed guard at home. Besides, they're not going to be able to keep up and it would be more of a hike.'

Shirley was adamant: no guards, no go.

For the first 20 minutes, it was like a lovely Sunday amble through Newlands Forest back home – all pretty and foresty, with dappled sunlight coming through the trees. Fearsome jungle race? What fearsome jungle race?

Then that snake appeared.

Fortunately, the guards weren't too far behind and I literally jumped into the one guy's arms. The monster slithered away and I was left with two guards wearing I-told-you-so smirks.

The next day, Shirley organised a half-day survival course for the competitors, presented by the Brazilian military. Standing front and centre, and listening attentively with his notepad and pencil at the ready, was one Ryan Sandes. It was a very different Ryan Sandes from the one who had started out life 27 years earlier ...

I saw first light at Kingsbury Hospital, in Claremont, Cape Town, on 10 March 1982. I was my mother's 21st-birthday present and, if you can believe her, I was the 'golden child', the perfect son throughout my childhood. Obviously my sister disagrees.

Apparently, I took my time making an entrance, and halfway through the birth my mother recalls changing her mind about the entire idea of motherhood. It was way too painful and she was totally over it (my sister always smirks at this point in the story). Having got this far, however, Frankie – that's my mom – decided she may as well finish the job, and I came out looking not very 'golden' at all. Sporting pitch-black hair and looking a bit like a gorilla, I was almost swapped at birth. True story! Because my surname is often pronounced 'Saunders', I was mixed up with another swarthy kid whose actual surname was Saunders, and my mother ended up breastfeeding this little imposter for the first day. Luckily, after about a week, all my hair fell out and the handsome Sandes genes became a little more recognisable.

My mom's more the free-spirited type and my dad, Chris, is a lot more conservative. I suspect I may have been a bit of a mistake, but the unplanned adventure into parenthood didn't seem to bother either of them, especially not my mom. Unlike her sister, who was a straight-A student, my mom was the wild child and at 16 chose to leave school and head for an Israeli kibbutz. School wasn't her thing, and I think her school pretty much echoed that sentiment.

My dad's your typical South African male. He likes his sports – particularly rugby – and he played flank for Hamilton Rugby Club in Green Point, where he hung out with the boys in the pub after matches. Obviously not my mom's vibe at all. Still, if you want proof that opposites attract, my parents are it. Clearly, there was enough attraction going on for them to tie the knot when my mom was only 20 years old and my dad 28. Maybe, in light of what would happen later, they were too young – but I guess that was an era when people got married far younger. And had their kids too – because not long after they were married, I came along.

For the most part, I was a healthy toddler, although a nasty fall when I was about one or two years old almost ruined any chance of a sporting career. We were holidaying in Arniston – a little seaside town about three hours from Cape Town – when I fell and bashed open my knee. My whole leg seized up, and I ended up in hospital for quite a while. At the time, the doctor told my mom there was a possibility I would never walk properly again. Quite a big call to make, I think. Fortunately, I've never been one to be told what I'm incapable of, and I did walk again. In later years I even learnt to run a bit.

I grew up in Hout Bay in a house right at the end of Valley Road. Back then, Hout Bay felt more like a small fishing village than the bustling and busy suburb it is today. We stayed near the top of the Hout Bay Valley – on the border of Oranjekloof Nature Reserve – and it was actually pretty rural. I spent most of my time outside with our next-door neighbour's kid, Sean Thomson, riding around on our BMX bikes. He's the son of my dad's business partner, and Sean and I have remained lifelong friends – he was one of my best mates at my wedding. But a career in BMXing wasn't for me, as, not being able to steer properly, I remember going straight through a couple of neighbourhood fences.

Sean was always a lot better and faster than me. I didn't like that much. Even then I was super-competitive. At any birthday party I had to win at least one prize in the various party games. I still clearly remember coming home crying the one day because I didn't win the 'pass the parcel' prize. There were even a few parties where I refused to leave without some kind of prize. I think the birthday kids' poor moms eventually just wrapped something up and gave it to me.

My parents also had a hand in fuelling my hunger for winning. Back then, my dad was doing a fair amount of road running. He was a member of the Atlantic Athletic Club, and ran marathons and a couple of Two Oceans Ultra-Marathons. The race route used to come through Hout Bay and we would cheer him on. My parents even got me kids' running shoes and had running kit made up to match my dad's white and royal-blue club colours. I used to wear his medals and run around in the garden pretending I had won.

My grandparents were also a big part of my life as I grew up, particularly my mother's parents. As my mother had me so young, they were often around to help her. My mom was always close to her parents and some of my earliest childhood memories are of spending time with them over weekends walking in Tokai Forest with their dogs.

I was particularly close to my mom's father, Nick Stander. He always felt like a kindred spirit. He was an Afrikaner from up north – Louis Trichardt – and he was an all-or-nothing kind of guy. Nick's mom died when he was quite young and he inherited a whole bunch of money. Instead of saving or investing it, he simply took all his mates on a holiday to the UK and promptly blew all the money. Apparently, he had to bet on a horse to get enough money to pay for his ticket home. The upside to it all was that he met my grandmother, Sheila, while he was there, which in my book is score one for the School of 'All or Nothing'.

That story made a big impression on me. I've embraced the attitude, and the first race I did in the Gobi Desert was something along those lines. Obviously it wasn't quite as maverick as my granddad's trip to England (and I didn't find a wife in the Gobi), but I used every cent I'd ever earned to pay for that trip.

All or nothing.

Nick was a free spirit who didn't take life too seriously, and I reckon there's definitely a lot of that in me. Not quite as much maybe. But enough.

My gran eventually came back with him to South Africa, and they became estate agents who moved around quite a bit, living in Hout Bay, Constantia and all over Cape Town's southern suburbs.

I guess you could say there was also quite a selfish side to Nick, and at times he didn't, to put it bluntly, appear to really give a shit. He took a lot of financial risks – blowing his inheritance being a prime example – but, luckily for them, my grandmother was a bit more savvy and often had to hold things together. He was much more of a dreamer. They rented a farm in Arniston, for example, which was entirely his decision, but, financially, it wasn't the smartest move. They should have been putting money away for their retirement instead. The story goes that when my dad first met my mom, Nick gave them a bit of a lecture about financial planning – my dad is fairly straight down the line – but they looked at him like he was crazy.

For all his faults, I've always felt a very strong bond with my grandfather. He was the first person who introduced me to nature, and the earliest memories I have of Nick are of him being really proud of his garden and getting me to help him prune his roses – this was when my grandparents were staying in Constantia. They lived in the Eagles' Nest area, which – especially back then – was quite rural. Later, when they moved to Franschhoek, I would spend all my spare time with Nick in the vineyards during my school holidays. He always took pride in how neat and well cared for his vines were. Nick treated plants and trees almost as if they were people, and I think he indirectly passed on this strong connection with nature to me.

When I'm out there on my own, running on some beautiful trail, feeling free and at one with my environment, it's often Nick who will pop into my head. I wouldn't say I'm the religious type, but I'm definitely spiritual, and my granddad and I have had the odd conversation out there. I definitely feel like he's watching over me in some sense. Even a couple of times during races, when I've been tired and have wanted to start walking on a big climb, I would just picture him standing there telling me to flippin' sort myself out and keep going.

Unfortunately – and I guess hardly surprisingly, given the way he lived his life – Nick never really looked after his health. He always looked older than he actually was and, in my grandparents' final years, my mom's sister, Juliet, and her second husband, Eddie, basically took care of them and they stayed in a house Eddie owned in Cape St Francis. My grandfather had a stroke and, because he lived quite far from a major hospital, he deteriorated quickly and passed away. Still, he was someone who made the most of his life, and I will always admire him for that.

I was also close to Juliet when I was younger. Interestingly, she of the straight As at school turned into a party-loving New York model. She came back to South Africa married to a guy called Chris Seldon, who was apparently a fairly famous musician-slash-model. To a young Ryan Sandes, Juliet definitely seemed to be from another, far more exotic and interesting planet. And it was a planet my grandparents definitely did not approve of. I really liked spending time with her and Chris, though. They seemed like people to whom the rules just did not apply. I remember once wanting to go bareback horse riding – I was tiny and my mom said there was no way I could go. But Chris just snuck off with me in tow.

Those early memories of my childhood were happy ones. By the time I was four, my sister, Ashleigh, had arrived and right from the start I gave this new little upstart a hard time. I dropped her on her head. Literally. She was a few months old and lying in one of those rocking cradles. My mom was outside and Ashleigh was bawling so loudly, I decided to rock the cradle a bit. She kept on screaming, so I rocked it a bit harder. Cue more screaming ... and more vigorous rocking ... until she was catapulted out the front. Her injuries were serious enough for my parents to be quite worried, but she recovered quickly enough. So they say.

Yet Ashleigh's head was in for more. It was a few years later and I had been given a small motorbike to mess around with on the farm. My mom was riding it – I think she was trying to show me how it worked – and my sister ran in front of her. My mother got a big fright and instead of pulling the brakes, she accelerated and kind of half ramped over my sister's head. Yes, Ashleigh was in the wars. And continues to be. Just before my wedding in 2014, she went mountain biking for the first time, and promptly fell and broke her wrist. We have some cool family wedding pics of her and her cast, as she was also one of the bridesmaids.

Despite my earlier attempts, Ashleigh managed to make it past toddlerhood and, while we have always been close, there's been an element of competitiveness about our relationship. When I first started getting recognition for my running, I think it got to her a little and we went through a bit of a phase. But now she's chilled with it and one of my biggest supporters. She's also taken up running in the last few years, to the point where she did the 2015 Two Oceans Ultra-Marathon with her husband, Brad. I'm pretty proud of her for that, and she listens to my running advice, even allowing me to put together a few training programmes for her. But that's about the sum total of the advice Ashleigh takes from me – she's quite fiery (which suits her occupation as a lawyer well) and claims to have inherited the brains among the Sandes siblings. I like to tell her she's a little bit of a know-it-all – just like her mother (I might have to duck for cover after they read this!).

Having a sister didn't entirely ruin my childhood, and I remember some great family camping trips to Beaverlac in the Cederberg. But the holiday that stands out the most is definitely the one to the UK – it was the first time I had ever flown anywhere, and my dad bought me one of those little portable Nintendo computer games to keep his energetic little son occupied during the long-haul flight. We were off to England to visit my dad's family. He grew up there, and his father, Robert, worked for British Rail until they emigrated to South Africa when my dad was about 13. After my dad finished school, his mother (Audrey), father and sister went back to England, but my dad stayed behind and went to the University of Cape Town (UCT).

I could never work out why my dad's family went back after my grandfather retired. My dad, on the other hand, enjoyed South Africa. He spent most of his schooling here and was settled, with good mates, and I think he much preferred the better weather and outdoor lifestyle.

I met Robert, my paternal grandfather, only four or five times. They used to come out here once a year for a month or so, but he passed away three years after that holiday to the UK. Audrey, my grandmother on my dad's side, is still alive, though. She's a tough lady – in her nineties now and still going strong.

Unfortunately, that holiday turned out to be the last for the Sandes family unit, as our lives would change fundamentally a year or so later.

My parents got divorced.

There were no big dramas or bitterness. They had just drifted apart. My mom, for example, spent her free time on the beach or riding her horse, whereas my dad was more into hanging out with his rugby mates. When they first met, I think they shared the same student-type partying and drinking kind of lifestyle, but the reality of having two kids and the demands of domestic life was a different story.

By the time my dad realised he needed to change some things to save their marriage, I think it was simply too late. My mom had already met someone else and she wanted a divorce. It was a really rough period in my dad's life. His father also passed away around the same time, so within the space of a year he'd lost his dad as well as his wife and kids. He was also retrenched, prompting him to start his own construction company.

I saw my dad only over weekends, but I could see how he was struggling with all the changes in his life. It was tough for me as well – maybe less so for Ashleigh, as she was still too young to understand what was going on – but I gained a lot of respect for my dad for the way he turned his life around. He built up his company (which he still runs today) and he rebuilt his life.

My life was also turned upside down. In 1991 my mom moved us to Franschhoek. Not quite the exclusive and upmarket area it is now, this little town in the Cape Winelands seemed like the other end of the world. Her parents – specifically my grandfather – were managing a farm out there, and I think she wanted to get away from Hout Bay and have the support of her folks.

Until then, for my first two years of school, I had been at SACS – the oldest school in the country, founded in 1829 and situated in the shadow of Table Mountain and Devil's Peak. I loved it there. I had lots of friends – loads of kids from Hout Bay went there – and I felt at home. Besides being called into the headmaster's office a couple of times for my hair being too long (thanks to my hippy mother), I had a great time at SACS. I did quite well at swimming, competing successfully in inter-school galas, and I generally felt like I belonged.

Franschhoek Junior School was completely different, though. It was a big culture shock to go from SACS, with its proud rules and traditions, to Franschhoek Junior, where you wore khaki shorts, a shirt and, only if you felt like it, shoes. It was also a lot more Afrikaans, and they didn't do swimming as a sport. In my grade, there were only two or three English-speaking kids, so I had to learn to speak Afrikaans pretty quickly. Divorce, like English, wasn't exactly common in Franschhoek either, and having divorced parents meant I ended up feeling like an outcast most of the time. To be honest, I wasn't trying too hard to fit in either. It was very near the end of the apartheid era and I associated apartheid with Afrikaners. I was proud to have some roots in England. Fortunately, I've long since abandoned that point of view.

Having divorced parents embarrassed me and I resented my mom for the situation. Looking back now, this was very unfair. To me, it seemed that *she* was the one who had wanted the divorce, thus breaking up the family. I would see my dad only every second weekend and, as mentioned before, I could see how heartbroken he was. And I really didn't like my mother's new boyfriend. My little sister called him 'dad', which freaked me out a bit. In my aggrieved, young opinion, he was a loser who he didn't have much money and was living off my dad, who was still supporting my mom. To be fair, though, he was very good to my mom – they shared a passion for horse riding and ended up being together for about eight years.

But some good also came out of the divorce. My parents bought me that small motorbike on which I could ride around on the farm (by now I'd mastered the art of not riding through fences) and, because my grandfather was managing the farm, I also spent a lot of time with him in his pick-up, driving around to check up on the vines. I always looked forward to seeing him. If my mom told me I would be spending the weekend with them, I was always stoked to go and see my grandfather. He passed away when I was about 12, and I still miss him dearly.

During this sad period, I also spent a lot of time with my godmother, Tanya Townsend. I used to call her Aunty Black and White because her house was black and white. I'd spend weekends there to escape what was happening in my own home. She was a very good friend of my mom's, and used to come and stay with us in Franschhoek.

Tanya was like my second mom and, during those first few years of my parents' divorce, she was someone who offered me not only refuge, but stability as well. There were times when I really resented my mom, and Tanya didn't think much of my mom's boyfriend either, so we had a lot in common. I felt I could really trust, confide in and talk to her about this mess my life had become. I idolised her a little, or maybe what she had in her life. To me, as a kid, her life seemed really perfect – it was as if she had everything going for her.

And then that part of my life was shattered too. Tanya died. For most of her life she'd worked really hard, running a very successful film-production company called Townsend Productions. The demands of her career meant she rarely had time for a personal life and couldn't seem to find the right guy. Eventually she did. She became pregnant … and was then diagnosed with cancer. She died shortly after having her baby. I remember sitting on her bed and saying goodbye to her. It was heartbreaking, devastating beyond words. Here was someone who had worked her whole life to be successful – and then this happened. Maybe she had neglected her health in the drive to make a success of her business – I don't know – but it was the first of a couple of lessons growing up that would show me how fragile life could be.

Looking back, the whole Franschhoek experience also taught me a crucial life lesson. I'd had a sheltered and privileged life up till then, and the move there made me understand that life doesn't necessarily hand you everything on a platter. My introduction to reality was seeing my parents divorce, moving to Franschhoek and having to make new friends.

After a couple of years my mom began to miss Cape Town and all of her friends, and property was starting to get too expensive for us there. So we moved back. It wasn't exactly a fresh start, as we bought a house in Hout Bay, but I was definitely happy about the whole thing. I went back to SACS for Grade 5, which on one level was great, but difficult on another. Although my parents' divorce was a source of embarrassment for me in Franschhoek, one advantage of going to school there was that no one knew my background and I didn't have too much explaining to do. But my old friends were all still at SACS and I had to fill them in on everything that had happened.

Nonetheless, SACS was a much better fit for me and, as it was a strong rugby-playing school, I started to get more involved in that sport. I was one of the smallest kids in my grade – not ideal for a rugby player – and in primary school and my early high-school years, I mostly played for the B-team. Like my dad, I played flank. (For those of you who don't know much about rugby, the flank is the small, tenacious player who really gets stuck in.) I spent much of the time believing I should be in the A-team. I did actually make the A-team in my U14 year, but then broke my collarbone... not that I let on to anyone on the field that I'd possibly broken it. My mom was on the sidelines watching, and I was more petrified of her running onto the field – because, had she known, she would have – than of the excruciating pain. With little black dots of pain swimming across my vision, I managed to haul myself up and walk off the field as upright as I could manage.

Another setback to my rugby ambitions was when I was 16 and it was found I had Scheuermann's Disease, a syndrome characterised by excessive forward curvature of the spine. It's just one of those things growing kids can get and, unfortunately, I got it. I remember having a lot of back pain and feeling really sore. The doctor sent me for X-rays, after which he explained the condition to me. I was devastated. As I grew, my spine began to straighten out, but at that time in my life, when I lived for rugby, it was very tough not being able to play for a whole year.

I trained hard, though, and being super-competitive I was back playing rugby the following year. I did a lot of training on my own – running and gym work to build extra muscle – and, up until about Grade 10, I honestly believed I could be a Springbok rugby player. I was like one of those little dogs that doesn't realise it's half the size of the others and takes them all on. It was typical of me – all out and wearing my heart on my sleeve. For me, it's always been all or nothing. At least when it comes to sport. It's the one area where I've always been able to express myself. I'm not good at that in my day-to-day life – and I'm sure my family and wife will agree – but rugby, and now running, has definitely allowed me to do that.

Looking back on those rugby days now, I know I had some talent, but not enough to have made it as a pro. The bottom line is that if I had been that talented I would have probably progressed further. It's definitely not something I'm bitter about. In fact, it was a pretty significant process for me to go through. All that effort and will power it took to recover from my injuries and make sure I was fitter than the bigger guys taught me the value of hard work. You can be as talented as you like, but without putting in the hard yards, you will ultimately not be successful.

In my final couple of years at school, I was playing more for the A-team. Because the coach wanted a heavier forward pack, I'd often be one of the reserves and then, at half-time, I'd get called on. Playing A-team high-school rugby was also a bit of a wake-up call for me. We were now up against some of the top Afrikaans schools, like Boland Landbou and Paul Roos, and those guys were huge! A lot bigger than us English guys from the southern suburbs. In fact, my A-team debut was against Boland Landbou, and that year their whole team had made the provincial Craven Week side, including some of their B-team.

They smashed us. I think they put about 35 points on us. Just complete annihilation. I remember going into the ruck with the ambitious idea of trying to steal the ball, and then getting pulled out and flung aside. I tried it again, and this time they just jumped all over me. I also remember playing against future Bok star Schalk Burger a couple of times. Our tactic was to just kick him as many times as possible in the loose ruck to make sure he went off the field quickly!

My standout rugby memory, though, was going on tour to New Zealand and Australia. The Aussie schools in Perth and Sydney weren't that strong, and we won our games easily, but the Kiwi schools were another story. For one thing, these kids were big. If I thought the Afrikaans guys were big, this was a whole other level of big. I remember warming up for one game against a school in Christchurch, looking across at the other team doing the same and saying to my mate, 'They're pretty big, but not that big. They're like one of the big Afrikaans teams, that's all.' We carried on doing our drills until their coach came over to us and said, 'No, no, you are on the wrong field. This is the junior school. That's the high school over there.'

Our actual opponents turned out to be significantly bigger. This was one game in which I was happy to be on the bench for the first half. We were completely intimidated and they were 50 points up at one stage. I remember running between two of the centres and putting my hand over the tackle trying to offload the ball, and one of them basically garrotted me from the side. I thought I was dead. I could barely breathe for five minutes and was unable to swallow food properly for a week afterwards. After a while, though, we realised they weren't all that tough and we came to within five points in the end.

They scared the hell out of me off the field too. The boy who hosted me in Christchurch (each member of our touring party was hosted by a family) picked me up in this very beaten-up Ford. He took off down the road, driving super-fast and talking to me at the same time. The next minute, this car pulls up next to us on the gravel road, and starts hooting like crazy. My host ignored him until, at a robot, the car starts to bump us from behind. Turned out it was this boy's dad and they both happened to compete in demolition-derby stock-car races.

New Zealand was pretty rough, but not as tough as having to explain to your friends that your folks were now back living in the same house. Not as a couple, but living under the same roof – my mom downstairs and my dad upstairs. My mom had broken up with her boyfriend and my dad didn't have a partner. It made sense for them. They continued to lead separate lives, and it was obviously a situation that worked for them because that's still the set-up today.

My mom's been with her current boyfriend, Cassie Carstens, for close to 20 years now. He also lives in Hout Bay, and is chilled with the situation. My mom can be a little – how do I put this without getting slapped? – 'difficult' sometimes and I reckon Cassie is more than happy to have his space. And my dad is really good friends with Cassie too, so it all just seems to work. My mom also has a place in Cape St Francis, and she and Cassie will go there for a few weeks and then she'll come back to the Hout Bay house.

I'm sometimes asked if my parents' divorce had a big effect on me – I guess journalists look for an interesting back story to explain their subject matter – but I honestly don't think it shaped me that much. It was a tough time, for sure, but it's not something that has made me into a particular kind of person. In the catalogue of things that can make a lasting and life-altering impression on a young mind, that isn't one of the worst by a long shot. If anything, it made me realise that life's real. Like many kids in South Africa then, I grew up spoilt by the life we led. You live in this little bubble, and it's only when you leave school that you understand there's actually more to life and that it's not that easy. The divorce meant I learnt this little lesson earlier rather than later.

Maybe it's been a little dysfunctional at times, but my family have always been really important to me. We've always been very close and, like they say, blood is thicker than water. My family set-up may be a little unusual, but they're the only family I have and I love them. They did, after all, put up with my party years …

STUFF I'VE LEARNT

The importance of balance in life

The one great privilege about being an ultra-trail runner is that it gives you a helluva lot of time to think about things. Spending four or five hours running on a mountain gives you plenty of time to ponder the complexities of life. When I think about my godmother, Tanya, on one of my long runs, it makes me realise how important balance is in one's life.

There have been times in my career as an athlete when I've put too much pressure on myself. Running is the career I've chosen and, for the most part, I love it. It excites and motivates me, but the racing part, if I'm completely honest, is not something that fuels my soul. Racing to me is a job. It's something that fires up my competitive nature and I'm always determined to do well, but it does feel like a job. This is why I need to make sure I stay connected with what it is about running that ultimately fuels my soul, as should you.

2

FROM PARTY SHOES TO RUNNING SHOES

It's possible, if they have read the opening chapter, that one or two of my mates might put a hand in front of their mouths and cough, 'Bullshit.' If I led you to believe my formative years were all about stoically enduring family dramas and an obsessive dedication to rugby training, I duly apologise.

There may also have been a few parties in between all of that.

It started when I was about 16, on a school rugby tour to Italy. I had just been told that I had Scheuermann's Disease, so I couldn't actually play, but everything had been paid for, so I was allowed to tag along. Turns out the Italians start drinking from a far younger age than us, and apparently taking a bunch of wide-eyed, foreign teenage boys to a bar was perfectly acceptable, if not expected. Back home I might have had the odd beer with my parents, but these guys gave us free rein – circumstances we accepted with enthusiasm. I had a lot of fun on that tour. And none of it involved actual rugby.

Back home I was also spending a lot of time on Llandudno beach, where I'd go bodyboarding and hang out with my schoolmates. Frank Solomon, John Barker-Goldie, Markus Phitides, Nicholas Owen, John Catlin, Thomas Catlin, Calum Hannay, Kyle Sarkas, Micah Sarkas, Greg Louw, Nick Taylor and Bourne Buirski were the guys in the crew. They gave me the nickname 'Hedgie' and still use it to this day.

My hair was quite long, until one day I had it cut short and spiky. Someone remarked that it looked like a hedgehog sitting on my head and, as is often the case with boys of that age, the nickname stuck like chewing gum to a sneaker. Not that I minded. In fact, I quite liked it and even used to go around drawing this little dog cartoon I called the 'Hedgie Dog' – I think I picked it up from a skating magazine – with the words 'make shit happen' underneath.

Don't judge me.

I choose to blame it on the exuberance of youth. And beer. We'd drink quite a lot of it and then egg each other on to do some silly stuff. One time it involved actual eggs.

It was a Friday night, and John and I had already had a few beers when we decided to gatecrash an awards ceremony at Herschel (an all-girls private school). It may have been revenge for something they had done to us – pranks like this would often happen between these southern-suburbs high schools – but I took it one step too far.

During the ceremony I ran into the hall, yelled my head off and threw eggs at the stage. Fortunately, the beer affected my aim and no one got hit, which could have been pretty painful, given that I was hurling the eggs from the back of the hall. I believe one did almost hit the deputy head girl.

It was a stupid thing to do. I was clearly going to be bust. I knew quite a few of the girls at Herschel and, sure enough, the following Monday I was called into our headmaster's office. Gordon Law was his name. Smart guy. The first thing he said to me was, 'On a scale of one to ten, how honest are you?'

'Seven or eight?' was my speculative and slightly shaky reply.

He then asked me if I was the one who had lobbed the eggs at Herschel. What could I say? I often got into trouble back then, but I did always try to be honest. Fortunately, Mr Law was a mate of my dad's through rugby, and I suspect that bought me a little leniency, because all I got was a couple of detentions and a directive to personally apologise to Herschel's headmistress. She was pretty cool about it. She could obviously see how nervous I was standing there in her office, and she said my honesty was appreciated and thanked me for coming.

Another incident involved running over some poor unfortunate parent's car. This guy had come to pick up his daughter at a party we were attending. Again, there might have been beer involved. I started to run towards his parked car. He saw me running towards him, and I could tell he was thinking, 'No ... he isn't ...'

But yes, I was.

I vaulted up onto the bonnet, ran across the roof and jumped off the back. I remember thinking while sailing through the air, 'This is quite a cool feeling ...' In retrospect, my interest in trail running might've been born right there and then – I get the same feeling running down a mountain really fast and launching off a rock. Some of the guys I'm competing against now were probably taking part in cross-country races and track meetings back then. I was busy running over cars.

And while we are on the subject of cars, I might as well confess to writing off my car. It was the year after I'd finished matric, and I had returned to my alma mater for my first SACS Old Boys' dinner. Of course, being back with all my mates recalling our glory days, I had too much to drink and crashed my car coming down Dean Street, in Newlands. The scary thing was I could not remember even driving it. My poor mother was super-freaked about it. She was always going on about drunk driving, and was happy to pick me up if I was over the limit. I still feel ashamed when I think back to this, and it remains one of the big regrets in my life. I let my mother down badly.

My plan all along was to enrol for a BSc in construction studies at UCT the following year, in 2002, but, until then, I was determined to spend a year packing in as much of a good time as I possibly could. And this carefree, alcohol-fuelled life really got going when I headed off to the USA with one of my Llandudno beach friends, John Barker-Goldie.

He's a really big-hearted guy, but a little crazy too. We'd all get up to some naughty shit, but John was on another level, especially when he'd had a few drinks. Many years later, during a Proteas cricket series against the West Indies in the Caribbean, he was the guy who streaked naked across the pitch. It even impressed the South African team's own bad boy, Herschelle Gibbs, who congratulated him on Twitter.

John and I had heard that a ski season in the Colorado towns of Aspen and nearby Vail was a big jol, and after being at school for

12 years hanging out with the same people, I was looking for some new adventures. I knew being employed at these ski resorts was pretty hard work, but it also meant I could do a lot of snowboarding and partying with the other – no doubt similarly enthusiastic – employees.

I obtained a student visa, did an online interview with the Aspen Skiing Company and was given a job as a ski-lift operator, starting in December 2000. One minor problem was that, unlike John, I'd never been snowboarding before. Typical of John, though, he didn't think that constituted much of a problem, and he bought me a board and shoved me into a lift. I fell flat on my face as soon as it stopped.

I had no clue, but being fearless youngsters, we went down one of the tougher runs first time out, neither of us wearing helmets. I had no control. I couldn't turn or slow myself down, but I could go straight and fast. The only way for me to stop was to deliberately fall. I was just beginning to get the hang of it when I caught an edge, pitched myself backwards, hit my head and knocked myself clean out. I woke up butt naked in hospital after the nursing staff, for some reason, had cut off my clothes. John was sitting there laughing at me. The next day I had to go out and buy some new snowboarding kit. And a helmet.

I also got a second job. I needed to make enough money to not only get me through the rest of my gap year, but also to fund my travels, and that included getting myself to Bali. I eventually found further employment at a fruit-and-veg store. I claimed that I had grown up on a farm (sort of true) and knew all about produce (not even vaguely true), but they bought it and I was employed for four months earning relatively decent money for a student.

We then moved from Aspen to Vail, where John had a lot of older friends he knew from school. I found work at a sports shop, and it was only in the final month of the ski season that I really joined in the serious partying. The action usually took place high up on the mountain.

On one particular day we were higher up than usual. The only reason I can remember that day is thanks to the video footage – my personal recollections are a little hazy. It was the last day of the ski season. I had a video camera with me and I was determined to document proceedings. John and I were quite a bit younger than the guys we were hanging out with, and they liked to mess us around. Sure enough, they offered us a bag of mushrooms – not the kind in your Spur burger sauce. According to the video footage, I asked how many of these hallucinogenic 'shrooms one should take.

'The whole bag,' was the jokey reply.

So I did.

It didn't take too long for it to kick in … and for me to have left this planet for another.

I tried snowboarding back down, but I basically fell all the way. By then I'd lost John, only to find out a few hours later that he was in jail for having tried to sneak into a club (you had to be over 21, which we weren't). I managed to bail him out the next day.

On the whole, the ski-lift operator work was boring as hell. It was a long shift – 7 a.m. to 5 p.m. – standing out in the cold, helping people into the lifts and maintaining the area. But every now and then a famous person would come through. I remember seeing US Vice-President Al Gore, as well as Cameron Diaz (although I didn't recognise her at first: she looks quite different without make-up).

John and I left Vail in April and headed for Mexico, the home of tequila. The other reason for our trip south of the border was the legendary big-wave surf spot of Puerto Escondido. Much like my first snowboarding sesh, I bit off way more than I could chew and nearly drowned the first time out on my bodyboard. I made the rookie mistake of catching the first wave of a big set, which swallowed me whole and threw me over the falls. The rest of the set then landed on my head. I just paddled back to shore after that.

John and I also discovered another delight in Mexico, called mescal, which is a drink similar to tequila but quite a bit stronger. After one night of heavy drinking, things started to unravel. We'd been knocking back mescal to the point where we could barely talk and then decided to go out on the town. I remember standing in a queue to get into some bar, and I could see the switch flip in John's head. Things were about to get a little crazy. He was getting into an argument with some big Mexican, and I was like, 'Okay, cool. See you later.'

I went back to where we were staying and woke up the next morning to find John passed out in his underpants, bleeding, with broken glass everywhere. He'd managed to get himself mugged, after which he had tried to crawl through our room's slat-glass windows, which had clearly broken. That was the last party we had. I flew home via Los Angeles and then travelled to Bali for a couple of months.

All credit to John, though. He did a few more ski seasons, but then pulled himself out of a pretty deep hole and went into rehab to face his demons. He was either going to get himself killed or he needed to change. Today he has a family and is doing well. He works offshore on oil rigs and is married with three little girls. Tash, his wife, is fantastic; she can properly put John in his place. John's a great dad to his kids, and it's flippin' impressive to see how he's grown and how strong-minded he is. It's been seven years now, and he hasn't touched a drink – not an easy thing to do when your mates still party pretty hard. When the guys down beers, he downs water. I had some good times with John, but we probably did push that envelope a little too far. These days we've reconnected again, and he often pops around with some fresh fish he's caught on the charter boat in which he has shares.

Like John, I also had my own hole to climb out of. It wasn't as deep as John's, and my exit wasn't as sudden either.

When I got back from two months in Bali in mid-2001, I enrolled at UCT to do that BSc, as planned. Although that didn't put an end to my party persona, it did put the brakes on it a little. My dad had done the same degree, and over the years I'd developed both an interest in and an understanding of what the construction industry was all about. During my degree I worked for his construction company in my spare time, and this helped make varsity fairly easy. The commerce subjects – accounting and economics – were a little harder, as was engineering drawing, but I found university a lot more practical than school and enjoyed it more. I worked hard, but could get by fairly easily.

My plan was to do a post-grad honours degree in quantity surveying (again, like my dad), though it took a little longer than usual thanks to another gap year I took after the second year of my undergraduate degree. It wasn't quite as wild as my North American adventure with John, mainly because I had met a girl. Robyn was her name, and I fell for her in a pretty big way. Despite UCT advising against it, given my honours-degree ambitions, I stuck to my belief in the School of What the Hell, You Only Live Once, and we travelled to London, through parts of Europe and to Thailand.

Besides, there was another far more serious and tragic reason that had fuelled my allegiance to this school of thought.

In 2003, my maternal grandmother was murdered on the farm in Franschhoek. I'm not going to go into too much detail, but it was an attempted robbery by some local youngsters that went wrong. They also lived on the farm, and had heard via my gran's domestic worker that she had recently earned commission on a house she had sold (my gran was an estate agent). The guys – high on drugs – broke into her house and demanded the commission they thought was in the house somewhere. They ransacked the house and the attic, but ended up just taking her cellphone. They tried to steal her car, but were too high to even manage that. The stolen cellphone was how the police tracked them down and eventually caught them.

For a couple of years afterwards, I was extremely angry at what had happened. I guess, living in South Africa, we are reminded on a daily basis of how brutal human beings can be. It's not something I will ever forget, but it is something I have been able to let go of. I hold dear the memories of my gran, but it's not something I want to dwell on too much here. It was a very tough time for our family and, of course, especially for my mom and her siblings. It was a process of healing for all of us, and running has definitely helped me. Being out on the trails, running, breathing and just letting your body go, has helped me deal with some of life's tougher tests. It gives me time to think about things, and inevitably I come to the conclusion that life is too short to keep anger locked inside.

In 2006 I returned to start my honours year and graduated second in my class. Turns out I was coming second in Robyn's life too, and we split up.

Whereas before I was kind of proud to be known as someone who loved having a good time, by my final year at UCT it began to bother me that I had developed this reputation as a party-animal-slash-piss-cat. It got to me. It wasn't how I wanted to be known. Even through all the partying, I'd still gone on the odd run to keep fit. In the UK and during that second gap year with Robyn I'd run a little, and in my final year at UCT, I began to up the kilometres. I was staying with my folks in Hout Bay then, and I'd take the dogs for a run on the dunes behind the house.

With my dad having run seven Two Oceans Ultra Marathons, running was obviously part of my upbringing. Witnessing him participate in all those races, watching the Comrades on TV and seeing the Argus Cycle Tour come past our doorstep every year, meant endurance sport was embedded in my psyche.

A couple of mates with whom I was studying were taking part in the 2006 Knysna Forest Half Marathon and, having done a few short runs with them, I figured what the hell and duly entered. Running two or three kays in the dunes and a couple of runs up and down Valley Road with mates probably wasn't the ideal training for a half marathon, but I backed myself. The race took place during the town's renowned Oyster Festival – which was basically less about actual oysters and more about having one massive party – a fact I knew all too well, having participated in the festivities many times before. (My family had a house in Plettenberg Bay, and during my high-school years we used to go up there every December and over June/July, when the festival was on.)

Sitting down at a computer in the UCT library, I googled the website, only to discover the entries for the half marathon had already closed. You could still enter the full marathon, though. What the heck. Half marathon ... marathon ... same thing. I punched in my details and entered. My dad had always run marathons – I should have a go too. Besides, it would be cool to see what my times were like compared to his. He'd never broken that sub-three-hour holy grail, and I was keen to see how close I could get. I didn't give it a helluva lot of thought at the time. Six weeks before the race, though, I reckoned it was probably best to put in a little extra training. This was a 40-something-kilometre race, after all.

Apart from those runs up and down Valley Road, I remember doing one long run up Chapman's Peak, and back home up Valley Road. We're talking 18 or 19 kays max. And then off I went to Knysna. Understandably, my old Llandudno beach mates thought it was a big joke.

About four days before the race, I started feeling fluey and decided to subscribe to that old wives' tale that swore by slugging back a few drams of whisky to banish the malady. Clearly, this myth originated in Scotland. So I drank a half-jack of whisky and resolutely made sure I didn't have a big night before the race, drinking only three or four beers.

Despite my attempts at self-medication, I didn't feel great at the starting line. If I'd been doing the race now, I probably wouldn't have run it, but back then I wasn't too fazed. Besides, as soon as the gun went off, the competitive side of me kicked in.

Other parts of my psyche also kicked in: running in front of me was this rather attractive babe wearing little red hot pants. She could run, too. The pace was a lot quicker than I was used to, but, interestingly, I realised that if I just focused on those hot pants – just sort of zoomed in – I could stay with her. I found out later that she was the leading woman, who eventually won the race. Anyway, my eyes managed to hang on until about 30 kays, when the route headed up a steep climb to the Pezula Resort. The wheels came off and I had to walk it. Any chance of a sub-three was properly out the window.

Still, I remember running down the other side to the finish and feeling pretty chuffed. I'd done it. Stuff all you mates in Cape Town: look who's laughing now. I felt a new sensation too … fulfilment. My official finishing time was 3:28:45. I came 76th in the men's category with minimal training. I didn't even get rat-faced that night – one or two beers, and that was it for me. I was happy with that.

Analysing that race now, I think being a little naive really helped.

I know that for most runners completing a marathon is a big deal. And it is. You generally need to put a lot of mental energy and training into running a marathon. My light-hearted approach had its advantages too, though. Given what I'd later achieve, I obviously had some potential. I was pretty headstrong and there were those red hot pants, but I think not stressing too much about the race, and going in with a carefree and open mind, helped a lot too.

My legs were shot the next day, but it was a nice kind of sore. I walked around the festival with a bit of a limp, but I could see a bunch of people walking the same way. I felt like I was part of a new crew. Instead of walking around with a hangover, my limp meant I'd actually achieved something. That was cool.

I also began to seriously think about a sub-three marathon time. Although my dad had never managed it, I reckoned with some proper training, I could give it a crack. I set myself a goal, but the problem is, it kind of consumes me when I do that. With the sub-three in mind, I joined local running club Hout Bay Harriers and started pounding the pavements in earnest. I was getting fitter, but I was also starting to pick up a whole bunch of injuries – iliotibial band (ITB) pain in my knees and sore ankles. Clearly, my body wasn't quite strong enough yet to handle what I wanted it to do.

In early 2007, I entered and ran the Cape Peninsula Marathon. Halfway through, a tendon in my ankle flared up, and I basically limped through the second half of the race. Still, I finished in 3:08, which I was quite pleased with, given the slow second half. It only egged me on more. I knew I could do it.

So I entered the West Coast Marathon a few months later, and had a proper go. I was on track for a fast time too. Everything was perfect. Then, just before the finish I started cramping. I clocked in at 3:01. I was pretty bummed, but in hindsight it's probably a good thing. I suspect if I'd ticked that sub-three box, accomplished that goal, I might well have thought, 'Well, that's my running done' and moved on to something else.

Instead, almost by chance, I started trail running.

A few of the guys at Hout Bay Harriers – Andrew Tunstall and Eric

Tollner, both very accomplished amateur athletes – were into trail running and I spent a lot of time training with them, particularly with Andrew. They convinced me that I should enter the Old Fisherman's Trail Challenge – one of Cape Town's original trail races, which traverses the mountains from Hout Bay to Fish Hoek. At one point during the race I think I was even in fourth place, but I somehow missed clocking in at one of the checkpoints and the race marshals sent me back up the mountain to get the requisite tick.

By now, running brought me the same highs as partying, plus it felt healthy and like I was achieving something, and doing something credible and good. It made me feel as if I had a place in this world. I spent a lot more time running with Andrew and Eric on the weekends and a lot less time partying with my friends. But, optimistically and rather stupidly, I was still trying to combine the two.

One evening, I attended a friend's birthday party at a bar in Camps Bay. After having been out till four in the morning, I got home, put on my running kit and arrived just in time to meet the guys for a training run to prepare for the Hout Bay Trail Challenge. I was still drunk. Among the little group was Warren Pettersen – one of the best South African runners of his generation. He had won the Paris Half Marathon and was now also doing quite a lot of trail running.

I stayed with him for about two or three kays before I had to pull over and puke. I managed to catch Warren on the downhill, though – mostly because he wasn't the best technical runner, but afterwards I just felt like an idiot. Like I had embarrassed myself.

There was another occasion: I'd entered a local 15-kilometre race, which I'd been looking forward to for weeks. I had even laid out all my kit on the bed the night before, congratulating myself on some excellent prep. Then I went out to meet my mates for a couple of drinks … and inevitably hit it way too hard. I remember my alarm going off the next morning and just thinking 'aah, stuff it' and going back to sleep.

I woke up later feeling really crappy – physically and emotionally. As I said, I'm the type of person who, once I set myself a goal, I have to achieve it no matter what. And here I'd let myself down badly. Again. It wasn't a major race, but I felt pretty stupid nonetheless.

Gradually, though, the partying began to happen less and less. I was spending more time doing three-hour Saturday-morning runs and, to do these at Andrew's pace, there was no way I could go out on a Friday night. So, I'd go out only on Saturdays, but then we started running on Sundays as well, and not wanting to feel crappy for these runs I basically stopped partying altogether. The rewards – the endorphins – were great and I began to see that there just might be a little bit of a place in the world for me. I was achieving things and doing well. It was great not waking up every Sunday feeling hungover. Instead, I began to feel really healthy. By late 2007, Party Ryan had left the bar.

It was also around this time that I got my first – and, to date, only – day job, working for Faircape Property Developers. I was thrown in the deep end there, which left even less time to party. It was quite a shock to the system – working a nine-to-five job, I mean. The party life was pretty much out of my system by now.

At first, I really enjoyed working there. I progressed quickly and found myself sitting in on meetings and being accountable for some sizeable decisions on multimillion-rand projects. The CEO of the company, Mike Vietri, put in long hours – he'd be there before any of us and leave way after we'd gone home. I never got it. To me, this guy had made enough money to retire many times over, but still here he was, stressing and working like mad. All his employees would be, like, 'Why the hell is this dude running around like this, about to have a heart attack?'

Of course I get it now. He was just super-passionate about what he did. And when you feel like that about something, you see things in a different way. You can pick up on the small mistakes immediately because the people who work for you are rarely as passionate. To them, it's just a job.

I think, subconsciously, I understood what was driving him. I began to realise that I would never feel about this industry the same way Mike did. It wasn't my passion. And while I still wasn't entirely sure what was, that space was beginning to become increasingly occupied by something far simpler, but also something that required as much dedication to become successful at it – trail running.

On one of those days at work – it was late October 2007 – some recreational browsing on the internet made me stumble across a series of ultra-distance races called 4 Deserts. 'Hmm,' I thought …

STUFF I'VE LEARNT

Relax a little more – be flexible

Endurance athletes – and I mean weekend warriors to the elite – can get too tense about the race they're about to do. You worry too much about what can go wrong, instead of focusing on what can go right. 'Control the controllables and don't stress the variables' might be a bit of a cliché, but it's also an invaluable piece of advice.

One thing that Knysna taught me – and it's a lesson I've learnt a few times in my subsequent career – is that I do best when I'm as relaxed as possible and running for the pure enjoyment of it. When I start to focus on the racing element and start worrying about a particular competitor, or what my sponsors might or might not want, it doesn't work.

Your prep is obviously key, but don't get too stressed if something goes wrong on race day. If you're at the starting line of a half marathon and realise you didn't pack your gels, don't stress. It's just 21 kilometres, and you can drink some Coke and water at the water point. It will give you exactly the same boost and, worst-case scenario, you're marginally slower than you may have been if you had slurped down a gel on the run. You've got to go with the flow. I think people get way too regimented – as if you have these six steps you must follow to run a sub-three marathon, and if one of them goes wrong, it's like, 'Oh no, this is it. It's all over.' Just go with the flow.

Sure, a game plan is necessary, I agree, but you've got to be flexible too. When you run, you've got to be relaxed. If you're not relaxed, you are not going to do well.

And have a glass of wine

If you're a typical weekend warrior who is serious about the endurance sport you do – be it running, cycling, paddling or whatever – I wouldn't get concerned about alcohol intake.

Everything in moderation, obviously, and smashing a bottle of whisky isn't smart, but if you enjoy a glass of wine with supper or the odd beer, then by all means do it. Besides, red wine contains antioxidants and it also relaxes you a little and helps you sleep. I definitely don't feel it's a bad thing.

In some ways, weekend warriors are very similar to elite athletes – especially if you are training for an ultra-long or multistage race. The stress and strain you put on your mind and body with all the training, plus work and family life, are similar to the load an elite athlete asks his or her body to endure. It's therefore good to give yourself the occasional physical and mental break. If, for example, you have been training your butt off for a race like the eight-day Cape Epic mountain-bike race, take time off to let your hair down for a night. Go catch up with your mates and have a couple of beers. It's going to prevent you from getting stale and stagnated.

When I'm close to a race and really focused, I don't drink, but otherwise I'll happily have two or three glasses of red wine a week. Having a beer after a race is also very much part of the ultra-running scene, and I like that. We run together, and then we have a beer together.

3

SANDES OF THE GOBI

I'm not entirely sure why I was looking for a foreign trail race that day. Maybe I was missing the carefree student lifestyle that my nine-to-five job no longer afforded. I loved travelling, so maybe I was missing that too. Trail running was beginning to represent freedom to me, and I guess doing a race overseas would be a great mix of the two. I remember thinking, 'Don't go and run something like the London Marathon – let's make it a proper adventure.'

One place I'd always wanted to go to was South America, and it was with that in mind that Google's little algorithm bots popped up the 4 Deserts Series website. Their next race was the Atacama Crossing in Chile the following February – a seven-day stage race that covered 250 kilometres through what looked like some pretty gnarly country. And it was self-supported, meaning I would have to carry all the food and equipment I would need for the entire race.

A quick scan of the website's 'Quick Facts' page revealed eyebrow-raising info: 'The driest place on Earth – it is fifty times more arid than California's Death Valley'; 'temperatures range widely and the desert climate can be extremely hot during the day and extremely cold at night'; and 'the Atacama Desert has the most lunar-like landscape on Earth and is frequently used by NASA to test its planetary rover vehicles'.

An almost casual mention, too, was the fact that the entire race is held at least 2.3 kilometres above sea level. Which was basically 2.3 kilometres higher than where I lived and trained. Not ideal.

What the hell. That living-on-the-edge attitude that fuelled my party days was still in me ... so I filled in the entry form and hit the send button. The deposit fee was quite steep – $1 200 – but I had been saving up. Time to go big or go home.

Straight-up, my old party mates told me I was nuts. The trail guys I ran with seemed to be a little more open-minded – though I wasn't as close with my running mates yet, so maybe behind my back they were also pointing to their temples and making little circles. My dad – the first person I told – was also slightly sceptical. Being a runner and a sportsman himself, he understood me better than anyone, but I think even he was a little unconvinced. Understandably so. On an apparent whim, his son had just entered a 250-kilometre, self-supported, multi-day race, despite the fact that he'd never even run an ultra-distance road or trail race.

He had a good point. So I started training.

Like I've said, once I set a goal for myself, I'm 100 per cent committed. And that has its positives and its negatives. In this instance, the negatives came out on top. I was suddenly spending all my spare time running. And it wasn't smart running, either. There was no structured training programme or routine. No build for two weeks, then back off and have a rest day. No interval training. Instead, it was balls-to-the-wall stuff. When I wasn't working or sleeping, I was running. And that can only lead to one thing ... injury.

After six weeks of pounding the roads and trails, my legs – especially my ITB – began to hurt. Initially I thought perhaps there was an issue with the running shoes I was wearing, and that I might need orthotic inserts or something. I booked an appointment with orthotic specialist Jen Rorrison who, knowing the race I had in mind and being the smart person that she is, instead recommended that I see running coach Ian Waddell. Right away Ian and I got on pretty well. He seemed open to different approaches and wasn't the 'my way or the highway' type, which would definitely not have worked for me.

Our initial discussion, in hindsight, was a little amusing –

Ian: 'You're going to run how far?'

Me: '250 kilometres. But it's over seven days, though.'

Ian: 'And the furthest you've ever run is?'

Me: '42.2 kilometres, on the road. And on trail, 35 kilometres.'

Ian: 'Ryan, I think you need to reassess this. The race is in three months and you have no real training programme. And you're injured. Back off a bit. Rather enter a race later in the year. You need to recover, get strong and let's get you training properly.'

He was right. Luckily, the 4 Deserts organisers allowed me to change my entry to the next race on the calendar – the Gobi March – scheduled for June 2008.

This gave me an extra three months to heal up and get in some smart and focused training. Clearly, I would need to up my game quite seriously. For one thing, the total race entry fee was $3 200, which was close to R40 000 then, and that's a sizeable financial commitment for someone who is in the first year of his first job.

The training was hard. Really hard. I still look back at that time and regard it – mentally at least – as the toughest prep I've ever had to do. Every fifth week, Ian had me running four-day blocks, where I'd run for three or four hours at a time, and one day it would be five hours. What made those runs especially tough was that I'd be carrying a backpack weighing 10 kilograms, and wearing two or three jackets to simulate the conditions I would have to endure in the Gobi. Remember, this was a self-supported race, and I'd be hauling all my food and gear with me through every stage.

And then there was the desert heat. As well as wearing the extra layers, I'd start my runs at 9 or 10 a.m., which meant I'd be running through Cape Town's midday summer temperatures, which, although they average around the mid-20s, can get into the mid-30s as well.

Working a nine-to-five job meant my major runs were on a Saturday and Sunday. Saturday would be a fairly long run – around three hours plus – and then Sunday a little bit shorter, around two or three hours. And then, at least once a month, I'd do those blocks: a long one on Friday afternoon, the usual Saturday and Sunday, and then another two and a half hours first thing Monday morning. That Monday-morning run was a killer. Apart from being knackered from the previous three days, I'd have to get up at 4 a.m. or so to get the run in and still be at work by 7.30 or 8 a.m. The week after the four-day block I'd take it fairly easy. Basically, the programme saw me build for three weeks, do the block and then take one week easy.

During a regular week I'd try to get in a little bit of quality running. I'd leave the backpack at home – running with it all the time reduces your speed – and usually on Tuesdays and Thursdays I would run twice a day. An hour in the morning and maybe an hour or 90 minutes in the evening, and then I'd always have at least two rest days a week. I began to be a big believer in rest.

Of course, the other issue I would have to deal with in this race was sand. And no endurance athlete I've ever come across – runner or mountain biker – likes sand. To condition my legs, I did many a run along Noordhoek Beach in Cape Town – a beach that must stretch for about eight kays from end to end.

So, yes, the training was tough, both physically and mentally. Of the proverbial highs and lows there were plenty. For one thing, I battled getting used to a heavy backpack. Apart from the added weight that puts pressure on your legs, it also kills your shoulders. I've seen a lot of strong runners make the mistake of thinking it'll be fine to do a few training runs with the pack a couple of weeks before a stage race. Your back takes a beating, trust me, and initially I would get some really hectic chafing on my lower back, and my shoulders would also get rubbed raw from the weight of the pack. I was also constantly tired, and then there was the added pressure of a full day's work at Faircape. They knew I liked to run in my free time, but they had no idea how much of it I was actually doing.

Those block sessions I did still stand out for me. I remember running from Hout Bay along the coastal road to Camps Bay, cutting up towards Kloof Nek and up to the lower cable-car station, and then following the trails all the way around Table Mountain to Constantia Nek ... and being completely buggered. I had to call my mom and ask her to come and pick me up.

There I was, lying on my back, thinking, 'How the hell am I going to get through the flippin' Gobi?!' This was only the Saturday run. I still had the Sunday and Monday to do, and here I was phoning my mother. You can't phone your mommy in the Gobi. In the race I'd have to do four 4.5-hour-plus runs and then a monster 100-kilometre run on Day 5. I seriously started to think I'd bitten off quite a bit more than I could chew.

It didn't help that this was a time when I'd usually be on the beach chilling with my mates. Except here I was running along the coastal road from Hout Bay to Sea Point and back, and below me, there the bastards were having a good time on the beach. It would be 35 °C, they're in their baggies, and I'm running past wearing a heavy backpack and two jackets. I'd also have two extra T-shirts with me, so that I could change them when they got too soaked in sweat. Because the jacket's cuffs would seal in the moisture, I'd eventually feel all this water sloshing around inside. I'd have to stop and empty out what felt like half a litre of sweat.

Once or twice I even ran with a beanie on my head, but that was beginning to feel a little over the top and weird. I got some very odd looks from people who drove past me – especially those big tourist buses, of which there are plenty driving around during the Cape summer. I remember passing a bunch of picnickers up Chapman's Peak Drive who'd clearly been enjoying a few glasses of wine in the hot summer sun, and a rather loud and rhetorical 'Wat de fok doen jy?!' was hurled my way. Even if you don't speak Afrikaans, I'm pretty sure you can figure out the sentiment.

From a nutrition point of view, apart from making sure I kept hydrated, I was using a supplement called Perpetuem, made by Hammer Nutrition. It's a white powder consisting mostly of carbohydrates, with added protein, fat and sugar. I'd mix it into a paste with some water, which I'd keep in little bottles. I'd use two to three of these bottles on a four-hour run. I'd also suck back a couple of Hammer gels on each run. I was running with around eight litres of water in my pack's water bladder – for added weight and to keep hydrated. So, no, I never ran out of water. I used Perpetuem for quite a long time, and it was only at the beginning of 2014 that I stopped. It didn't seem to sit well in my stomach any more. I think after eight years the body said enough's enough.

With Ian's wise counsel, all the training began to pay off, and by May/June I had developed some confidence in the fact that I might just be able to finish this race. Apart from one or two blocks where I was too shattered to do the Monday-morning run, I hadn't had any major setbacks. Ian felt like we'd put in the hard yards, and mentally I was ready. My mother dropped me off at the airport. I remember feeling pretty good about the race. Or maybe I was just super-naive. I still didn't really know what I was getting myself into.

My flight there certainly brought that point home.

My limited budget meant I had to opt for the cheapest possible flights, and that meant a series of connections from Cape Town that took in Joburg, Dubai, Faisalabad and eventually Kashgar, in China. The Dubai stop was a two-day layover, and I figured I may as well get in a little desert-climate training while there. Unfortunately, my hotel was right next to a massive 12-lane highway, and the only piece of land that wasn't concrete was this grass verge in the middle of it. I literally ran for 10 kays on this lane of grass in between two six-lane highways. A little silly perhaps, but it was the only bit of trail I could find.

Faisalabad proved interesting too. Remember that Perpetuem I was telling you about? The white powder? Well, the Pakistani authorities were very interested in that ... and not because they were endurance-sport athletes. It didn't help that I also had Recoverite in my bag – a recovery drink powder that's also white.

All this was packed in my main bag, which was checked in all the way through to Kashgar, but the Pakistanis insisted, despite my pro-testations, that I couldn't wait in the transit lounge before my flight to China. I would have to get my bag out of holding in Faisalabad Airport, clear customs and then come in again through customs to catch the connecting flight. In other words, a monumental pain in the butt. I tried to explain how much easier it would be for all of us if I spent the 20-hour layover in the airport, rather than having to cart my big bag around their lovely city. They were having none of it. I'd like to say it was the language barrier, but I think they just wanted to dick me around. Besides, my protestations had only served to make them suspicious about the contents of the bag in question.

Eventually I was ushered into a small side room while some uniformed person went off to locate the offending bag from wherever it is that airports keep such in-transit items. And so, my small packets of white powder were discovered. It was only then that I realised what it could all mean.

Initially they wanted to prod and poke holes in the packets – ones that I'd carefully prepared for each stage. I was like, 'Whoa! No, no, no, let me open it.' I was trying to explain to them that it was a nutritional supplement for running, but it was all going way over their heads. Plus, adhering strictly to Customs Official Rule No. 5, they were trying to make me feel as uncomfortable as possible.

I was starting to get a little bit worried.

Eventually I grabbed some of the powder and put it in my mouth, trying to gesticulate that it was for energy (but not *that* kind of energy). One official then tasted a little bit too – which probably isn't in the Customs Official Rulebook – but, happily, the light bulbs seemed to go on, and they realised I wasn't transporting high-grade heroin. There was a bit of a laugh – more of the nervous kind coming from me – and they let me close the bag up ... and then *still* kicked me out of the airport. I had to sit outside on my bag, being hassled by millions of people, until my flight to Kashgar.

Kashgar – not a city known for its beauty. Situated in north-west China, it's right on the Mongolian border, and it feels and looks like a total throwback to communist Russia *circa* 1970. I'd travelled a bit, but nothing quite prepared me for this. As I'd arrived on the Wednesday and we didn't have to meet with the race organisers until the Friday, there was some time to kill and I figured I may as well take in some of the local culture. I wandered into a market and slowly began to realise that the only thing you could buy was various bits of animal. Not a place I would suggest you stroll through if you're an animal lover or a vegetarian – some of the stuff I saw in that market made my stomach turn. They were also betting on fights between what looked like a hedgehog and a scorpion. Obviously my money was on the hedgehog.

I went on a couple of small training runs – 10-kilometre loops – both to keep my legs loose and because I find it's the best way to discover or explore a new city. It gives you a real feeling for what a city's about (even if some of it, like that market, turns out to be a little disturbing), and you experience first-hand interaction with the locals. Mostly, though, I spent the time hanging out in my hotel room. I'd go online or read. I was reading one of Dean Karnazes's books – he's one of the legends of ultra-distance running, someone whom I'd long admired, and of course he very kindly wrote a foreword for this book. In 2007, *Time* magazine named him as one of the top 100 most influential people. I also slept a lot. I wasn't sure how much sleep I'd be getting during the race, so I figured I may as well stockpile while I could.

The Olympics were being held in Beijing, China, that year, and the day before the Gobi March started, the Olympic torch procession came through Kashgar. And even that turned out to be something of a weird experience. The hotel's management stuck notes under the doors warning us to keep our curtains closed, and not to look out any windows when the procession came past. The Chinese military had snipers on the lookout, as apparently there might be anti-government agents looking to disrupt proceedings. If we peeped out a window, we might get shot. I thought it highly unlikely a potential terrorist would be staying in the best hotel in town, but the Chinese soldiers didn't seem to be the types interested in my thoughts and opinions on military paranoia, so I never asked.

Besides, I had other, more pressing issues on my mind: my inaugural ultra-distance trail race. We registered on the Friday evening, and it was the first time to get an idea of the other athletes. I was obviously a total unknown, so no one paid me any attention. There were some names I recognised – a few athletes from Hong Kong and China, plus the guys who had come first and second at the Atacama Crossing earlier in the year (the race I'd originally wanted to enter). The runner who came second was Welshman Rob James, and the guy who came first was none other than … Dean Karnazes.

I'd like to say it didn't faze me much, but it was pretty intimidating. On the Saturday morning, everyone had a big breakfast together and it was then that the butterflies really set in. It was a four-hour trip in a 15-bus convoy to the start, where we'd kick off on the Sunday morning, and I remember watching the remnants of civilisation slowly disappearing as we entered the desert. The last thing we saw was this massive graveyard. It brought the point home just how unknown the territory was – geographically, physically and mentally – that I was heading into.

But now it was time to focus on myself. Sure, there were some big names around me, but I had put in the training and I just needed to zone in on doing the best I could. In the back of my mind I was hoping for a top-20 finish, but I wasn't aiming to beat any particular athletes. I just wanted to get to the finish line as quickly as possible. If that was good enough for a top-20 position, then great.

I did make one crucial, Spanish-flavoured mistake, though. Once the buses arrived at the start camp, we were assigned to a 10-man tent that we would share with the same competitors for the entire race. I was assigned to one occupied by eight Spaniards – all of them really good mates and all of whom snored like a herd of Iberian bulls. For the whole night. That, and the fact that I had thought the Gobi Desert would be sandy, so I hadn't bothered packing a sleeping mat for what turned out to be one big rock field, meant I barely slept a wink that first night. The nerves didn't help either.

I woke up the next morning with legs like jelly and feeling nauseous – I couldn't even eat breakfast – and doubts creeping around inside my head. I'd spent around R60 000 on this race – money I could've used for a two-month holiday surfing and partying with my mates in Indonesia. Was this what I wanted to do?

For the opening 40-kilometre stage there was a bit of pomp and ceremony from the local community. The mayor made a speech, and there was a parade and drum beating while local horsemen galloped around in full traditional regalia, which all meant that by the time the starting gun went off, it was quite late – around 9 a.m.

Predictably, some guys went flying off in front, but I just stuck to my rhythm and began ticking off the checkpoints. Initially I was quite far back, but I slowly started picking guys off. I even passed Dean. I think it was quite early on, and we ran together for a few kays before I pushed on. That was quite a cool feeling, a nice little confidence builder, so I kept up my pace. Not too quick, but I was feeling pretty relaxed and strong.

I had no idea where I was in the field until I got to the last checkpoint, around eight kilometres from the finish. The medical crew asked me how I was feeling – I gave them the thumbs up – and they almost casually mentioned that I was in second place. Cue wide eyes. I was hoping for a top 20, maybe sneak into the top 10, but this was a proper surprise. And that's when the adrenalin and my competitiveness kicked in full blast.

The guy in first place was only about four minutes ahead, and for me that meant game on. I started running hard. Not the smartest thing to do on Day 1 of a very long race, but the red mist came down and I didn't care ... I wanted that stage win.

The guy leading was the appropriately named Chinese hard man, Stone Tsang. I'd heard of him – he does a lot of the mountain races and was one of the favourites. With three kays to go, I came over this horizon and saw him up ahead. He wasn't happy – bad cramps. He even asked me for some help and pointed to the top compartment of his backpack. That's where he kept his salt tablets, and he wanted me to get them out so he didn't have to stop running.

A little cheeky perhaps, asking the guy who is about to pass you for help, but I could see Stone was done, so I helped out. And then put the hammer down. I remember looking behind me and there was no one in sight, and then looking up ahead to the cliffs and seeing the race village. There was about one kay to go and I knew I had it in the bag. It was super-emotional. I don't often express my feelings, but there were tears running down my face. Relief was part of it, but also thinking back to all the training I'd done and all the people who had told me I was mad to enter. This was a pretty powerful confirmation of my self-belief and determination.

Obviously I was on a complete high afterwards. There were some interviews and word spread around the race camp that I had won the stage, so I was getting a lot of congrats. There were a few other South Africans in the race, and one of them – Paul Liebenberg – and I got on particularly well, and we'd become fairly good friends over the next couple of races. Paul came over and had a chat with me – he'd had a fair amount of experience of these multiday races, and he helped me out a lot during the rest of the race.

Yes – the rest of the race. There was still a way to go, and I had no idea whether I'd overcooked it by finishing guns blazing. The camp was small and there was a lot of talk going around about my out-of-the-blue result. I heard from Paul that a lot of the guys reckoned I wasn't going to finish Day 2.

One individual who certainly wasn't even going to start Day 2 was some Canadian chap who came in about seventh, finishing like he was doing a 10-kilometre time trial. Clearly, his mission had been to beat Dean, which he had done by basically sprinting the last few kilometres. At the finish he was going ballistic – completely pumped and loud-mouthing his achievement. Twenty minutes later, he wasn't feeling too well, and was going to lie down. Next thing, I saw the whole medical team rushing to his tent. He'd started convulsing. Apparently he had got his nutrition completely wrong during the race, only drinking water and not taking any additional food. His muscles had basically started eating each other. It was serious. He was on the verge of renal failure and it was touch-and-go for a few hours. Fortunately, the medics stabilised him, and he was taken back to a hospital in Kashgar, where he recovered after a couple of days.

That freaked me out properly. I did not want to be that guy.

Still, I slept a little better that second night. My Spanish compadres continued to snore up a storm, but I was pretty knackered. Determined to keep it real, I started Day 2 with zero expectations. The previous day's win was rad, but I was still heading off into the unknown. After the first checkpoint, I started to feel a bit better and kind of picked it up. For most of the time, I was running in the top 10, and by the time we got to the final checkpoint, there were only three of us in the lead group.

We got to a bit of climb and the other guys just seemed to have nothing left in the tank, so I made a bit of a move to see if I could pull away. No one followed me. Again, my adrenalin started pumping and suddenly the prospect of two wins was on the cards. It was balls-to-the-wall time, and I ran as hard as I could to the finish. Amazingly, I had won another stage!

I remember waking up on Day 3 feeling really stiff and sore, but within 10 kays I started to get some life back into the legs. The one easy thing about the Gobi March – if you can even say that – is that it's not the most mountainous of routes. There's probably only about 2000 metres of climbing over the entire race, but it does have its own unique challenges. One of which was trying to work out where the actual route was. In theory, it's staked out by these little pink flags every 100 metres or so, but when you got to the sections close to a local village, you'd see the kids waving the same little pink flags. They'd obviously pulled them out of the ground and, while they meant to be all encouraging and supportive, we didn't know where the hell to go. I'd run past them shouting for directions, but no one understood a word and they'd just smile and wave. Competitors would inevitably get lost, and on more than one occasion I had to circle twice around some village before I figured out which direction I should be heading.

Those villages were a surreal experience. They're literally out in the middle of nowhere, really basic set-ups, except they all had these massive satellite dishes on the roofs. How they even powered them I don't know, but it's progress, I guess, and it couldn't help but make me feel a little sad. As much as it does help us, development was also screwing up the world. And there I was, employed by a property-development company, running through a very remote community and not being happy with what I was seeing. Surreal. Ironic.

The 38 kilometres of the third stage followed the by-now familiar pattern. I'd start conservatively and then work my way through to the front of the field. This time, though, I was involved in a sprint to the finish with a Chilean. There was no need for it – he was pretty far behind overall, but I couldn't help myself.

I remember getting to the last checkpoint and one of the officials saying there was 'only five to go'. Thinking he meant five kays, I filled up only one of my water bottles – but, of course, he meant five miles, so for the last few kays I had no more water. The finish was also at the top of a peak, and those remaining kilometres took longer than I expected. The Chilean guy – Juan Encina – caught up with me with about two kays to go and overtook me ... but I hung on. We were neck and neck for the last 300 metres, gunning it at full pace. We crossed the line together, both of us dipping, Usain Bolt–style. Pretty stupid, given the race we were doing, but, hey, it's what guys do. I was given the win – it must've been by a ball hair – but I was happy to take it.

The other competitors were treating me a lot differently now. I wasn't this young gun cruising onto the scene, only to blow out after Day 2. I was also suddenly getting a ton of support messages from all over the world. My daily blog post on the 4 Deserts website received some amazing comments.

What wasn't so amazing, however, was how I was beginning to smell. As it was a self-supported race, I had to carry everything I needed for the full seven days in a pack that I would run with. And that meant packing as light as possible. A nice fresh pair of shorts and shirt to put on each day was not an option. One set would have to do. And you couldn't wash them. At the end of each stage, you'd get a ration of water that was enough to cook the dehydrated food you were carrying and to rehydrate your body. They were really strict with water.

It was mandatory to take two shirts, but I would run in the one and sleep in the other – at least that way I had a semi-clean one to sleep in. My running shirt, on the other hand, could literally stand up by itself after the second day. It was lightweight, breathable synthetic fibre, which got encrusted with salt.

For the first time in my life, I had had to think really carefully about what kit I was going to use. I needed apparel that was comfortable, durable and light. That last quality was particularly important. I did a fair amount of research and, as one should always do, tested various items in the weeks and months leading up to the event. I was running in New Balance shoes back then, and one piece of advice I picked up online was to run in shoes one and a half to two sizes too big, as your feet swell up during a long desert race. It was the first time I've ever had a pair of shoes that were too big for me, but the advice turned out to be spot on.

Chafing was a big issue too, and even though I was running in thigh-length lycra tights, I still had a big tub of petroleum jelly with me to make sure I didn't end up with raw skin where you definitely don't want it.

But, yes, the smell was the worst.

The Gobi March is not an event to attract the opposite sex. Especially on the last day. I'm sure I smelt pretty horrendous after Day 3 and 4, but you grow used to the smell and you tend not to notice it. By Day 6, however, even your own stink is inescapable. That's the rest day after the long Day 5 and before Day 7's shortish run to the finish. You're sitting around the race village and everyone stinks to high heaven. But by then I was like, 'Okay ... enough already. Let's get this done and get the hell out of here.'

With that attitude in mind, I won the fourth stage as well – by about two or three minutes. It was another 40-kilometre stage and this time there was no sprint finish or anything like that, thank goodness. By Day 4 I was starting to feel pretty good. The soreness and stiffness I had felt at the beginning had gone. This is a common thing in multiday endurance sport. It would always be like that for me in the subsequent races I ran, and I know from my wife, Vanessa, who's done two Cape Epic mountain-bike races, that she and her fellow competitors in that race feel the same. Day 1 you're usually quite fresh, but Day 2 and 3 are always the worst. By Day 4 your body just seems to get into it and you kind of settle into a groove.

While we're on the subject, remember to not totally take your foot off the gas in the week leading up to a multiday race. You don't want to rest up and do nothing. After all the training you've done, your body has got used to running, riding or paddling at least every day. Stop completely for anything longer than three or four days, and it is going to think it's time to switch off and rest. In the week leading up to the big race, rather do a few short, slow efforts and then, the day before, a quick little higher-intensity activation run. This keeps your body sharp and focused. I've seen guys do all the right training and then make the mistake of resting up for five days before, and having a total nightmare on Day 1.

On Day 4, everyone was running fairly conservatively, given what awaited us on Day 5. That was the race's queen stage – around 80 kilometres, and it's where the Gobi March would be won or lost. I was feeling pretty good after Day 4, which was more than I could say for the Spaniards ...

The group snoring had got so bad that they were actually starting to fight among themselves, punching one another and throwing shoes around in the middle of the night to shut the other person up. Even I was getting in on the action. The altitude makes you get up to pee in the middle of the night, and I'd make sure to walk past the guy who was snoring the loudest and give him a little bit of a kick, so that he turned over and stopped the chainsaw. One word of advice: If you're ever staying in a tented race village, pack earplugs. You won't believe how much snoring, farting and talking in your sleep goes on.

Day 5 began with a very early start. We had to be up at 4 a.m. for a bus trip of one and a half hours to get us from the camp to where the stage would start. I was feeling good, but the wait was pretty nerve-wracking. They also staggered the start for this long stage with the slower guys setting off first and the faster guys last, so everyone goes through the checkpoints at the same time and they have to keep some of them open all day.

That meant I only started four or five hours after the front guys had gone. The pressure was definitely starting to build now. I had gone from being a nobody to actually being able to win this flippin' thing. Paul helped a lot to keep me in the right frame of mind. He told me to keep doing what I'd done every day – to take it easy and not do anything rash. If I blew up on the long stage, my seven-minute lead meant nothing. Chatting to him, with a couple of Afrikaans words thrown in here and there, made me feel a lot more at home in this very foreign environment. Still, I'd never run 80 kays before. Plus, we'd also be running in the real heat of the day, which, in the Gobi, was around 3 to 4 p.m. – a time I'd usually be finishing the other stages.

A group of 30 of us started in the final batch, and my plan was to try to stick to whoever was at the front and not let them get too far ahead. Encina, the Chilean, took off hard, and initially I hung with Tsang, who was in second place overall. But my 18-minute lead over Encina, who was in third, could disappear if I let him get too far ahead, so I took off too. I caught him after about 30 kays or so, and suddenly it was game on. We started racing quite hard, mostly because he was trying his best to drop me. He must have figured that this long day was his big chance, and on some downhills we must've been running under four minutes a kay. He would take off and I would sit behind him, and then on the flats I'd try to surge ahead. It was proper backwards and forwards stuff the whole time – obviously a stupid waste of energy.

I started to feel it too. I remember getting to around 50 kilometres and not feeling great at all. I was determined not to let slip, though – I would fall down dead before I gave up. And, fortunately, that's when I discovered my latent ultra-distance-race mojo – that zone where nothing else matters but winning. Nothing. After all the messages of encouragement I'd received, I felt like I was representing my country and I wasn't going to let anyone down.

At about the 55-kilometre mark, Encina started to slow down – thankfully, because I was starting to seriously overheat. I don't think I had been drinking and eating enough. It was only later on that I worked out that pouring water over your head, the back of the neck and your upper body really cools you down.

By the 60-kilometre checkpoint I was completely out of it. As soon as I stopped running, everything started to spin. The medical crew were talking to us and I had to hold onto one of the gazebo's poles. I kept looking down at my bottles, worried that they would pull me out of the race. My vision was a bit blurry and my thoughts even more so. I avoided any more medics, filled up my water bottles and took off.

Encina was still following me. By now it was so unbelievably hot and I was so knackered that I didn't know if I was going to manage another 10 metres or fall over and collapse. Whatever happened, I wasn't going to stop. Eventually, Encina dropped off a bit ... but then, out of the corner of my eye, I saw Stone Tsang come up my shoulder. That really rocked me. Here I was in a really bad state, feeling super-nauseous and on the verge of puking – and my closest rival was about to trot past me.

Somehow I hung on. This was new territory for me. I was pushing past mental boundaries I didn't even know existed. I didn't think it was possible to run for another 10 metres. But I did. You just keep doing it. Focusing on the next 10 seconds. It's pretty scary looking back at it now – I kind of get angry thinking I was basically prepared to die out there to win a race. Why? But in that situation, at that time, it made perfect sense.

Fortunately, I didn't die. In fact, I started to feel a bit better. The ambient temperature dropped a little, and I managed to pull myself together. Arriving at the last checkpoint just as Stone Tsang was leaving, I caught him with five kays to go. We ran together for a while and then, with a few kays left, I could see it was now his turn to hit the wall; he was really battling. I upped my pace, pulled away and won the stage!

Cue massive relief. I hadn't just won the stage and probably the race ... I had survived.

I remember just lying there at the finish line – it must've been for over an hour – feeling incredibly nauseous and with a massive headache. I couldn't get anything down and was really concerned that the medics would have to put me on a drip, which would've meant a time penalty, so I went to lie down behind the tents where no one could see me. After an hour and a half, I managed to drink something, and later I had a little soup. I had a rough night's sleep, getting cold sweats, and couldn't eat anything until the next morning at breakfast. It wasn't until the Leadville Trail 100 Run in 2011 that I would push myself that close to the limit again.

Fortunately, Day 6 was a rest day for everyone, with the final stage being a short 10-kilometre run. Like the Tour de France, whoever was leading after the penultimate stage pretty much has it in the bag, providing there's no major disasters. People were already congratulating me, and Stone Tsang, Juan Encina and I decided to run the final stage together.

Again, they staggered the start, and when we crossed the finish line in some little village, all the competitors had already finished and were there to congratulate us. In the end I had beaten Tsang by 31 minutes and Encina by 41 minutes. The South Africans and I shared a couple of beers and some proper food, which was pretty cool. After a week of eating horrible freeze-dried meals, ProNutro, Perpetuem and Recover-ite, it tasted like the best food in the world.

The joy of winning, rather annoyingly, quickly dissipated and the real world intruded once again. I knew that would inevitably happen, but I didn't quite anticipate it would happen on the bus trip back to Kashgar. It was a long trip, and for the first hour everyone on the bus was making loads of noise, and my head was still spinning with what had happened to me over the past week. But after a while it quietened down as people tried to catch up on some sleep, and I remember staring out of the window feeling super-stoked. Then, I felt this massive emptiness set in. I'd spent the last six months training for this race, and it had filled up most of my head space. What now?

There was one thing that, at least temporarily, kept my existential crisis at bay – Faisalabad. Yup, before I could share my unexpected triumph with friends and family back home, and figure out my future, I still had one more challenge to face: I had to go through Faisalabad again. Except this time I had a one-day layover, which meant I had to find a hotel.

I had to go through the usual song and dance with my mates at the airport. This time their customs comedy crew wanted to confiscate my trophy, but I was so proud of this thing, there was no chance I was going to give it up. Besides, you don't get any prize money for winning any of the 4 Desert Series races, which made this trophy especially valuable.

Hello, world! As a baby with my mom and dad

With my grandfather, Nick, and grandmother, Sheila. They lived around the corner from us, so we had a close relationship. I was their first grandchild, and they really spoilt me

On my uncle Michael's farm in Franschhoek with my grandfather, Nick, his dog Ernest, and Michael. It was the school holidays and they were harvesting grapes. I spent many hours cruising around with my grandfather in his bakkie listening to his old war stories

What do you think of my running kit? My dad's Red Hill Marathon medal is around my neck and the club licence is half pinned to my side. This was my first taste of 'winning' a big race – or at least I thought so in my head. I insisted that my mom take this photo of me

With my aunt Juliet, my mom's sister. She had just got back from New York and was dating a guy called Chris, who was in a rock band. In my eyes she was super cool. To this day I still have that leather jacket I was wearing … maybe when I hit 40, I will join a band

On our smallholding in Hout Bay, where I grew up. My mom, sister and my mom's horse Storm, who was basically her third child. My mom arranged to have these professional photos done, but I hated every minute of it. Look at my cool haircut! I finally got rid of it in Standard 7 and got the nickname 'Hedgie' with my shorter, spikey hair

My final high-school rugby game, for SACS's first team vs SACS Old Boys. I have so many memories of that field

At Cape Town International Airport with John Barker-Goldie, about to depart on a gap year that included a ski season in Aspen, USA. We thought we were bulletproof and life was good. I was homesick two days later

KNYSNA FOREST MARATHON 2006

My first marathon. This was about three kilometres into the race on the first little climb. I guess this is where it all started

With Vanessa and Jonty Rhodes just before the Featherbed trail run. I had met Vanessa two days earlier and we decided to run one of the Featherbed races together. It went a little slower than I was used to, but I spent a lot of time following Vanessa, admiring her stride

With Vanessa just before the 2011 Laureus Awards in Abu Dhabi. It was a pretty surreal experience, and just a few seconds before the photo was taken, we were walking up the red carpet with some of the biggest sporting names imaginable. I was shitting myself, as I had to do a live interview with Kevin Spacey during the ceremony

She is a keeper. Recce'ing the Fish River Canyon with Vanessa before my 2012 record attempt. We fought over her sleeping mat at night, as I was too hardcore to take a mat and ended up wanting to share hers

It's the small things in life that count. Thandi and I won the five-kilometre K9 Search & Rescue Association's fundraiser race. I am not sure who was more stoked, her or I. This will go down as one of my more special race victories. Our rosette is still on the fridge

© Craig Kolesky

The 2012 Pre-Salomon Skyrun on Balloch Farm with Thandi, aka T-dog. I was out there preparing for the race and Ness and T-dog joined me. Thandi knows when there is a fire, she gets to eat meat. We spent 10 days on Balloch Farm and I have some epic memories of our stay

Post–Big Bay park run with two of my heroes, Elana Meyer and Bruce Fordyce. Bruce is a real character and had everyone in hysterics

Surfing in Jeffreys Bay during the 2014 Oakley X Over competition. I never imagined a 30-minute surf heat could be so tiring. So much fun, though!

© Craig Kolesky

© Anja Aucamp

With my groomsmen before the wedding: (from left to right) Frank, Sean, Ryan and John. These guys are legends. I was still feeling quite relaxed here, standing in my undies. But once I put my suit on, I started to feel a bit more nervous and started sweating

© Anja Aucamp

Our big day… We ran overtime with our photos, so I figured it would be quicker to run back to the reception through a few fields instead of driving back to the venue in our wedding car

They started shoving this state-of-the-art narcotics detector – a stick with a nail on the end – through all my running shoes. I could basically throw them away afterwards. Fortunately, they had not had access to this piece of hi-tech equipment when I passed through there the first time. And, once again, realising I still wasn't an international drug smuggler, they somewhat reluctantly let me go.

For my night in Faisalabad I'd pre-booked two hotels, thinking I'd be clever and hedge my bets in case one was a little sketchy. After all, what you see on the internet and what you get in real life are often two very different things, and I was willing to bet this especially applied to Faisalabad accommodation. Walking out of the airport building in my spongier-than-usual running shoes, I hailed a taxi and instructed the driver to go to hotel number one. No, no, he said. Very sadly, that one had closed down. I then pointed him to hotel number two. Very tragically, and somewhat coincidentally, that one had burnt down only very recently. However, there was this one hotel that he could strongly recommend. Right. Obviously he was getting a kickback or something from this establishment but, being tired and just wanting a room, I went with the flow.

Unfortunately for him, he drove right past hotel number one – it was a Holiday Inn, I think – which I immediately recognised, and I made him stop.

I can't see myself going to Faisalabad on holiday any time soon.

STUFF I'VE LEARNT

One grain of sand ... and one training session at a time

For the Gobi, I did some training in the Hout Bay sand dunes. On a Tuesday and a Thursday I would do some short repeats up and down the dunes. After one particular session, sitting there and getting my breath back, it struck me how much the dunes would change from one week to the next. I'd watch the wind blow a few grains of sand in front of me, and then when I returned the next week, the whole dune would've changed shape and moved.

One grain of sand at a time leads to the whole dune completely shifting. This was the mantra I took to the Gobi Desert race. Being my first race, at times the whole thing felt completely overwhelming. Two weeks into my training with Ian, I felt so tired I didn't know if I was coming or going, and I still had another big week of training to go. It felt like a massive mountain I could never climb.

Thinking back to those grains of sand helped, though. It helped to break it all down into small steps and just focus on getting through one training session at a time. I tried to block the rest out of my mind and maintain my focus on the moment. Small steps – one grain of sand at a time. Basic Psychology 101, sure, but it works.

Training for Gobi

I was using a five-week cycle that was based on the following approach:

Week 1	
Monday	Rest day
Tuesday double sesh	Morning: steady run for 1 hour
	Evening: more of a quality run – 6 x 1 km repeats (10 x 1 km if I was feeling energetic) If I wasn't up for this – and until I turned pro, that was fairly often – I'd just do an ordinary run.

Wednesday	Low-intensity, easy 45-minute run
Thursday double sesh	Morning: again, a steady run for 1 hour
	Evening: more quality, so hill repeats or other shorter stuff based on time – 1 minute hard, 2 minutes easy
Friday	Rest day
Saturday	Long, steady run with race gear and a heavy backpack
Sunday	Same as Saturday, but about 70% of the distance

Weeks 2 and 3

The training is the same as for Week 1, except to up the intensity and distance a little as you get fitter.

It should be sufficient to do 90 minutes in the evening session on Tuesdays and Thursdays, and up the weekend distance runs to around 5 hours for the Saturday run.

Week 4

This would include the dreaded four-day block:

Monday	Rest day
Tuesday double sesh	Morning: steady run for 1 hour
	Evening: 6 x 1 km repeats (10 x 1 km if I was feeling energetic)
Wednesday	Low-intensity, easy 45-minute run
Thursday	Rest day
Friday	Long, steady 3-hour run
Saturday	Long, steady 4.5-hour run
Sunday	Long, steady 5-hour run
Monday	Long, steady 2.5-hour (sometimes 3-hour) run

Week 5
This would be a recovery week:

Tuesday	Rest day
Wednesday	Rest day
Thursday	Rest day
Friday	Very gentle run
Saturday	Little longer run, with some quality stuff
Sunday	Same as Saturday

It was only after the Sahara Race that I started consistently doing the quality runs – intervals and hill repeats – so don't beat yourself up if you don't have the time or are sometimes too tired to do them.

How to run in sand (but be careful not to pick up bad habits)

Running in sand is an art, and it's as much about your head as it is about your feet.

The head part

You've got to be super-relaxed. You can't fight it. It's almost like swimming against the current. If you fight it, you're going to get fatigued pretty quickly. You've just got to go with the flow and try not to resist it.

Stay relaxed and accept that every now and again your foot is going to slide backwards, and you're going to have to run an extra two steps to make up for the ground you've lost.

The actual technique

You need to shorten your stride and kind of shuffle a bit more. To get more grip and contact area with the sand, it also helps to adjust the angle of your foot's contact with the sand. You need to be more duck-footed, if you know what I mean.

The downside

Run too often in sand with a pack on your back – like I did in those first few years – and you begin to develop some bad habits. Your running form suffers. Apart from running too duck-footed – good for sand, bad for actual trail – the addition of the pack means you tend to run with your weight further back. You run very open-chested and with your ribs flared, whereas it's more efficient on a firm surface to run with your weight further forward and your core muscles more engaged.

4

AND MORE SAND

Looking back at it now from the perspective of a professional athlete, that Gobi race was the key to it all. To be even more specific, it was all about Day 1. That first stage made me realise what I was capable of – it spurred me on and allowed me to push as hard as I did during the long Day 5 stage. If I hadn't won Gobi, I wouldn't have got sponsorship to do the Sahara race. If I hadn't done Sahara, I wouldn't have spent as much time as I did with Dean Karnazes running through that North African desert. And if I hadn't done that and got the advice I did, I probably would not have become a full-time athlete. So, yes, winning Gobi was key.

The other thing about Gobi was how spot on all my training and prep had been. Through some planning, but mostly through fluke, I had somehow managed to do everything the experts now recommend as preparation for an ultra-distance endurance race. I did all the right research, I got there a week beforehand, I spent a lot of time on my own and I didn't eat any dodgy food. Somehow I just seemed to get in the mindset – it just came automatically. Speak to a coach now and they're, like, oh, you've got to get there a week before the race ... you've got to do this ... you have to do that. Somehow, for Gobi, I managed to get it all right. I had a plan. I trained. And I executed. Now all I had to do was apply that strategy to the rest of my life.

Getting back home was a bit of a comedown after all the drama of the Gobi. Not surprisingly, life back here seemed a little mundane. I even began to miss my customs-official mates in Faisalabad. My family and friends were obviously stoked that I had won – a little gobsmacked too, obviously – and I was given a massive welcome when I got back home. The win also generated a fair amount of interest from the South African media – probably more than any other trail race or athlete had achieved. The local newspapers ran stories, and the main running magazine – *Runner's World* – did a feature on me. Obviously, it wasn't like winning an Olympic gold medal or something that changes your life overnight, but I was definitely getting some recognition.

My work colleagues at Faircape took a little more notice of me as well, but they were still a little bemused by it all. 'Why the hell would you want to do something like that?' and 'What are you running from, bru?' were the commonly posed questions-slash-attempted humour. They were chuffed for me too, though, and my big boss, Mike Vietri, the MD and founder of Faircape, loved it when I mentioned the company in some of the press interviews.

Then this germ of an idea began to form ...

Spending some time with Dean Karnazes during Gobi, and after reading his book and seeing what he had achieved, made me realise that nothing is impossible. It wasn't like I thought I could now definitely do this on a full-time basis – that would happen after the Sahara Race – but the cogs definitely started turning.

There I was, four days after winning a major international race, back in the office sitting in a meeting and getting crapped on because I was behind with all my work. It was weird. The week before I was on the other side of the planet living this nomadic existence in the desert, and now I was feeling the pressures of a nine-to-five corporate job. 'Back to reality,' as they say.

Don't get me wrong, there's nothing wrong with a nine-to-five job – even as a pro athlete, that's essentially still my work ethic – but it needed to be a nine-to-five job that I loved and was passionate about. Making someone else happy wasn't what I wanted to do with my life. I just didn't have the same desire, focus and drive with this career path that I once had. Granted, I never really had much of it to start with, but by now even *that* had left the building.

I wasn't hating my job, but it was a typical corporate environment, which meant that if you wanted to get ahead, you had to put in the long hours. I wanted to put in long hours and get ahead – just not in construction.

For a week or so it didn't look like it would be in trail running either.

After getting back from the Gobi, all my mates at Hout Bay Harriers wanted to run with me and, after conquering a 250-kilometre desert race, I was feeling pretty good. At least, I thought I was. So I entered the Hout Bay Trail Challenge. It did not go well. The race is one of the oldest trail runs in South Africa and circumnavigates the mountains around Hout Bay. It's a tough event – around 35 kilometres long with 1 800 metres of climbing.

The wheels came off early on. There's me thinking, 'Phhht ... 35 kays is a walk in the park after Gobi', but going up the first climb – Karbonkelberg – I could feel I had nothing in my legs. It's not like I could hide either: news had spread that I was running, and I remember being in the lead pack when one of the guys asked, 'So where's this Ryan Sandes guy?' I had to pipe up and say hello. By the time we got to the Llandudno ravine, I was in real trouble. I simply did not have the legs and my race went completely pear-shaped. So, yes ... that did not bode well for making this my career.

Fortunately, I was also hearing talk that I was this one-hit wonder who'd fluked a win at the Gobi March thanks to luck and a weak field. Nothing like a little trash talk behind my back to get my motivation levels up! Next on the 4 Deserts calendar was the Sahara Race – another seven-day, six-stage, 250-kilometre race through the hottest and sandiest desert on the planet. A good result there should shut them up. Besides, I'd always wanted to see the pyramids.

To enter and start in Cairo, however, would take money – something of which I had very little after Gobi. Fortunately, my uncle Michael – my mom's brother – came to my rescue. His company, Cape Kingdom, not only sponsored my entry fee, but publicist Kelly Burke, who was doing some work for them, also began to help me out. A lot more people now began to know about my plans.

That included my employers at Faircape Property Developers. Running was front and centre now. I would leave work at 5 p.m. on the button, whereas most of the guys would be there until 7 p.m. My success at Gobi meant that my direct boss, Andrew Slingsby, was quite lenient with me as far as work hours went. I'd sometimes also come in late after a morning training session. But one of the directors, Stephen Frankel, got a little irate from time to time, especially if I was behind on my admin. I'd be heading out the office before anyone else, and I'd see Steve look at his watch and say, 'Hey, where are you going? It's payments – are all your payments done?'

'No,' I'd say, looking a little sad, 'but I've got to run.'

He'd lose his shit, but there was nothing he could do, as Andrew had let me go. Sorry about that, Steve. I feel a little bad about that now. You guys were good to me, and I do appreciate it.

I was starting to close the door on Faircape – and no doubt they were doing the same on me – but my Gobi success had begun to open a few new ones. One of them led into the office of Professor Tim Noakes. South Africa's world-renowned expert in sports medicine and training allowed me to use the facilities of the Sports Science Institute of South Africa, of which he is a co-founder.

They had an environmental chamber – a room with a treadmill, in which they could control the heat and humidity. In return for my being allowed to use it, his team would conduct some tests on me. Fair trade, I thought. A little piece of hell it may have been, but it was a massive help to my training programme. It was winter and running in the Cape's wet, 12 to 15 °C climate wasn't ideal preparation for a race in a dry desert, where the temperature – even in November (which is autumn there), when the race was held – would be around 40 °C and higher.

The sessions in that room were pretty brutal. They lasted anywhere between 40 minutes and two hours, during which I'd do my slow-broiled hamster impression, running on the treadmill and staring at the wall in front of me. As good as the physical training was, though, the mental prep was even better. As I'd discover, running in the dry desert heat is suffocating – like you're running with a paper bag over your head – but by the time I got to the starting line in Egypt, I was ready for it and at peace with the conditions I would face.

What I wasn't ready for was the rubber glove and anal thermometer. Yes ... the part of Prof. Noakes's job that doesn't get talked about much. His team were interested in my core temperature, and initially presented me with said probe. I politely declined. Luckily for all involved, they got hold of a capsule-sized device that I could swallow, which would then transmit all the data they needed.

Other than that, I was still following my coach Ian Waddell's training programme, though by now I was a little more used to those four-day blocks. One area I did step up was the quality days, where I did hill repeats or interval sessions. For Gobi, I'd often be too knackered after the block days, so I'd skip them. For Sahara, though, I was able to get in plenty more.

I did some sand training as well, but not too much. Certainly no more than I did for Gobi (which, ironically, turned out to have very little in the way of actual sand). I would do the odd run in the Hout Bay sand dunes and on Noordhoek Beach. Because the sand works your legs a lot, and given the high mileage I was doing, Ian had warned me that I was in danger of picking up some injuries. Because of that I'd do only a couple of key sessions in the sand. During four-day block weekends, for example, I would do only half the day's run on the sand. I'd run from Hout Bay, over Chapman's Peak to Noordhoek, run up and down Noordhoek Beach a couple of times, and then head back home over Chappies to Hout Bay.

It was pretty hectic at work in the week before I left for Cairo – there was a lot to sort out before I could walk out the door. Fortunately, once in Cairo, I had three days on my own, which always helps me to get into my head space and do all the pre-race prep I need.

My first few hours in Cairo were, however, very far from that head space. What a mental city! Seriously. The traffic is nuts. Just the drive from the airport to the hotel totally freaked me out. The traffic jams are epic, and everyone is driving through the alleyways and narrow streets trying to find a short cut. My driver's tactic was simply to push pedestrians out of the way. Look, he did it fairly gently, but still. We even saw one guy attempt what could only have been suicide – either that, or he figured he was safer out of the car than inside it. He jumped out of a moving taxi and began running into oncoming traffic. Cars were hooting and swerving all over the show, people were swearing … just general mayhem. In terms of traffic, Cairo was the worst I'd ever seen. It really made me appreciate home.

There was definitely more pressure going into this event. I was now a bona fide favourite and I could feel the crosshairs on my back. I now also had a sponsor, and they needed to see a return of some kind on their investment. Then there was that 'one-hit wonder' tag with which I'd been labelled in some quarters back home. And it didn't help that on a gentle training run through Cairo I somehow tweaked one hammie, and right up to the start it was feeling pretty tight and sore.

Day 1 started just outside Cairo – about an hour's bus trip – and, much to my relief, right from the gun I felt pretty good. My hammie wasn't bothering me and, with the experience of Gobi under my belt, I had more of a plan. By now I'd worked out that with a multiday race, it's best to get a good lead on Day 1. It sets you up for the rest of the race and allows you to then run with your nearest competitor and, if he blows up, push on and put more time on him.

It was quite chilly at the start – 8 or 9 °C – but it warmed up pretty quickly and, within the space of half an hour, it was in the high 20s. By the time the stage was over, it would be above 40 °C. I think the highest recorded temperature during the race was 48 °C.

I ran with a couple of guys for the first five kays after the start, but then decided to put my head down and go for it. My hammie was feeling okay, and for most of the 38-kilometre stage I was out on my own, managing the heat well, thanks to that chamber of hell back at the Sports Science Institute. Not all the guys were handling it, though. They were okay for the first 20 kays, when the racing was quite tight, but in the second half of the stage, the heat got to them and they just fell apart.

I won't bore you with too much detail on each stage, but basically my strategy worked a treat. I won the first stage comfortably – and every stage after that. I coped well with the heat and sand, and a couple of extra items in my race kit – a cap with a neck flap, gaiters over my ankles and shoes to keep the sand out – helped a lot. I did get a few blisters during the race, as the heat makes your feet swell, but that wasn't too much of an issue. After having walked around barefoot for most of my life, my feet are naturally pretty tough.

Unlike those of some other competitors. By Day 4, they wouldn't allow film crews in the medic tent any more. It was just getting too disgusting – people's feet were a mess. After the next 4 Deserts race I would do, in the Atacama, a local airline wouldn't let a whole bunch of competitors onto the return flight. They were turned away by the ground staff, who told them that their bloody and swollen feet were not allowed on board. Apparently, they had to wait in Chile for an extra week.

Mentally, it's quite taxing to be out there running on your own for the 40-odd kays of each of those first four stages. I'd look back and there'd be no one behind me and nothing in front – you're just following these pink flags dotted among the white sand all around as far as the eye can see. Plus, being out in front feels a bit like a hunted animal. You wonder if you're going fast enough and whether someone's catching up with you.

The sand isn't easy either. Despite all the mental prep and the training I'd done on Noordhoek Beach, it still didn't quite prepare me for the Saharan dunes. Every now and again you'd hit these hectic sand mountains where you take four paces forward and slide back two. Slow going. And then you'd be running along the ridge line of some sand dunes that looked like a knife's edge. One wrong step and you'd slide down the side.

What helped keep it real for me, though, was that I knew I was having a much easier time of it than some of the others in the field. These guys needed to draw on mental-strength reserves way deeper than I had to.

One such person was Jack Denness. This Englishman had run the legendary 135-mile Badwater Ultramarathon in California's Death

Valley. This single-stage race goes by the name of the 'World's Toughest Foot Race'. No arguments here. Now, at the age 73, Jack was running the Sahara Race. I think he had tried it before, but didn't finish. Then, in 2008, Jack made it, crossing the line in stage six after spending 63 hours and 7 minutes running through the desert. That was 33 hours longer than it took me. And all this at 73!

Jack is a real character too. He got completely boozed at the awards ceremony afterwards – the last man still sitting at his table at 1 a.m. with his pint of beer when everyone else had faded. Jack's 80 now and still running ultra-distance races. What a legend!

The one thing about an ultra-endurance race is that it will find you out if you don't put in the prep beforehand. Training only in a cold climate – even if you put in the requisite miles – will not prepare you for the desert heat. Not even close. One guy in the Sahara Race got so dehydrated that he wandered off course and the organisers had to send a 4 x 4 out into the dunes to find him. He was so out of it that he thought the race officials were part of al-Qaeda or something, and were trying to take him hostage. They had to force him into the car and sedate him because he kept trying to jump out.

Towards the end, the race village starts to look like a bit of a war zone as well. For the first two or three days some of the competitors just push too hard. Their egos get in the way and, because they've seriously undertrained and have underestimated the race, they don't pace themselves properly. The officials are always carting people off to hospital. The Jungle Marathon – we'll get into that in Chapter 5 – was the worst. The heat and humidity were unbelievable. After the first day there were guys falling out of their hammocks and convulsing.

One person who had got his training and prep spot on again was fellow Saffer Paul Liebenberg. He had a great result at the Sahara Race, finishing fifth, and Paul and I resumed the friendship we'd begun at the Gobi March. Another unlikely friendship I struck up was with two runners with whom I shared a tent during the race: Simone Bishop and Kimberly Dods, two very well-groomed women from Johannesburg. They were slow but steady runners, finishing the first two stages near the back of the field. Interestingly, they always finished the day looking tired, but exceptionally well made-up.

On Day 3 and 4 the wheels started to come off a bit, and they finished the stages looking completely broken. Both kept on complaining about how heavy their packs were starting to feel, but they never ate much, so they couldn't have been carrying too much food. Eventually Paul pulled me aside and said I'd better help them out because there was no way they'd be able to finish the 100-kilometre-long stage unless we helped lighten their packs. So I did.

In their packs there wasn't much in the way of food, but what there was made me laugh out loud. Each had a huge vanity bag filled with make-up. I was like, 'Ladies, you have to toss this stuff! Seriously.' Simone wouldn't budge, but Kimberly agreed to get rid of two of the three different types of eyeliner/mascara/lipstick she carried. To their credit, they both finished smelling and looking a lot better than I did. I've since met up with Simone at a number of races. She did Atacama and Antarctica with me, so I got to know her and her husband, Mark, pretty well.

After winning stage four, I knew that the race was probably in the bag. I just had to get through the long stage, which in this race was 100 kilometres – the longest distance I would've run up to that point. And through the desert, too. My only worry was illness. In endurance events, stomach viruses often do the rounds through a race village and you never know ... I could wake up on the morning of the long stage with hectic gastro. Fortunately, though, that didn't happen, and I was able to spend a lot of time running with the man lying in second and someone who was fast becoming a bit of a mentor: Mr Dean Karnazes. By then I had a three-hour lead, so there was little incentive for either of us to race, and the route was pretty flat too. I think we initially talked about running the first half of the day together, but we were at the front of the field so we just kept on running and chatting.

I think it was mostly me asking questions and Dean, being Dean, was only too happy to impart some of the knowledge he'd built up over the years. His advice on how to manage a potential career as a full-time athlete was particularly valuable. Through him, I was made to understand that representing your brand(s) didn't mean you just got to train, sleep and race, and then your sponsor picked up all your bills. He explained how hard he worked on that side of his career – how, for example, before the Gobi March, he had been involved in a big project with his sponsor, The North Face, which required him to do a whole bunch of roadshows across America. Not ideal prep for a 250-kilometre stage race, but still Dean was there, running. It's something he loves to do, and people love to see him doing it. Even if he wasn't in the kind of shape to win it, he was still giving The North Face the kind of positive exposure they are after.

We finished the 100 kilometres together. It was pretty cool, and something that forged an ongoing friendship. Whenever I'm on the US West Coast, I always go to San Francisco to say hi to Dean and join him for a run on his home trails.

With the long stage over, the race was definitely in the bag now. After the rest day on Day 6, all that was left was the short 10-kilometre final stage. They'd organised for us to finish at the Pyramids of Giza, which meant a long five-hour bus trip to get us within the required 10 kays of this ancient wonder. The big pyramids in the background obviously made for cool finishing shots, but to get there we first had to run this crazy route that saw us cross roads and run through alleyways. Not something I enjoyed, given my experiences with Egyptian driving habits up till that point. I remember running down an alleyway trying to find the route marker flags, and there were motorbikes bombing out of side alleys. I even had to dodge a horse at one point. It was total chaos. Guys were getting lost and running around the wrong pyramid. Looking back, it was hilarious.

Fortunately, the stage then headed back onto the sand, where the marker flags stood out more, making the route easier to follow. I crossed the finish line. I'd won again! And, this time, by a far more convincing margin. The naysayers back home would have to shut up now. Say what you like about how competitive the field was or wasn't – what you couldn't dispute was that I was becoming a better athlete.

For me, personally, the great thing about winning the Sahara Race was that it didn't leave me with that same empty feeling I had had after Gobi. There wasn't that 'now what?' vibe. I now knew what I wanted, and that was to be a professional athlete. I wanted to give it a real bash.

Dean was super-helpful throughout this whole period. In the weeks after the race we exchanged emails and he was very encouraging, talking about the potential he could see in me and how he'd love to see me tackle a 50- or 100-miler single-day race. Those events – the likes of Leadville and Western States – were the races that all the world's top ultra-distance runners dreamt of winning. It was cool to hear that from someone like Dean, and all his advice, on dealing with sponsors and establishing myself as a brand, really helped me see the bigger picture. He was such a huge inspiration, and I can never thank him enough.

I mean, we're talking about a guy who had done some track and cross country as a junior, but only really started running in his early 30s. The story goes that it was his birthday and, while getting boozed with mates, one of them dared him to run 30 miles or something like that. And he did it. He ended up running 30 miles, and had to phone his wife to come and fetch him at five in the morning. That was what started it for him. He eventually quit his well-paid job and became a full-time ultra-distance runner.

It was time for me to do the same.

After getting back home, I first spoke to my dad about my plans. He wasn't that keen on the idea to begin with. And he had a good point – the South African economy was very obviously heading into a recession, and this wasn't the smartest time to be quitting a well-paid job with promising career prospects.

We talked it through and, eventually, even though I think every bone in his body told him I shouldn't do this, he gave me his backing 100 per cent. My mom, on the other hand, was a lot easier to convince. She was all 'follow your heart, it's a great thing, live your life, live your dream', etcetera. It may have had something to do with the spirits too (my mom's a bit of a hippy). Every now and again she sees a clairvoyant, and a couple of years earlier the clairvoyant had said, 'Your son … I see a picture of him with a backpack on his back, travelling around the world.' Granted, that's a pretty safe call for any clairvoyant to make if she knows her client has a teenage son. The chances are high he'll take a gap year. And gap years tend to involve backpacks. Not that I was going to challenge this: if the clairvoyant was helping ease my transition into being a full-time trail runner, then she got the thumbs up from me.

I then spoke to Faircape, and we came to what I initially thought was a pretty good solution – I'd work half days for them. That way, I could get my training in, start to work on my sponsorships with a view to becoming a full-time pro, and still earn a salary. It sounded good in theory, but in practice it didn't work for either of us.

Being able to follow my passion for half the day meant that I was even less hassled about what happened at Faircape than ever. Whereas everyone else was running around super-busy and stressed, I was this chilled figure. Obviously, it frustrated them – it could only have. Guys like Mike and Steve are passionate about their work and putting in 110 per cent. Given what I have had to do to make my career work, I can now relate to that completely. I couldn't then, though.

I also realised that I was expected to do the same amount of work that I had been doing as a full-time employee, only now in half the time, and I was getting paid a lot less. So, after three months, in March 2009, I made the most significant decision of my career and resigned from Faircape.

Right. Cool. Time to take the plunge and go for it!

STUFF I'VE LEARNT

How to pack for a multiday race

The 4 Deserts organisers provide you with drinking water during the race and water to cook with, but that's about it. You have to carry some compulsory items: a sleeping bag, a hydration bladder, two headlamps, a multi-tool, a whistle, a survival bag, a mirror, a compass, some sunscreen, a cap, some gloves, some medical items, a warm jacket and the kit you will run in.

The rest is optional, but I would also take the following:

- Food. Most of the stuff you need to pack is food. For these 4 Desert races I would pack ProNutro and coffee powder for the morning, Perpetuem (by Hammer Nutrition) to run with, and then after the race some recovery powder, like Recoverite (also made by Hammer Nutrition), with maybe a bit of protein powder added in. For the evening, I would carry freeze-dried meals. I'd also carry quite a lot of teabags and one or two sweets.
- Clothing. There's no point in taking any other clothing than is mandatory. I would run in the same clothes the whole time.
- No sleeping mat and no pillow. It doesn't exactly make for a comfortable night's sleep, but you get used to it.
- And one pair of running shoes. Yes, it's a bit of a risk because, if they break, your race is basically toast. In the Atacama race, one guy put his shoes next to the fire to dry and, when he woke up the next morning, one of them had melted. Because he was one of the back-markers, I think the organisers helped him out. But if he had been one of the front-runners, it would have meant the end of his race.

For those first few races, my backpack weighed around 10 kilograms. By the time I did the Madagascar race in 2014, my backpack weighed 6 kilograms, so I've streamlined it quite a bit.

How to run in sand

There's definitely an art to running in sand – whether it's on the beach or through a desert. There's a mental and a technical side to it ...

Go with the flow

You have to accept the fact that forward progress is not going to be easy and efficient. It's a big ask, I know. Endurance-sport athletes hate having to dish out more energy reserves than they absolutely have to, but, like cycling into the wind or swimming against a current, when you're running in sand you simply have to make peace with this inevitability. Every step you take sees you slide back a little, or if you're running up a dune, it sees you slide back a lot.

If you're running along the side of a dune, at a camber, your outside foot is always going to be sliding down, so just kind of go with it. Stubbornly stick with a 'this is my line and I will hold it no matter what' attitude, and you're going to burn up way too much energy.

Adjust your cadence

Instead of taking big, heavy strides, adopt a shorter, faster cadence. This will mean your footfalls are also lighter. Also run with your feet pointing out a little more. This gives you more grip in the dunes. But, and this is a big but ...

Don't adopt bad habits

I picked up a lot of bad habits running in sand, the worst of which was a duck-footed running style. It's okay for the sand, but don't do what I did and let that become how you always run. As all my initial stage races were run in deserts, and because all the training I did for them involved sand, I unwittingly adopted a permanent duck-footed footfall. It's something I've worked very hard to correct.

The art of the sneaky pee

Dean Karnazes taught me many things, including how to take a leak on the run. It was during Sahara that I first noticed this particular skill of his. We were running and chatting along a fairly smooth gravel road when I glanced sideways and noticed that he wasn't just running and talking to me, but running and talking to me, *and* peeing. And no spillage either. What a pro! I wanted to be a pro too, and clearly, if you wanted to be a pro, you had to be able to pee on the run. It took two years of fairly messy trial and error, but I finally mastered the 'Art of the Sneaky Pee'. (Needless to say, this applies to men only.)

The how

Obviously the key objective here is not to pee on yourself, and that means two crucial external factors that come into play: 1) wind direction; and 2) the nature of the terrain. Pissing into the wind, metaphorically or physically, is never a good idea. If the wind is blowing, you definitely want it at your back. Secondly, this is not something you want to attempt on uneven, rocky terrain. I don't even have to explain that one.

Once you've ascertained the wind direction and terrain, what you want to do is slow down a little, run slightly sort of sideways and – while making sure there are no runners on the side you've chosen – aim a confident and strong stream into the nearby vegetation.

It's this last bit that's the most difficult. Stage fright aside, physically it's quite hard to get whatever muscles control this body function to work while you are moving. Your body is so used to peeing when it's motionless that to do it while running, or even walking, requires practice.

The why

It does save you time. I probably need to pee three or four times during a 100-miler race and, if a pee stop will take, say, 30 seconds, that's about two minutes you've lost over the race distance. Plus, if you stop, it also gives your competitors the opportunity to suddenly put down the hammer and open up a gap. That's not something you want late in a race, when catching up is always that much harder.

5

REDEMPTION IN THE JUNGLE

From a sponsorship point of view, my new career got off to a great start. I had signed with ProNutro earlier in 2009. Sports-gear manufacturer Salomon – who remain one of my main sponsors – then signed me up, and I picked up a couple of others, too. All I needed now was another win in my first race as a full-time professional to cement the venture. Turns out there was one happening right on my doorstep – the Namibia 2009 Race. Although this is not part of the 4 Deserts Series, it was also organised by the RacingThePlanet crowd, and was one of their so-called 'roving races'.

Things were really looking up. In theory, it should all have been easier. I didn't have to travel far to a strange and inhospitable country (the Fish River Canyon, where the Namibia Race was held, is 800 kilometres north of Cape Town), and I was, after all, dominating the series. On paper, a third win on the trot looked a good bet.

That was the theory. In practice, it didn't quite feel like that.

Arriving at the start of the race, I sensed something unfamiliar: intense pressure. After my previous two wins, I was definitely the out-and-out favourite, and with this event being so close to home, I was also getting a lot more media attention. Plus, I now had some big sponsors and, although there never once was any kind of pressure from them, I was nevertheless carrying this inescapable weight of expectation. For someone who calculates every gram in his backpack during a race, this wasn't a pleasant sensation.

True to the 4 Deserts format, Namibia was another seven-day, six-stage race and the route seemed pretty cool. We started on the edge of the Fish River Canyon and finished at Walvis Bay – you basically run through the canyon and then head towards the coast. There was a lot of variety in the route too, which runs through the hot and rocky canyon floor, and the hot and steep sand dunes. There was no variety in the weather, though.

My main competition was Spain's Salvador Calvo Redondo, who'd won a RacingThePlanet event in Vietnam the year before. He was a decent ultra-trail runner, but I reckoned I had his number. I felt good at the starting line, and he and I ran together for the first 20 kays until we got to a steep climb that takes you back out of the canyon. Salvador began to pull away and, try as I might, I just couldn't stick with the guy. It really knocked me psychologically. Instead of accepting that he was stronger on the steep climbs and waiting for the flat section, where I'd be likely to catch him again, my head dropped and I let myself slide into a mental hole. And when that happens, usually your day is done. I also went over on my right ankle and overstretched the ligaments, which didn't help. Even second place was now a concern for me, and I kept on looking behind me, expecting to see the field catching up. You cannot run with that kind of negative energy, and I limped to the finish line just in front of the third-placed runner, Italy's Marco Olmo, and a massive 24 minutes behind Salvador. I was feeling pretty sorry for myself. This was not how I had scripted it.

Perhaps I'd gone a little soft, or maybe I'd underestimated things because the race was so close to home. The conditions also turned out to be a little tougher than I had expected. It got close to freezing at night, and wouldn't be much past 5 °C each morning at the start. We'd go from that to 35 °C within half an hour of racing. To save weight, I didn't pack a sleeping mat either, which in this particular case was a bad call. We were basically sleeping on very rocky ground. That, along with the cold, meant I was getting precious little sleep. Actually, it got so cold that I ended up spooning the guy next to me. You just don't care any more – it's basic survival. Notably, my mate, Rob Graham, took spooning to the next level. He claims it was because there was a slope in the ground, and he's sticking to that story.

So, after minimal sleep on that first night, I woke up the next morning with the recent interviews I'd given in my short running career bouncing around in my head. When asked about what motivates and drives me, I'd sagely talk about what to do when life's little challenges slap you on the back of the head. Every time you get knocked down, you have to get up again … you get knocked down eight times, you get up nine times: that type of thing. Time for me to practise what I had preached, which is sometimes pretty difficult to do.

Despite the fact that Mr Unbeatable 4 Deserts Kingpin had just had his butt handed to him, I needed to get back into a positive frame of mind and focus on the next stage. It was a new day, there were still five stages to go, and even though I had dropped plenty of time to the guy in the lead, there was still a chance I could make that up, especially with the long 100-kilometre stage still to come.

On Day 2 I tried to forget about Salvador and focus more on just relaxing and running through the beautiful Namibian countryside. I saw loads of wildlife – zebra, giraffe, oryx, ostrich – and the terrain suited me a little better too. I could open up my legs on some of the flat sections.

But it was still very rocky, with the odd 60-metre-high dune thrown in. However, during the second half of the 38-kilometre stage, I turned on the gas and broke away. I managed to put 10 minutes on Salvador. A much better day for me, and a way better day than the one experienced by Japanese runner Kenji Ohi. Running near the back of the field, Kenji took a wrong turn just two kays from the finish and disappeared off into the night. At about 10 p.m. they sent out a search party, but no one could find him. They eventually did, the next morning, but the unfortunate runner had had to spend the night out in the bush. Not only was the temperature around 5 °C, but there was some hungry wildlife roaming about. 'I was very scared the whole night because I could hear animal noises,' Kenji is on record as saying.

Also part of the official record is the fact that some of the front-runners were found to not be carrying all the mandatory kit. I won't mention any names here, but I was not one of them. Not carrying all the required kit means you're running with a lighter pack, and that obviously gives you an advantage, especially up steep climbs. It also helps to have several of one's countrymen in the race, too. When you arrive at the finish line and the organisers want to know why half your kit is missing, you can claim to not speak a word of English and that you need to wait for your mates to finish, so that they can translate for you. And then, when they arrive, suddenly all the missing gear starts to miraculously reappear. Dodgy. Very dodgy. I sympathise with the organisers, because it's tough to police everything, but if you're a rule-obeying athlete, it's pretty frustrating to witness.

Some of the foreign guys also liked to ignore the designated race route and follow, let's call it the 'more efficient', line. And I'm not talking back-markers here, but the guys at the sharp end of the field. On one day during the Namibia race, we were running through the dunes where the flag-marked route looped around a lot, but one of the guys simply ignored the markers and ran the straightest, most direct line he could. He knew we could see what he was doing and I even called him out on it, but he basically didn't give a shit. I think it's a European thing. In their races it's accepted that sometimes you just basically cut a few corners on the trail if you can.

I remember Kílian Jornet inadvertently getting into a little trouble at a race in the US because, being such a skilled mountain runner, he simply ran a line straight down the mountain instead of following the trail's switchbacks. It was part of the Skyrunning Series and in the European races they allow that, so he didn't think he was doing anything wrong. In the end, they reached a compromise and Kílian was awarded the Skyrunning Series points, but not the race win.

The remainder of the race was a bit of a ding-dong battle between Salvador and me. We shared the honours the next day and, going into the long 100-kilometre stage, which for this race was on Day 4, he still had a 19-minute lead over me. Right from the start we went hard in a cat-and-mouse battle to see who would break first. The first 15 kilometres were up and down sand dunes and my legs were already tired, but I was not prepared to back down and kept pushing. At 30 kays, though, I hit a bit of a wall and began to flag. I'd been here before during both the Gobi and Sahara races but, unlike then, when I was in the lead, now I was finding it extremely tough to push through the pain barrier. I began to look around, hoping I wouldn't be caught by Marco, who was still in third.

Time to dig deeper than ever.

I managed to regroup, and coming into the 50-kilometre checkpoint, I saw Salvador sitting there, looking like he was taking strain. I went past, but that didn't last too long. I had miscalculated my water intake, and there was more of a gap to the 70-kilometre water point than I had anticipated ... idiot. Not only did I run out of water, but I also made the mistake of eating a stick of droëwors (dried sausage), which simply absorbed any water that was still in my system. I ended up having to walk the final three kilometres to the next water point. And Salvador passed me again. The ambient temperature had soared to 43 °C, and in those circumstances it's amazing what three kays with no water can do to you. I was in a bad way, feeling light-headed, seeing stars and stuff. For a while, I thought my race was done. I was in total survival mode. I went straight for a water bottle and downed it. I poured another over my head. Strictly speaking, you are only allowed one bottle of water at a checkpoint, but they must've seen the feral look in my eyes and did nothing.

After getting rehydrated and slurping back a couple of gels, I managed to regroup for the second time and caught up with Salvador at the 75-kilometre mark. It seemed like he was tiring, so I surged to see if I could put a gap between us – the sandy, less technical ground suited me. He hung on, though, and by the 80-kilometre mark we were both taking strain. I kept up the speed, hoping he would crack, but just before the 90-kilometre mark, my legs were waving the white flag. For the first time, after battling it out for over 200 kilometres, Salvador and I started chatting – though with my non-existent Spanish and his few words of English, it wasn't much of a conversation. Still, we called a truce and ran the final 10 kilometres together and finished arm in arm in a time of 11:30. It was slow for 100 kilometres, but it was brutal terrain and the temperature had made it a very hard day out.

After a rest day, the sixth stage was a short but challenging 21 kays, and again I didn't have a great day. After failing to put time on Salvador during the long stage, the race was pretty much over. Feeling pretty flat, I finished a minute behind him. The last stage was, as always, a short one, and we ran those 10 kilometres together.

I'd run my first race as a professional ... and lost. That's how I saw it, anyway. Of course, second place was still something to be proud of, but I couldn't help feeling that I had failed. And I had failed on my home turf. It hurt.

I had let the pressure get to me or, to put it more accurately, I had placed too much pressure on myself. Neither my sponsors nor my supporters had done it. I had simply taken it all on board and applied it myself. No disrespect to Salvador – he's a very strong and technical runner – but I lost that race mentally. Instead of going with the flow after that initial setback on the first climb, I just fell apart completely and started thinking the worst. In the end, I could not claw back the time I had lost on that first day.

In hindsight, I was probably overthinking everything and getting deeper and deeper into a bad mental space from which I couldn't quite extricate myself. I wasn't running with anywhere near the freedom and the gut instinct I had going at the Gobi March and Sahara Race. It was best to file this under 'Experience Gained' and look ahead to my next endeavour – one that would take me into the steaming jungles of South America for what would turn out to be probably the hardest and strangest race I'd ever do.

The following year, in 2010, I'd earmarked the Atacama Crossing and The Last Desert race in Antarctica as the 4 Deserts events in which I wanted to compete. The Antarctica race happens only every two years, and I also needed to try to find a bigger sponsor to fund the steep $10 000 entry fee. But there was still time for another race in 2009, and, after Namibia's disappointments, I was looking for a little running redemption.

It came in the form of the Jungle Marathon. Held in the Brazilian rainforest, the 242-kilometre race is a six-day, five-stage event that wasn't part of the 4 Deserts Series, but I'd heard the odd story about it. These whispered tales were usually accompanied by wide eyes and the shaking of heads by all who told and heard them. I couldn't glean much info from the runners I'd met during the 4 Deserts races – all I'd get was a nervous laugh and a 'just go and do it and you'll find out'. The race had gained a degree of notoriety and press attention after the BBC had run a three-part documentary on it. The second episode had ended with one of the competitors nearly dying from heat exhaustion. You see the guy being stretchered off-camera and then suddenly someone shouts, 'Oh no, I think we've lost him!! I think he's dead!!' And then, smart film-makers that they are, they ended the episode at that point and everyone had to wait another week to see if the poor bloke had made it or not. Apparently, after that, interest in the race really took off, and the organisers now have people all over the world wanting to enter.

And one of them was me.

Seriously, how tough could it be after what I'd done? 'Voted by CNN as "The World's Toughest Endurance Race" ... Temperatures of 40 °C ... Humidity of 99% ... Primary jungle with a dense canopy covering and not a chink of daylight ... Swamp crossings where anacondas lurk ... River crossings with caiman and piranhas as companions' – these were the warnings plastered on the front page of their website. Right. Whatever. Things are always being hyped up. Besides, I had heard Salvador was entering the race as well. Revenge? What, me? Never!

I clicked on the 'Enter' button.

I'd been reading Lance Armstrong's book about his recovery from cancer, and it helped motivate me to take on the jungle after my Namibian setback. I realise that you can't compare fighting back from cancer with being miserable about a second place in a desert race, but his description of those first post-chemo rides he took on a stationary bike inspired me. In the wake of the big doping scandal and Lance becoming something of a pariah with a – justifiably – tough punishment dished out, I couldn't help but admire his determination to overcome a massive challenge like cancer. Reading about how, in his prep for the Tour de France, he would ride a route three times to pinpoint every little bump in the road really resonated with me; it made me want to become far more specific in my training too.

I started doing a lot more quality work that was more race-specific. After a little research on the Jungle Marathon, I worked out that the race had lots of small climbs and some huge river crossings. In a couple of stages, they start you on the one side of a river and you have to swim a few hundred metres across before the actual running can even begin. To get used to swimming with a fully laden backpack, I went to the Silvermine dam above Tokai, in Cape Town, to make sure I didn't completely sink, and I also did a little bit of swimming at the gym. Running-wise, I did a lot more hill repeats and shorter, sharper stuff – like really short 50- or 100-metre climbs up and down. I was determined to do well in this race, which, in my head, at that point, meant first place.

As I mentioned in Chapter 1, the race takes place in the Floresta Nacional do Tapajós in northern Brazil. Getting there was a bit of a trek – a flight from South Africa to São Paulo, a connecting flight to Manaus, and then another to the town of Santarém. From there, it was a boat trip up the Amazon to the start.

Before the race started, we were given a brief survival course by the local Brazilian military, who pointed out all the dangerous elements of the jungle – which turned out to be most of it. Even the trees. Touch the wrong tree, and it can kill you. At least that's what they said. I remember lying in my hammock that night and not being able to sleep. You can't sleep on the ground because there are too many insects – the ground's like a highway of termites. I was too scared to go to the toilet because there were just eyes – red eyes – all around ... just looking at me. I ended up taking a bottle to pee in at night because it was just too gnarly to go to the toilet.

And remember all that hype on their website about piranhas and caiman crocs at the river crossings? Well, they showed some underwater video footage from previous races, and there they were, swimming among the competitors. 'Don't worry,' said the military guy, 'they're actually more scared of you than you need to be of them.' Sure.

There were a few more things I had to worry about too. A few weeks before the start, my right hamstring started to play up. I rarely picked up much in the way of niggles, but the hammie started to get quite sore and then, on top of everything, I sprained both my ankles on Day 1 of the race.

The problem was that, although the route was marked with bio-degradable orange tape, things biodegrade so quickly in the jungle that half the time the tape would turn greeny-brown and just fade into the foliage. And the actual jungle itself is incredibly dense. You can vaguely make out the trail, but the floor is covered with leaves, so you can't really make out where the roots or holes are. You just plant your foot and hope for the best. Unfortunately, luck wasn't with me that first day and I went over on both ankles. In fact, my right ankle was so swollen that it couldn't flex sideways any more, even if I went over on it again. It's like the body protected itself through the swelling. I would still stand in holes or slip, but it never got any worse. The drugs helped too. I had Myprodol painkillers with me and was having to take a couple every few hours. The natural endorphins helped too, and I found that the more swollen the ankle got, the less painful it was. I've learnt now that if I tweak my ankle and it doesn't swell up, then I need to start worrying. Still, through the whole race I was running with this fear in the back of my mind that I would injure my ankles further. The terrain was so sketchy.

The fear in the front of my mind was what the jungle's resident wildlife might do to me. I remember running a few metres behind Salvador, with US runner Mike Wolfe just ahead of both of us, when suddenly Mike started screaming and shouting. He'd been attacked by some or other vindictive swarm of insects, and I'd get that sick feeling in my stomach, knowing that we were up next on the menu. A couple of times I ran under fallen trees and my backpack knocked the rotting bark as I ducked underneath, which dislodged all these fire ants that would fall on my back and start biting me. It's like getting stung … very painful!

I also saw at least two or three snakes every day, as well as a couple of these massive rodents called capybaras. They look like seals with legs and they can run bloody fast. If you see one of them sprinting out of the dense foliage in your direction, you shit yourself. At least I wasn't still out there running after sundown, as I had finished the stages by then, but some of the slower guys reported seeing jaguars too.

One totally unexpected 'snake' belonged to a French competitor who, as it turned out, was also a male stripper. Apparently he had a show booked in Paris soon after the race and had decided to keep his tool-in-trade well maintained during the race. That involved a thorough shave, which unfortunately backfired, as it caused him such bad bollock chafe that he had to withdraw or risk compromising his entire livelihood.

The other snakes to watch out for were some of the local runners. Up until then, in its four-year history, the Jungle Marathon had only been won by local athletes. They were obviously very familiar with both the terrain, the route and the short cuts. Poor Shirley, the founder, had her hands full with them. By 2009, Shirley had separated the race into two categories – one for locals and one for foreigners. The foreign guys would get really annoyed when one of the locals would come running over the finish line, drinking an ice-cold Coke. They would be like, 'Where the hell did you get that from?!', and the runner would claim he'd carried it with him, which was total nonsense. Clearly, they were being seconded somewhere along the route, but that kind of stuff was really difficult to regulate. Shirley had my sympathies, and I never made a big deal about it.

After the first two days I had built up a 10-minute lead, but that wasn't any guarantee of a win. The nasties could always get you. The previous year, some poor guy had grabbed onto a branch that was unfortunately also home to a particularly venomous spider, which promptly bit him. That was his race done right there. What could end more than your race was a local species of rattlesnake that's known to kill around 100 people each year in Brazil. Remember, it's a long boat trip to the nearest town, so getting bitten means there is a good chance you won't make it. How someone hasn't died in that race yet is a miracle, to be perfectly honest.

After I'd finished the second day, I was lying in my hammock as most of the field began to come in, including a big group of UK soldiers. They were high-fiving each other at the finish line, only for them to start having fits a couple of hours later. They'd contracted severe heatstroke and had to be evacuated that night. Apparently, some of them were properly messed up. One guy, I later heard, ended up with some form of brain damage.

Like with all these multistage races, it all came down to Day 5's long stage. It began with a 250-metre swim before we headed into the jungle. Despite my niggling hammie and swollen ankles, I was having a very good race. Going into the long stage, I had built up a comfortable two-hour lead on the foreign guys and 45 minutes on the top local athlete.

This stage was 89 kilometres long but fairly flat, and the second half of the stage saw us in open terrain along the coast. I spent most of the long stage running with Mike Wolfe, until the heat saw him back off a little. It was as hot as the desert races I'd done, but the big difference here was the humidity. Unlike the dry heat of the Gobi or Sahara, which evaporated sweat quickly and helped cool you down a little, here the humidity was like a blanket.

It didn't help that, while running on my own up front, I managed to 'miss' a water point. Either I was so far ahead that the organisers hadn't set it up yet, or there was a little local subterfuge going on. Whatever the case, I ended up becoming spectacularly dehydrated. About a kilometre out from the next water point, I couldn't take it any more and came across this little creek full of green water. I dropped to my knees and started drinking the water. I knew it was the worst thing I could possibly do and the potential of contracting 10 kinds of rare tropical diseases was very high, but I didn't care.

But, whether it was luck or my strong constitution, I didn't get ill and actually crossed the finish line so far ahead of everyone else that it caught Shirley and her crew off guard. They hadn't even got there yet, and it was up to my mate, Greg Fell from film production company The African Attachment, who was shooting a documentary about me, to film me crossing the line and zoom in on my watch to record the time.

The final stage was 32 kilometres, and by now no one had the energy to make up the time gap I had built up. My hamstring was still bothering me and had got a lot more painful towards the end of the race – like someone had kneed me in the side of the leg and given me 'dead leg' – but my race mode had well and truly taken over. I wanted this win badly. Still, there was a lot going through my mind. Manage your ankle and hamstring, don't get lost and, of course, don't get bitten by a snake.

There was quite a steep climb on the final 10-kay stretch, and as I was hauling my tired body over yet another tree, I got half stuck, fell over and face-planted. As I extricated my head from the mud, I found myself looking into this massive dark hole right in front of me ... and these two red eyes were staring straight back. Another snake. That obviously got me going again pretty quickly, and with the adrenalin pumping through my veins, I crossed the finish line. I ended up winning comfortably, having beaten the locals and, more importantly, my Namibian nemesis, Salvador Redondo.

I think I was in the right space mentally and sufficiently motivated to not let the conditions get the better of me. It was a very, very tough race – technical and energy sapping. For example, Day 2 was only 24 kilometres, but not only was it hilly, there were times when I was wading chest deep through a swamp or falling face down in thick, black mud. One minute I was running on hard-packed ground, the next I was somersaulting into a mud pit. I lost my Oakleys in that pit and had to spend the rest of the race without any eye protection.

Not an ideal situation for my new eyewear sponsor.

All in all, 2009 was a great learning curve for me. I suffered my first loss in an international event, returned to win the next one, and I had also begun to experience the ups and downs of finding and maintaining sponsorships. In my line of work, there is very little in the way of prize money, so making a living depends completely on the sponsor deals I secure.

As I mentioned, at the start of the year I'd secured a deal with ProNutro, but it wasn't exactly working for me. Simply getting a monthly cheque wasn't how I wanted my relationships with sponsors to work. I wanted to develop a partnership that would help elevate my profile, grow the sport, and give that company the exposure in return. ProNutro never seemed keen to leverage their association with me, and then the marketing manager I was dealing with left, and I pretty much never heard from them again, as they didn't renew the contract.

It was a bit of a blow, given my plans to do Antarctica in 2010. My relationship with Salomon was beginning to grow, but I still needed a bigger corporate sponsor if my plans were going to work out. And that's when Trevor McLean-Anderson, the MD of Axis House – a mining services and consumables company – stepped in. A keen runner himself, Trevor was keen to build a state-of-the-art gym and training facility in Hout Bay, and had heard me chatting to a couple of guys from the Hout Bay Harriers running club about my financial issues. He approched me, said he was keen to help, and that I should swing by his office the next day to chat. I wasn't sure how serious he was – I've heard that line from so many people and then, when you get hold of them, it's more often a case of 'actually, let's meet next year'. I didn't think anything of it until he sent me a message the next morning to set up the meeting. Off I duly went – genuinely taken aback by how serious he was – and showed him my proposal. He looked at it and was like, 'Geez, how are you going get by on this? This is really cutting it fine. Tell you what. Let's double it, see how you do over the next 12 months, and then take it from there.'

Trevor would go and build that gym, and two years later, with a little planning input from me, I'm proud to say that the well-known Velocity Sports Lab opened its doors.

Suddenly I had enough money to actually live on each month *and* do the Antarctica race. No more stressing about funds: that was a massive relief. Velocity Sports Lab remains a sponsor of mine and their logo takes pride of place on my running kit. It's pretty discreet branding but, for Trevor, the association factor with Velocity is more important than having anything in your face. Trevor and I have become good mates, and I'm very thankful for his role in my career.

STUFF I'VE LEARNT

Knowing what you're in for can be a bad thing

There are some trails that I simply do not like. Whenever I run them, it feels like a struggle and I'm inevitably slow. It's partly psychological – you know you're slow in this section, so subconsciously you hold back – and partly that your running style is simply not suited to it.

Llandudno ravine is a good example. I had a really bad experience running up there during the 2009 Hout Bay Trail Challenge, and every time I ran it again, all those bad thoughts came flooding back. It took me two years to put that bogey to rest.

So ... don't listen to the hype

Endurance athletes can't help themselves when it comes to scaring their peers. They feel compelled to tell others how unbelievably tough a particular event, stage or climb is and, as a result, whatever it is they're hyping up becomes this scary monster for the rest of us.

Don't listen to this stuff. Sure, you need to know the general route and its length, but don't get caught up in the drama. It's a philosophy I've often applied to the races I've done – sometimes it's been on purpose, and other times because I've been a little naive. Take that emergency training course the Brazilian military gave us before the start of the Jungle Marathon. I listened to most of it but, to be honest, I left with about two hours to go. I knew that if I heard more of what could potentially kill me out there in the jungle, it would do my head in. It was really hectic and beginning to freak me out.

For Gobi, I also didn't quite know what I was in for, but that was more naivety than an active choice not to know. Still, the result was the same. I went in fresh and unafraid of what I might encounter.

Cold water over your head

I'd heard people talk about this, but I felt the benefits first-hand during the Namibia race. It was incredibly hot during the long stage, and my core temperature had increased to a point where I was feeling physically ill – nauseous and dangerously light-headed. I didn't know then that it was because my core temperature was simply too high, but instinctively I reached for a bottle of really cold water and poured it over my head.

It quickly reduced my core temperature, and it was literally like flipping a switch. I went from not feeling great to suddenly feeling pretty good, and I took off after race leader Salvador Redondo.

One of the most extreme applications of this was used by American ultra-distance star Scott Jurek while competing in the legendary Badwater Ultramarathon, in which competitors run 135 miles (217 kilometres) through California's Death Valley, where the temperature regularly soars past 50 °C. Scott won the race in 2005 and 2006, with his support team carrying a tub the size of a bath filled with ice water in which they immersed him to keep his core temperature in check.

How to get, and stay, sponsored

Many trail runners have approached me for advice on how to obtain sponsors. They've seen me do it and are keen to do the same. And why not? From the outside it looks like a cool lifestyle – basically you get paid to run all day, right? Well, that's not quite how it works.

Winning races doesn't necessarily get you sponsors. It's really all about what you can offer a sponsor – it is about developing your public image and working hard on creating a strong relationship with your sponsors.

At its most fundamental level, a brand – and let's use my shoes and gear sponsor, Salomon, as an example – is in the business of selling something. And the reason they sponsor anybody is because that person will help Salomon sell more clothes and shoes. It's a simple return on an investment equation. So ...

Develop a following

The more media attention and the more of a social-media following an athlete gets, the more gear that athlete's sponsors will sell. It's about marketing. You are part of a sponsor's marketing plan, and to be part of that marketing plan means you have to market yourself.

US athlete Anton Krupicka is a good example. He doesn't win a lot of races, but his sponsors, New Balance, don't mind. Anton's a very cool guy with his hippyish persona and at-one-with-nature approach, which really appeals to people. He's an intriguing individual. He even looks like Jesus with that long, fair hair and beard. It's inspirational stuff and he has developed a large following. It was also a perfect match for New Balance's range of minimalist running shoes, and he was used extensively in their clearly very successful campaign.

Tell it like it is

It's one thing doing well in a race and getting the media's attention, but keeping that attention is another thing altogether. Many times I've seen an athlete win a race and, in the interview afterwards, deliver all the predictable sound bites. That doesn't work for the media. They get a boring interview that no one will want to watch or read. And that doesn't work for a sponsor.

Real sports heroes are the ones with personality. And that means sharing their highs and their lows from the heart. It makes them real and human. Fans want to identify with someone, and if they're hearing the same old lines all the time, they can't identify with the athlete.

Trust me, it's hard sharing your failures with everyone, especially at the time. Failure is a bitter pill to swallow. But it's how you deal with setbacks that is the real test of your character, and that can be an inspiration and a motivation for others who are also facing challenges in their own lives, and who can identify with what you are going through.

Find a balance

It's not all about giving good media. Obviously, you also have to focus on your training and maintaining your fitness and competitive edge. Again, Dean Karnazes really set the template for us all. He wasn't winning as many races as a contemporary like Scott Jurek, but initially Dean got a lot more exposure than Scott. Later, Scott caught on and has successfully promoted his vegan diet regime with a very successful book called *Eat & Run*.

Finding that balance isn't easy. There are times when you have to focus more on your training, and that means you have to be selective and unfortunately say no to certain interviews. I've always tried to be as approachable as I can and make time for everyone, but sometimes it's not always possible.

You also have to balance the requirements of your sponsors. They will often need your direct involvement in a marketing and promotions strategy, and that time commitment could mean you're not perfectly prepared for every event you enter.

Believe in your brand

Don't agree to a sponsorship just for the money. If you don't believe in the product they are selling, the public will pick up on it. The whole deal will lack authenticity, and that's damaging for both you and the sponsor. I work with brands like Velocity Sports Lab, Salomon, Red Bull, Suunto, Oakley and Cross Country Insurance. It means I can confidently talk about them in public and recommend them, knowing that they work for me.

That said, I'm not a salesperson for those brands – they wouldn't expect me to be. If, for example, someone comes to me for trail-shoe advice, expecting me to recommend Salomon regardless, that might not always be the case. You might have very wide feet, and then I'll probably point you to New Balance, who make shoes with wider toe boxes. It's cool with Salomon. They want real people using their products. They want authentic and respected brand ambassadors, not cardboard-cut-out sales people.

Develop a personal relationship with your sponsors

I've never had a manager, choosing instead to handle all my own professional affairs. There are obviously pros and cons to this – I'm not, for example, a financial whizz, but I've been able to get help where I need it. The big pro, though, is that I have been able to develop very close relationships with my sponsors. I know individuals in those brands very well, and they know me.

Together, we've been able to come up with projects like the Drakensberg Grand Traverse, which I did in 2014. Setting the fastest known time (FKT) across South Africa's mighty mountain range with my mate Ryno Griesel got a lot of media coverage – probably around 70 per cent of the total media coverage I got that year (you can read more about that particular adventure in Chapter 13).

Take a guy like Spaniard Kílian Jornet. This fellow Salomon athlete is arguably the best mountain trail runner in the world, but it's his free-running projects that have rocketed him to the world's attention – even more so than the many races he has won. He's currently planning an FKT up Everest. Imagine how much attention that's going to generate!

6

ANOTHER DESERT, BUT AN OASIS TOO

The end of 2009 felt like a watershed for me – like I might just be able to make a go of this 'being a pro-athlete' thing I'd so badly wanted. Financially, it looked possible, and when I say possible, I don't mean in a bulging-wallet kind of way, but more like at least I wouldn't have to supplement it delivering pizzas. I also began to feel like I was becoming a better athlete. With my coach, Ian's, help, I was doing more and more quality sessions. As I mentioned earlier, for the Gobi race I really just wanted to get through the training, and if I was supposed to do a 12-kay run with eight one-kay intervals, I'd often skip it. Now, through January and February 2010, not only was I doing these nausea-inducing sessions, but I was attacking them and applying a lot more focus and energy.

Not having a day job was such a game changer for me. It meant I not only had proper recovery time between sessions, which makes a massive difference, but I could also go off and do even more concentrated training specifically for a race. My next event was in March 2010 – the Atacama Crossing in Chile. This was another race in the 4 Deserts Series, and the key element to overcome here wasn't so much the dry heat of the desert, but the altitude.

It's one of the driest places on the planet – a 1 000-kilometre plateau on the Pacific Coast of South America, some parts of which have never seen any rain ... ever! But, more significantly, it's at an altitude of over 2 000 metres. And that's just over the threshold for altitude sickness. Going there straight from sea level and attempting to race is not advisable. My new pro athlete status, however, meant I was able to spend 10 days training up in the Drakensberg (South Africa's highest mountain range) before flying to South America. I had also decided that I was going to spend 10 days in La Paz, Bolivia, before the race – a city at an even higher altitude than the Atacama. I was really growing in confidence now. I could run faster for longer, and was generally just feeling a lot stronger.

As an athlete, I was in a good space – physically and mentally – but personally I wasn't feeling that great. As much as I valued that training up in the Drakensberg, I was also feeling pretty lonely. Over the preceding couple of years I had put so much energy into my career – training, trying to build my profile, the daily admin of answering emails, etcetera – that there was no space for anyone else in my life. Obviously I had my family and mates, but it's not quite the same, and during those 10 days in the Berg, for the first time in my life, I began to feel a deep loneliness. The last serious relationship I had had was in 2006, and that had ended badly. I was quite serious about it and thought she was too. Turns out she wasn't. After that there were some dabblings here and there, but as I started running more and more, that part of my life became harder and harder to incorporate. It's tough to include someone else in your life when you're as focused as I had become on my running. There are not too many women who are okay with the fact that their boyfriend is away most of the weekend, running on his own.

Although it helped with my fitness, spending a week on my own in Bolivia didn't help, and as super-focused as I was on the race ahead, I can remember sitting in that hotel room feeling pretty bleak. Fortunately, that would change further on that year, but we'll get to that later.

What helped me snap out of my 'little box of tissues' moment was news of a massive earthquake in Chile – it turned out to be the sixth largest ever recorded on the planet and, tragically, while just over 500 people lost their lives, given its size it was a miracle that number wasn't significantly higher.

We could feel its effects in Bolivia, where the country's comms were down for four or five hours. Naturally, the folks back home were very concerned, but I managed to eventually get hold of them. It also threw my travel plans into complete disarray, as all flights in and out of Chile had been cancelled. The Atacama race was suddenly looking like it might not happen.

After all the focused training I'd put in, giving up and flying back home wasn't an option either. I headed straight to the nearest bus station. The hotel concierge had told me I was wasting my time because everyone had the same plan and the buses would obviously be full, but I wasn't giving up just yet.

Sure enough, at the station I was told there were no more seats on buses to Chile, but I hung in there and eventually one passenger didn't turn up and I grabbed his spot. A few minutes into the journey, though, I began to regret my decision. The driver was a maniac. Perhaps that's unfair. Perhaps all Bolivian bus drivers drive like this, but I will not be using this particular public transport system ever again. It was a 37-hour trip, during at least 36 hours of which I was convinced I was going to die in the smoking wreck of a bus at the bottom of a deep Chilean ravine.

The guy would bomb down these steep passes, swerving onto the wrong side of the road, hooting at oncoming traffic and generally breaking just about every rule of the road. It's not like they swapped drivers either to prevent driver-fatigue accidents. No, this guy did 37 hours on the trot. He was so tired near the end, he was weaving all over the place. Interestingly, the other bus passengers didn't seem as freaked out as I was. Most of them dozed away while I stared wide-eyed into the night.

The other reason for vigilance was the roadblocks – and more specifically the soldiers at the roadblocks. They'd storm onto the bus brandishing automatic weapons, and start checking everyone's luggage and demanding passports. Fortunately, having travelled through Mexico a few years earlier, I learnt to only show my South African passport. Even though I have a British passport, thanks to my grandparents, my experience in Mexico taught me that British or American passports usually result in a request for bribes and an extra dose of hassle. But produce a South African passport and they leave you alone, because they think you have no money (which is an accurate assessment when you look at how much foreign currency the rand buys you these days).

To get into Chile, we went up this massive pass – around 4 000 metres – and stopped at the border post to get our passports stamped. Even just getting out and walking around made me a little light-headed and out of breath ... a bit worrying, given the race ahead. More of a worry, though, was the ongoing seismic activity in the region. The Bus Trip from Hell ended in Calama, where some of the other competitors and I had to spend the night before the organisers drove us to the town of San Pedro de Atacama, where the race was due to start.

The town is in a mining region and you could hear big explosions going off all the time, but while sitting in my hotel room on the fourth floor – busy writing a blog post, as I recall – what I thought was a really loud mining explosion turned out to be something a lot more dangerous. The whole hotel started shaking. When I heard screaming from below, I froze. It was a very large earth tremor, and while it only probably lasted five or six seconds, it seemed like minutes. I literally froze. Obviously, this is not what one wants to do during a quake – and I was highly annoyed with myself afterwards – but it stopped me dead in my blog. Luckily, it subsided before causing any structural damage, and I quickly bolted down the stairs and out of the building to join the other scared hotel guests outside.

Despite winning the Jungle Marathon relatively easily and feeling like I was in the best shape of my life, I was still a little angsty going into the Atacama race. The altitude had something to do with it and, sure, the earthquake had thrown me a bit (not to mention *that* bus ride), but I was also starting to feel a little of that pressure I'd felt in Namibia. My profile was continuing to grow and with quite a few TV networks filming the race, I was definitely getting the lion's share of attention. Having already won two of the 4 Deserts races, I was being talked up as possibly being the first person to win all four. It was a goal that was beginning to formulate in my head, too. Coming second here was never going to be good enough. Besides, if I did not win, the thought of going through all this drama again to come back and have another go wasn't exactly appealing.

It didn't help that another stomach bug – that scourge of any multiday race with a communal tented village – was doing the rounds, but, luckily, I managed to dodge that particular bullet. I still felt a little grim, though – altitude tends to have this effect if you're not fully accustomed to it. There was also some competition in the shape of American Eric LaHaie, who had won the 2009 Gobi March. At registration on the day before the start, I heard him chatting to one of his mates. He was talking up his chances big time.

What a stroke of luck. Just that little extra bit of motivation I needed.

By the next morning's start I was completely amped and ready to go. My body was feeling hundreds and seemed to be handling the altitude quite well now, plus Mr LaHaie had given me just enough of a poke in the ribs to turn my competitive-instincts dial up to 100.

San Pedro de Atacama lies at around 2 400 metres and the route profile showed that we'd get up to 3 000 metres on Day 1, but that was the highest point of the race. Most of the route was lower than 2 400 metres, which meant that if I survived and did well on Day 1, it would set me up for the rest of the race.

As it turned out, Day 1 went very well. For the first few kays of the 36-kilometre stage I stuck with Eric, but dropped him as we started to climb a ridge out of the first canyon. I could see he was struggling in the thin air, and I put the hammer down. I extended my lead through-out the stage, and ended up finishing 28 minutes ahead of him.

One thing that really stood out for me on that first stage was just how beautiful this place was. For most of the first day we ran through a river canyon, with very undesert-like green vegetation and an ice-blue river at the bottom. We had to cross it several times – the water was flippin' cold – but you'd soon warm up again in the heat. The Atacama Crossing was probably the most beautiful race I've run of all the 4 Deserts Series events. It's just surreal. It's not super-hot – never more than 36 or 37 °C – but it's incredibly dry. As mentioned,

NASA use it for testing because it's the closest thing to a Mars-like environment that we have on Earth. I remember running along this arid landscape and then looking up to see these massive ice-capped mountains. It's a truly breathtaking sight.

Day 2's scenery was a little more varied – more canyon stuff, but it also included running through an old mining tunnel, and we encountered some big dunes for the first time too. Unlike the African sand dunes, these South American ones are more brown in colour and the sand is a lot more powdery. It was another good day and I was now 45 minutes ahead of Eric.

For the next couple of stages it was basically the same story – I'd run with the other three or four front-runners for the first half of the stage, and then disappear off into the distance for the second half. From a terrain point of view, Day 4 was about as varied as it can get in a race. We started off running up a canyon, through some big dunes, and then into this luscious green valley along a river, through fruit orchards, a rocky plain, and then ... the infamous Atacama salt flats. They're pretty gnarly. The compacted salt is thick in some places, but every now and again your foot will break through the crust and it will cut your ankles and shins. And of course the old 'salt on the wound' saying means it would burn like crazy. It was particularly hot on these flats as well – around 40 °C – and pretty cold at night, now that I remember it. As always, trying to carry as light a pack as possible, I didn't have much in the way of warm clothes, and there may have been some involuntary spooning going on in our tent during this race.

Day 5 was the long day – around 80 kilometres of the same varied terrain and the same tactics from me. Actually, I did have some company on that stage – a few dogs. I had run through a little village and some dogs started following me. They ran with me for about 30 kays until the next checkpoint, when, luckily, some of the guys who helped around the camp managed to take them back. But they were happy to just cruise with me and then chill around the camp. I was also in total cruise mode by now. I had built up a lead of over five and a half hours over the rest of the field by the end of this long stage.

As usual, the next day was a rest day and the final stage was a short

9.6-kilometre run into San Pedro de Atacama. No one had run the Atacama Crossing in under 30 hours before, but I was aiming to break 24 hours. It meant I had to run the final stage in under 30 minutes – 10 sub-three-minute kays after running 230 kilometres through a high-altitude desert. It would be tough, but I was so full of confidence by now that I would have backed myself against Usain Bolt in the 100 metres.

Off the gun went. And off I went. This time I wasn't spending the first half hanging around with the rest of the field, but put my head down and opened up my stride from the start. I had to literally sprint the final two kays, but I ended up dipping under the 30-minute mark and won the race in 23:58:39. I'd beaten the record by six hours. Of all the places my running has taken me, San Pedro de Atacama is probably my favourite town, and the finish there was pretty special, with a big crowd and a police escort. Pity there wasn't someone special in my life with whom I could share the moment. Still, to date this was easily my best race.

Atacama ... tick.

Bring on The Last Desert race, in Antarctica, and my chance to become the first person to win all four of the races in the 4 Deserts Series.

That race at the South Pole was scheduled for November, though, and before then I had an appointment in Europe. I had been invited to attend my first Salomon Advanced Training Week in France.

Post-quake flights out of Chile were still in disarray, but via Santiago and Frankfurt I eventually managed to get to the small Provençal town of Bédoin in France, which, as most cyclists reading this will know, marks the start of the ascent up the mighty Mont Ventoux. The hardest of all the mythical Tour de France climbs, it's a 21.5-kilometre-long series of switchbacks, with many sections on a 10 to 12 per cent gradient. We took a drive up there and, trust me, TV cameras do not do justice to how steep the road really is.

My relationship with Salomon was growing stronger and stronger, and it was great to hang out with their other sponsored athletes from around the world. To swap experiences and hear from seasoned runners like Jono Wyatt, Julien Chorier, Kílian Jornet, Anna Frost, Thomas Lorblanchet, Ricky Lightfoot and François D'Haene was invaluable for me. In particular, so was spending time with guys like French mountain-running king Jornet and Kiwi 5 000-metre Olympian Wyatt, who showed me what you need to do to perform at that level.

Along with the athletes, Salomon's R&D and marketing teams were also in attendance, and we'd spend the week doing morning and afternoon training runs, where we'd test new equipment and generally just bond as a team. It wasn't as scientific and organised as the Advanced Training Weeks have progressed to now, but it was the perfect atmosphere for me to experience it for the first time. Back then, we would basically just do a five-kay loop in one pair of shoes and kit, come back, and do another in a different set of gear.

Naturally, throw a bunch of top competitive athletes together and a couple of egos are going to come out to play. We were cruising along on one of the morning runs, when suddenly one of the crew bolted off ahead, wanting to take a photo of the group running. Some of my Salomon teammates, however, thought he was trying to test us, and they went after him. Suddenly the group went from trotting along at 4:30 a kay to surging at 3:30 a kay all the way back to the hotel.

It wasn't a strict training-camp vibe either. There was a lot of free time and a lot of photo sessions, so it was more chilled. The following year it got a little more serious. It was more like a full-on training camp with three runs a day and detailed feedback on the gear each evening.

It was also really cool to start building a relationship with the R&D team – usually they were in their labs designing stuff for most of the year and we'd only communicate by email, so it was rewarding for both them and us to have these one-on-one sessions. It's great to meet the guy whose name you've been seeing in your inbox for the last 12 months. Plus, it's also pretty rewarding to see your design input appear in stores a couple of years later. I had some input on the shoes, but mostly on their 'skin bag' backpack. This was something of a revolution in running packs, and it only weighs 80 grams. You can carry water bottles in the front, as well as a hydration bladder in the back, and it's made of highly breathable material so it's comfortable to wear and doesn't chafe. I know I'm sounding like a salesman here, but this pack really is the business.

After this first Salomon Advanced Training Week, they also began making custom shoes specifically for me. I had been running in their S-Lab Series for a year, but because my feet were so wide, I'd always been in shoes that had quite a big gap in the front in order for me to feel comfortable. That could be a problem, though, for example in the Jungle Marathon, where I was constantly kicking roots and sometimes tripping and falling over. Now, however, with a last made specifically for my foot, all my running shoes have the requisite width without too much of a gap up front.

One of the great benefits of this first annual week with my fellow Salomon colleagues was that it began to shed some light on where my future might be heading. I was beginning to ponder a trail-running career beyond the 4 Deserts Series. If I won in Antarctica – and the odds were fairly good – I was keen on setting my sights on the next challenge. That appeared to be competing in single-stage, 100-mile trail races, which were big in the US, and the single-stage mountain races in Europe that Kílian had dominated. These events attracted the very best of the best endurance runners and, if I wanted to really see how good I was, this was where my future lay.

Greg Vollet, now Salomon's international team manager, was also there that week. He was new to the brand, but he would soon become instrumental in opening up some new avenues for me. After a couple of chats with him, I could see a whole new world beyond multiday desert racing. I wanted to go and try something new. I wanted to explore the mountains.

Before I could do that, though, I had some commitments back home. My exploits on the 4 Deserts Series meant I was now getting plenty of invites to do trail races back home. It was a bit of a tricky situation to handle, because obviously not all trail races suit me. Short distances aren't my strength at all, and it's amusing how many people don't get it. They see me as a trail runner, which means that whether the distance is 250 kilometres or 10 kilometres, I should be winning it. I think they see trail running as one discipline, and not as a sport with many different facets. It's a bit like expecting a marathoner to also be a decent 100-metre runner.

One of the four races I did say yes to was the ProNutro AfricanX Trail Run. This is a three-day stage race with a couple of 34-kilometre stages and a shorter final stage of 22 kilometres. It's also a team race, and I ran with South African trail runner Cas van Aardenne. It was a bit of a stuff-up, to be honest. Firstly, the final day got cancelled due to bad weather and, secondly, because I was just totally off the boil. I didn't feel great and was probably still a bit fatigued after Atacama, but I still gave it everything I had, and we ended up coming third. I felt bad because Cas had really trained hard for the event, and I was definitely the weaker link. Given my poor post–Gobi March effort at the Hout Bay Trail Challenge, I should've known better. But, again, coming back from the Atacama I was on such a high that I felt invincible.

It wasn't the result I was hoping for, especially because there was this ongoing vibe among some of the local runners that I was being overhyped, and that I was only doing well in the 4 Deserts Series because it wasn't very competitive. It seems to be a very South African thing. It always hurt me quite a bit … like if you do well, it's almost as if your neighbour wanted you to do badly. It's weird. The Americans, on the other hand, seem to have a different attitude. They'll be super-tight at the event and if the one guy wins, the other guy is really stoked for him.

Ironically, given my little moan about not being suited to shorter distances, I won my next races. They were all 12 kilometres. After AfricanX, I went to Knysna in July to run the Featherbed trail races over the Oyster Festival weekend. As I said, they didn't suit my strengths, but I always enjoy going back to Knysna – it's where it all started for me, after all – and I managed to win them, so it helped ease the disappointment of AfricanX a little.

As it turned out, Knysna would again be the place where something started for me. This time, though, it had nothing to do with running.

I was at race registration for the Featherbed and about to leave with

'Big Steve' Greeff, who runs Salomon's operations in the Western Cape, when Mark Collins, who owns Magnetic South Events, the company that runs the Featherbed, came running up to me, saying there was someone he really thought I should meet. I followed him outside … and there was this beautiful blonde called Vanessa Haywood. Mark must have had some kind of match-making mojo going on because Vanessa and I hit it off immediately. There was clearly an instant connection for both of us, and it was only when Big Steve started giving me the 'we've got to go now, pal' eyeball that we said goodbye. We exchanged numbers with a rather vague plan to meet up a few days later.

Vanessa is going to hate me for saying this, but she pretty much started messaging me the next day. Then, a few days later, I got another message, inviting me over for dinner. Obviously, I said yes. Hey, I had been single for a *long* time!

Big Steve wasn't all that pleased, though. I was supposed to go out with some of the Salomon guys and, with my best interests at heart, he started giving me a lecture about how a serious relationship wasn't good for my career. I was like, 'C'mon Steve, I'm just going for dinner.' And that's all it was. Dinner. Still, I got back quite late and Steve was kind of waiting up for me (we were sharing this little chalet). I let myself in quietly, only to find Steve in the living area, sitting on a little stool. Cue 101 questions about what I had got up to. 'We just had supper and chatted' was not the answer he wanted to hear.

He particularly didn't want to hear that I'd agreed to run one of the Featherbed races with Vanessa the next morning. The Featherbed is actually three races over the same day: a morning 12-kilometre race, which I won; a 12-kilometre midday race, which I did with Vanessa; and another 12-kilometre race in the late afternoon, which I also won.

The midday race with Vanessa was painfully slow, but in her defence she wasn't feeling too great and she is a lot quicker these days. We hung out together during that whole week, and things moved quickly – by the Friday we were pretty much a couple. That's how I remember it. Interestingly, Vanessa has a different take: 'By the Thursday evening I was like, "Ryan, are you ever going to kiss me or not?" He'll tell you he was playing hard to get, and that he wanted to take things slow because his career comes first. But actually he's just super-shy.'

Lies. All lies!

Nevertheless, things moved along a lot more quickly than either of us – and especially Big Steve – anticipated. Happily for me, I had someone who was not only prepared to put up with the long, solitary hours that came with my career, but who was also super-supportive. So super-supportive, in fact, that she would support me at my next race …

STUFF I'VE LEARNT

Trust your body

I never race with a heart-rate monitor. I might use one in training because my coach likes the feedback, but basically I prefer to listen to my own body.

I think a heart-rate monitor can make you a little lazy in this respect. You become too reliant on it, and you can lose touch with what your body is actually saying to you. Run without one and you'll begin to instinctively recognise what hear-rate zone you are in, and be able to push or slow down depending on where you want to be. And let's face it – these devices aren't always the most accurate. My resting heart rate is currently around 42 beats per minute, but I can push it up to about 195 or 196. On a recent training run, however, it was showing 200 beats per minute. Obviously, there was something wrong with the device. One could argue that the fact I'd just seen two Cape cobras on the trail in the space of three minutes had something to do with it. Still, 200 was a little on the high side. I did actually hit 200 properly once. It was back in 2008, when I was training in the environmental chamber before the Sahara Race, but your heart rate does drop as you get older and mine never gets close to that any more.

Always fill up your bottles

Even if your route map says there are only five kays to go from the last water point, I would still fill up my water bottles. You never know what you are in for. In my experience, those route maps and the accompanying pre-stage brief are sometimes spectacularly inaccurate. You hear that this particular bit is tricky – only it's not – and that it's five kays to the finish from the last water point … except it's more like eight.

This happened to me on Day 4 at the Atacama Crossing. We were told it was eight kays to the finish and fairly easy running over some hard-packed ground. Usually that would mean you'd only need one bottle and a couple of gels to get you through. Turns out that after running for another one and a half hours, going over one massive 100-metre dune after the next, I could eventually see the finish – except it was at the top of what looked, to me, like a mini– Mount Everest. Mentally, that breaks you and if you have no more sustenance, you're in a fair amount of trouble.

Trust me, I've learnt the hard way. Don't cut corners when it comes to stocking up on food and water. You might have further to go than you think, and then there's always variables, like the weather or equipment failure, which might add considerable time spent on a stage.

Adjusting to altitude

It's an age-old debate: for how long before an event held at altitude should you acclimatise? It's always been a widely discussed issue for rugby teams coming to Johannesburg for a big game. The city is, after all, 1 750 metres above sea level. Should you arrive a week before to get used to the conditions? Or should you jet in the same day and play the game before your body has time to realise what's hit it? The latter is a tactic the New Zealand teams have used with annoying success.

Fortunately, there's no debate when it comes to endurance sport events. If your regular training environment is anywhere close to sea level, you have to acclimatise your body to the loftier heights that will host the event you have entered. Without doing that, you have no chance.

Minimum time for acclimatising

Look, a lot does depend on genetics and some people are simply able to acclimatise quicker than others.

As a rough guide, however, I would say two weeks, depending on the height. Before the Atacama Crossing, which takes place at over 2 000 metres, I was in the Drakensberg for about 10 days and then in Bolivia for another 10 days. As it turned out, that worked well; so, ideally, I would recommend three weeks.

If you want to be serious about a 100-mile, single-stage race, like the legendary Leadville Trail 100 Run – an event held at the 3 200-metre mark – it's best to acclimatise in stages. I would say you almost need to spend three weeks at about 2 000 metres, before moving up to Leadville's altitude for another 10 days to two weeks.

Always going to be tougher

The reality is that unless you have grown up or lived for many years at altitude, you're never going to find it easy. Even when I've spent a few months training at altitude and subsequently won the race I was training for, I always felt uncomfortable, if not downright nauseous, during the race. Speak to someone like US ultra-distance legend Scott Jurek, who has lived at altitude, and he'll tell you that maybe once a month he'll have a day when he feels good, but it's never like you're running down at the coast or at lower altitudes, when you're feeling really good most of the time.

7

PROVING A POINT, MOVING ON ... AND THEN PROVING IT AGAIN

Next up was a local race a little more suited to my abilities – the 2010 Peninsula Ultra Fun Run (PUFfer). An 80-kilometre race over mountains from Cape Point to the V&A Waterfront, it's a hardcore trail run involving a lot of scrambling up and over steep ravines. It would be an interesting test to see if I actually had the ability to pursue my future mountain-running ambitions, and an opportunity to answer my local naysayers.

Maybe I'm exaggerating the negativity – I can be a little sensitive at times – but that's how I remember feeling about all the comments that were circulating. It was hard to read not just critical, but pretty disrespectful, stuff about me from the same people who had been so supportive when I had won the 4 Deserts Series.

Some of the online posts on certain forums were saying that I wasn't a real runner because I hadn't run that most famous of all South African road races, the iconic 90-kilometre Comrades Marathon. It was something of an old-school mentality that thought trail running shouldn't be taken seriously, and I guess a lot of people were pissed off because I was getting a lot of media attention – certainly more than the athletes who won the Comrades. I was seen as someone whose exploits were fuelled more by an effective PR machine than actual athletic ability. One journalist even listed the names of South African trail runners who she thought were better than me.

Some of the guys on that list were also pretty vocal in their opinions of me. I even had a 'moment' with one of them at the 2011 Otter African Trail Run – a 42-kilometre trail run along the well-known Otter hiking route between the Storms River mouth and the Groot River estuary in Nature's Valley (apologies, I'm skipping ahead here). I had been running behind him for ages, mostly because he wouldn't let me get past. The trail was narrow with dense vegetation on either side, which meant I couldn't pass without being overly aggressive. Eventually I thought 'stuff this!', and tried to squeeze by, but as I did he kind of stopped me from passing. It's not really in my nature to get into an argument with someone under these circumstances – especially during a trail run along the beautiful Garden Route – so I hung back for a while. I ran on his heels for another eight kays, and then finally slipped past and managed to win the race, setting a record time of 4:40:15.

Getting back to the PUFfer, this was my big opportunity to show the South African running community that I was the real deal. Besides, my new girlfriend was helping Big Steve crew for me, and of course I had to show her what a world-class athlete she was now involved with. It was a nice opportunity for her and Big Steve to bond too. After his fatherly speech in Knysna and his stated dislike for blondes, I figured the two of them needed to get to know each other a little better. Happily, after he saw her dedication to the task at hand, he had to concede that perhaps, possibly, maybe, she was okay.

There were a few big local names in the race and I started off conservatively, running in the front bunch, but not ready yet to make a break. The weather was an issue too – shortly into the race we were hit by a storm of biblical proportions, and it was clear not everyone around me was coping too well with these adverse conditions. I bided my time and then, just before Ou Kaapse Weg, made my move and pulled away.

I ended up winning the race an hour and 18 minutes ahead of the second-placed runner, and broke the course record by 16 minutes. Given the conditions we ran in that day, I was really chuffed with the result. It was a convincing statement that would silence those critics. In hindsight, I feel a bit stupid remembering how badly I had wanted to prove myself against my detractors back home, but that's just how it was. It was a process I had to go through – one of those little hurdles in life that help you to feel comfortable in your own skin.

The PUFfer was ideal prep for my next international race – the inaugural Trans-Alpine Run, which would take place two weeks later in Europe. I was running with fellow South African trail runner Linda Doke in the mixed category. The Trans-Alpine would be an interesting test for me – it's a 270-kilometre race run over eight stages from Germany, down through Austria, Switzerland and into Italy. Obviously, the distance and format suited me, but the terrain would be completely unfamiliar. In fact, it would be the polar opposite of my stage-racing experience thus far.

Linda was a strong runner, having twice won the 200-kilometre Cape Odyssey stage race from Hermanus to Boschendal wine farm, as well as being the reigning women's AfricanX champ (the one where I had blown so badly). As Team Salomon/Velocity Sports Lab, we were something of an unknown quantity to the European mountain-running community, but this 'under the radar' status suited both of us. It was going to be a tough race – not because we were undercooked or anything like that, but simply because we were both utterly inexperienced when it came to running through alpine mountains. It was towards the end of the European summer, so at least it wasn't ridiculously cold. Still, we were running through the Alps and they are nothing like the mountains back home. In Cape Town, running along Table Mountain, you can see the ocean on one side and the city on the other, but here all you can see from your mountain is more mountains. Plus, you are sliding all over the place in the snow.

Again, altitude would be a factor – the race takes place at an average of around 2 300 metres, with the highest point being just under 3 000 metres. With both of us living at sea level, the best way to acclimatise would be to head for the Drakensberg, which we did. We stayed at the Sani Pass Hotel, situated at just under 3 000 metres. Linda headed up there a few days before me, as I still had the PUFfer to do, and we trained there for a week. It was a week that presented some challenges ...

There was no running water in our chalets, and we had electricity only from 6 to 9 p.m., which meant that washing oneself involved boiling a kettle and using a bucket. I don't know about you, but getting naked when it's –3 °C outside, and pouring lukewarm water over yourself, is not something I enjoy. Having spent a week running in the desert without washing my clothes, however, meant I wasn't too fussed about my daily ablutions here either. Linda had to put up with an increasingly smelly running partner for a week.

On the upside, I wasn't sweating that much. Not only was it chilly, but being in recovery mode after the PUFfer, my daily runs weren't much longer than an hour or so. It also meant I got to spend some time in the hotel's famous pub, 'Africa's Highest Pub', chatting to locals and passing travellers, which was fun. Sani is a heaven for trail running at altitude, and I'll definitely be back ... but with a camping shower of some sorts.

Our time there paid off, and Linda and I did reasonably well in the Trans-Alpine, given our newbie status. We managed to finish third or fourth every day, and on the final stage we put in a big effort to finish second. That secured us third place overall in a time of 35:21:06.

It was a credible performance. I felt pretty strong throughout, but having seen what the European athletes could do in these mountains, it was clear I had some work to do if I wanted to be a real contender on this terrain. The fitness was there, but what I was sorely missing was experience.

My next event was also in the snow, but not the alpine kind. This was the type you find at the other end of the world ... Antarctica. The fourth race in the 4 Deserts Series, The Last Desert race would be a landmark event for me. If I won it, I'd be the first person to win all four of the 4 Deserts events, but with my sights now set beyond this series, it would also represent the end of a chapter. A few years down the line, I would return to do a few of RacingThePlanet's 'roving races', which they tag onto the 4 Deserts Series each year, but this would be my final 4 Deserts race. The series had been very good to me and it was instrumental in my becoming a professional athlete, but it was time to move on. I thought so, and I think the international trail-running community thought the same. It was time for this Ryan Sandes guy to show us what he could do in the big one-day mountain races and 100-milers.

To be honest, the whole 'be the first person to win all the 4 Deserts races' was more of a media spin than an actual goal of mine – I merely wanted to run all of them – but now that it was out there, I had to go for it. Besides, I would be travelling to Antarctica, and how many people get to do that in their lifetime?

Looking at the entry list, there didn't appear to be anyone who could trouble me, which brought with it its own pressures. And I knew I could run in the blazing heat of a desert, but I had very little idea how my body would respond to prolonged exposure and physical exertion in extreme cold weather. There were other external factors too, like coping with seasickness. During the race, the expedition ship would be our base, and the year before, Dean Karnazes had competed and suffered severely from seasickness. It got so bad, he almost had to pull out.

We boarded the expedition ship in Ushuaia, an Argentinian town that's part of the Tierra del Fuego archipelago – the southernmost tip of South America – and sailed through the famous Beagle Channel and Mackinlay Pass, before heading across the Drake Passage to the Antarctic land mass. The Drake Passage itself was an interesting experience. It's known to have some of the roughest seas in the world and, although we didn't quite experience its full wrath, there were a few occasions when we would be eating and suddenly our plates of food were hovering somewhere around our heads. The boat was designed for these waters, though, and all the tables were bolted to the floor and the chairs secured with chains.

We were thrown around a bit during the crossing, and I had to hold onto my bunk to stop myself from getting tossed out of bed, but on the whole it wasn't too scary. Fortunately, with the help of a special patch that you put behind your ear, I managed to dodge the seasick bullet, but not everyone was that lucky. All in all there were 80 competitors on the ship, and about 30 others who were either ship crew, media or part of the RacingThePlanet organisation.

Nearing Antarctica, the sea flattened and the wildlife was incredible. Albatross and petrels were gliding just above the swells, humpback whales and orcas were playing right next to the ship, and a killer whale was tossing its breakfast – an unlucky penguin – up in the air. I had a quiet chuckle when one of the competitors, while eating his bacon and eggs, remarked how cruel killer whales were as he witnessed nature in action. I wondered how the pig he was eating felt about this.

The race itself had its own unique challenges. Naturally, the elements were one, though I had a whole bag of specially made Salomon kit with me to deal with that (see the section on 'Stuff I've learnt' at the end of this chapter for more details), but the format was a unique one too. It wasn't a point-to-point race like the other 4 Deserts races. For this race, you get taken from island to island where each stage is being run, are given a fixed time for each stage, and then you have to run as many loops of the designated course as you can within the time allocated for that stage. The winner is therefore decided on total distance run rather than elapsed time.

As we approached King George Island for the first stage, I was amped to get going. After two days on the ship, I was getting a bad case of cabin fever and that starter's gun couldn't come soon enough. The stage was due to kick off at 6 a.m. I'd been up since 4 a.m. getting ready and was about to leave my cabin when they announced that the winds were too strong and the race start was going to be delayed. Would we ever get off the flippin' ship and actually run?

Finally, the weather played ball. It was suddenly all systems go and a scramble to get everyone into the Zodiacs and to the starting line. We were given a short briefing and the instruction that we had nine hours to run as many 14.5-kilometre loops as we could. Lining up, I felt weirdly nervous ... it was the same jelly-leg feeling I had had at the start of the Gobi March in 2008. Not what a three-time 4 Deserts winner should be experiencing. Maybe it was the cold.

Running loops is a little mind-numbing, but initially it wasn't too bad, as the loops were fairly long, but towards the end of the week the weather began to get worse, so they made the loops a lot shorter. There was a lot more snow too, making the going slow and very technical. It's not the ideal way to run an endurance race, but from a safety point of view, it's the only way to do it. The weather can close in very quickly, and you don't want to be trying to find a bunch of runners stuck out in an Antarctic blizzard. With the loop system, when the weather goes from sunny to a snowstorm in the space of 10 minutes, they can sound the siren and pull you off the course.

When you're in an environment like this, you kind of realise how insignificant and vulnerable we humans are. On average, the temperature during the race was around –15 °C, but it varied from –5 °C to around –20 °C ... and then you can probably add on another –10 °C for the wind chill. You might be feeling invincible after crossing the finish line to win a stage, but within the space of five minutes you can actually get hypothermia. It's quite humbling.

As I said, thanks to the folk at Salomon, I was quite well kitted out. Before all my races, I've always done my homework to make sure that I've got the right equipment, and I did some testing of prototype gear at Salomon's HQ in Annecy, France. Serge Chapuis and Patrick Leick were Salomon's R&D guys, and I think they get more excited about this stuff than any of the athletes.

Salomon has always been a big snow-sport brand, and they have a massive environmental chamber where you run on a treadmill and they use infrared scanners to see where you are getting cold. Serge would give me running tops with one half made from one material and the other from another material. I'd then run in the chamber to see which worked better. I could literally feel one side of my body getting colder than the other. As a final check, I did some more testing at the Canal Walk branch of local outdoor gear store Cape Union Mart. They have a cold-weather chamber, and it was useful to get an approximation of how my new gear would hold up.

The race was supposed to have six stages, but we ended up running only five. The vagaries of the weather also meant that the format needed to be flexible, and the idea was to try to get in as much mileage as possible in the first half of the week. The first islands you stop at are more runnable, but the further south you travel, the trickier it gets with colder conditions and deeper snow.

You're also on standby a lot of the time, and we had to be prepared to run at any time. There's sunlight for about 16 hours a day, so you could be woken up at 2 a.m. and be told that the next stage was going to get underway in two hours. Suddenly, you had to be up and brace yourself to jump into the small Zodiac and be ferried to whatever island was hosting the day's stage.

I started the first stage completely kitted out in all my new high-tech stuff, but after running for a kilometre I was getting so hot, I had to pull most of it off. I removed all my base layers and ran with the shell jacket and tights. I managed to run four loops of the 16-kilometre route within the allotted time, comfortably building up a lead. There wasn't much in the way of competition from the other runners, and the only thing that kept me on my toes was this bird. It obviously had a nest close to the trail route, and out of nowhere I was thumped on the back of the head. I hit the deck in fright. Turns out I'd been dive-bombed by a skua gull and every time I'd come past, it would line me up for another strafing run. The route did a figure of eight, so every loop I had to pass the damn thing twice, and every single time this flippin' maniac gull would have a go at me. It eventually got so hectic that I would grab handfuls of snow and make snowballs to fend it off.

At least the bird helped keep my concentration levels up because it became clear that as beautiful as this environment was – snow-white mountains, frozen blue ice lakes, a sky filled with birds, and penguins shuffling alongside the runners – it was also one where things can so easily go wrong. A couple of competitors had to drop out that first day, when they ran slightly off the route and dropped through an ice sheet. They only got their feet soaked, but that was enough. Within minutes, their feet got so cold that they had to pull out of the race.

Not such bad luck for me, and I had secured the start I wanted in case some of the other stages got cancelled due to bad weather. Stage two also took place on King George Island, but unfortunately the weather did not play along, and we were pulled off the course after 30 or 40 minutes. I was a bit bummed on the way back to the ship, but I felt a lot better knowing that I had a comfortable cushion of 14.5 kilometres after winning stage one.

Stage three was the long stage and it took place further south, on Deception Island, which is not only an active volcano, but also infamous for having been a whaling station in days gone by. They hunted so many whales that there are still whalebones sticking out of the ground all over the place. It's a fascinating place – a caldera – and the bay is almost completely surrounded by land, save for a single narrow opening out into the ocean. Once a day, the whole bay basically becomes this giant hot spring as volcanic activity heats up the water.

Unfortunately, not even the spectacular beauty of Deception Island could counter the drudgery of what was in store for us, as we embarked on one of the most unusual long-distance endurance stages on the planet. We had to run as many 2.5-kilometre loops as possible in 15 hours. You're basically running round and round in circles on an island of snow. It's as surreal as it sounds, believe me. The loop was mostly flat – actually the whole race is basically flat – with a couple of small climbs no more than 100 metres long. The only issue you had to worry about was the fact that it was very slippery, but I was wearing ice spikes to compensate. Conditions were not ideal, and we started off running in a blizzard.

Mentally, this was one of the toughest things I've had to do, especially because I couldn't get into my own head space – my running zone – and switch off. I was always passing people, which was distracting, and there was no actual goal to aim for, no finish line. We were all just going round and round like headless chickens, with very few visual clues as to how far ahead or behind you were. It was basically just a matter of gritting my teeth and getting through it. There was nothing enjoyable about it, and I had to dig really deep from loops 15 to 35. My legs felt flat, my feet ached, and I felt like I was running in slow motion.

As I finished loop 35, though, I was told we would be finishing the stage early due to a big low pressure moving in. It suddenly gave me this instant mental boost, and my legs felt recharged. Now I had a goal. I wanted to tick off 100 kilometres, and I needed to complete five more loops to get there before they called us in. I did it and felt really strong crossing the finish line. It is amazing how being in the right mental state can affect your physical performance.

Again, I won the stage comfortably ahead of the field and, bar any catastrophe, that was basically the race done and dusted. That said, the catastrophe almost happened on the Zodiac back to the expedition ship. I was pretty tired after running 100 kilometres, and on the little boat my core temperature suddenly dropped and I was wracked by uncontrollable shivers. I was clearly on the brink of hypothermia. Back on board, the only thing I could do was stand under a piping hot shower until I slowly began to warm up.

That evening we were briefed that the fourth and final stage would be held on a massive glacier called Dorian Bay. A glacier it might be, but icy it wasn't. The thing was covered in waist-deep snow, which was physically impossible to run through – the best you could do was a kind of fast shuffle. I figured out it was best to let someone run in front of me for the first few loops, which would compact the snow and create this narrow little path that I could then actually run along.

The final stage went to script, and it was just a matter of managing the elements and dealing with the endless loops. I proudly ran the last one with the South African flag flapping in the wind behind me, and even afforded myself the luxury of stopping once or twice to take in the panoramic views from the top of the glacier. As I ran down the final hill to the finish line, I was a mass of emotions and covered in goosebumps caused as much by the occasion as by the temperature.

And that was that: I had won The Last Desert race. And I had won it comfortably, completing 230.5 kilometres in the time allotted – around 37 kilometres more than my closest competitor. I was really happy with that.

If only it hadn't felt like such a big anticlimax. There was some pressure to win, to complete the set of 4 Deserts races, and I had done it here in the snow of the Antarctic with relative ease. Perhaps, if the victory had come after a close tussle with another runner, I would've felt more of a sense of achievement, but it hadn't.

It was a bittersweet moment for me. This was the bookend to a pivotal chapter in my life, but the race itself hadn't quite lived up to what I had hoped this significant moment would be. The Last Desert race was an awesome experience and it's something I'll remember for the rest of my life, but it also left me with a certain emptiness. I'd spent the last three years intensely focused on the 4 Deserts Series. It had started my career and shaped me into the person I am today.

Now what?

My basic plan was to have a crack at those European mountain races, but I didn't have the kind of detailed plan that had shaped the last few years. I guess I'm a bit of a control freak and, having had the whole of 2010 meticulously planned out, suddenly there was a big mountain in front of me – both metaphorically and physically – and I wasn't totally sure how I was going to get up and over it.

One thing I knew for sure, though, was that I was definitely done with 4 Deserts. However, a few well-intentioned people close to me weren't that sure. They weren't quite convinced that I had what it takes to make the next jump. Prof. Tim Noakes had publicly said that I was actually quite an ordinary athlete when you looked at my marathon times, but I think some people misinterpreted what he was saying. He was really making a point about my mental strength, and comparing a marathon athlete to an ultra-distance trail runner obviously isn't the same thing. There was consequently a lot of advice that I should maybe just stick to the multiday stage stuff because it's what I clearly excelled at, and I could keep winning.

To know me, though, is to know that it's not just all about winning. Obviously, I like to do well and the will to cross the line first was clearly a strong motivator in my successes, but I've always had a strong desire to try new experiences. Over the previous couple of years, I could see how I had improved as a runner and I wanted to keep evolving, both as an athlete and as a person.

Besides, it was still pissing me off that my achievements were being dissed, and that the 4 Deserts Series was seen as 'not that competitive' compared to the single-stage, 100-mile races. Sure, it was true

117

to a degree – and I had recognised that – but still, I'd beaten guys like Mike Wolfe, Marco Olmo (who had won the prestigious Ultra-Trail du Mont-Blanc twice), and Alberto Oviedo and Salvador Redondo, who'd both done well in one-day, big-mountain races. I might have silenced my local critics, but I still felt I needed to put a zip in the criticism coming from overseas.

I decided to enter the Ultra-Trail du Mont-Blanc, or the UTMB, as it's commonly called. Regarded as Europe's toughest trail race, it's held over a 167-kilometre route, with a cumulative 9 600-metre elevation gain, across the Alps through France, Italy and Switzerland.

Having secured my entry, I flew to France to be part of the next Salomon Advanced Training Week in Lamont, and again hooked up with Salomon's international team manager, Greg Vollet. Greg has always been a good sounding board for me and someone whose advice I've always valued. During the Advanced Training Week, we spent a lot of time chatting about my future, but he wasn't convinced that doing the UTMB was the right thing – at least not at that point in my career.

I kind of knew he was right. The Trans-Alpine Run with Linda had shown me that there was a lot I still needed to learn about running in the mountains, and Greg suggested that the Leadville Trail 100 Run in the Colorado Rockies would be a better alternative. It wasn't quite as mountainous as the UTMB, but the altitude at between 2 800 metres and 3 800 metres was a massive factor. It would be a good way to improve my mountain-running skills and gain experience, plus Salomon were also looking to make inroads into the American market, so there were commercial benefits for my sponsor too. It made a lot of sense. I withdrew from the UTMB and entered the 2011 Leadville Trail 100 Run, to be held in August the following year.

But, before that, I had a little engagement waiting for me in Abu Dhabi.

STUFF I'VE LEARNT

What to wear for an Antarctic stage race

This was the race apparel and footwear I used during The Last Desert race, in Antarctica:

Outer shell

You need one that is both fully waterproof and breathable. It's a key necessity in the Antarctic climate, because if you get too hot and start sweating, your sweat freezes and you run the risk of getting hypothermia.

Layers

I had four different types of base layers for both top and bottom, which ranged from relatively light to really thick and warm. I also had some standard alpine tights, which I used a lot in some of the early stages, plus my standard trail-running stuff, which included a windproof jacket and a lightweight waterproof one as well. I also had different types of thermal socks, and inner thermal and outer waterproof gloves.

Footwear

I was fortunate to have had specially developed running shoes made for me by Salomon's footwear guru, Patrick Leick. They were based on one of Salomon's standard shoes, but they were fully waterproof and had an ankle extension, like a hiking boot. They were great – not at all like a hiking boot, which is quite stiff, but light and very flexible. Initially, I tried some of the lighter Salomon alpine hiking boots, but they were too heavy and stiff for me.

I also had some ice spikes to clip onto the shoes if conditions became too icy, which is exactly what happened on the long stage. The downside was that all the ice would pack around the shoes, and I ended up running with an extra half a kilo on each foot. Not ideal when you're running 100 kilometres, but the extra grip the crampon spikes afforded was essential.

In the last five years, the various footwear brands, including Salomon, have started to make running shoes specifically for snow. Salomon further developed and modified the prototype I used during The Last Desert race into the S-Lab Snowcross, which you can now buy.

Don't accept sponsorship from a product you don't believe in

Just before the Antarctic race, I signed with Red Bull. You have to be a decent athlete to get picked up by Red Bull, so I was pretty chuffed that they approached me. I'd always liked the way they look at sponsorships. Red Bull likes to work with an athlete to develop not only their talents, but also the sport in which they're involved. By building up a tight and long-lasting relationship with the athlete, he or she will become an authentic brand ambassador because there's a shared goal. I also liked the way that they didn't sell branded merchandising – you had to earn it. Only Red Bull–sponsored athletes receive those iconic Red Bull caps. You can't buy them anywhere, and for an athlete they are a badge of honour.

Still, as progressive as they are in their approach to sponsorship, I wouldn't have signed on the dotted line if I didn't believe in their product. Red Bull gets a fair amount of flack because it is supposed to be bad for you, but, like coffee, only if you slug back too much are you going to feel a bit buzzy.

Red Bull definitely works for me during a race or long training runs. I mix it with water and drink it towards the end of the event or session. It's a tactic many endurance athletes make use of, as the caffeine gives you an energy burst and keeps you alert.

I know this sounds like I'm paying the bills here, but trust me, it's not in my nature to be involved with something in which I don't believe. It's six years down the line, and I'm still proudly wearing that Red Bull cap.

8

I WOULD RUN 100 KAYS AND THEN 100 MORE ... AND HATE IT

The year 2011 started off on a glamorous note, with an invite to attend the Laureus World Sports Awards to be held that year in Abu Dhabi. The call came out of the blue, saying I would be one of the featured athletes, and I reckoned, well, why the hell not. I had kind of heard of the Laureus Awards, but I'd never paid it too much attention. A Google search quickly educated me on what a big deal the annual awards ceremony actually was, and that my usual jeans-and-T-shirt attire wasn't going to cut it.

With my first ever bespoke tuxedo packed in my luggage and two complimentary first-class tickets in hand, Vanessa and I flew north for the daunting prospect of mingling with the world's top sportsmen and women, and some high-flying Hollywood celebs. They had requested some video footage of me from my 4 Deserts wins, and they were going to splice that into a live interview that would take place during the awards. Turns out Oscar-winning actor Kevin Spacey would be conducting the interview ... cue slight freak-out. Fortunately they gave me the questions beforehand, so I literally memorised the answers.

We'd arrived a couple of days ahead of the awards, as there was a series of functions, golf days and cocktail parties attached to the event as well. With The North Face 100 in Australia coming up soon after this, I was still trying to squeeze in some training – not easy in this part of the world. I didn't want to head out into the desert for fear of getting lost, so I ended up running along the centre island of this massive multi-lane highway that runs through Abu Dhabi. There's me running along amid thousands of cars on either side. Surreal.

But not as surreal as standing in front of a massive audience, during a global TV broadcast, talking to Kevin Spacey about my career. I was petrified he'd ask me something off the cuff, but happily he kept to the teleprompter script behind me and it all went off pretty smoothly.

It was really interesting for me to see how some of the top athletes conducted themselves too. There was an after-party as well, but guys like Spanish tennis superstar Rafael Nadal and world-title-winning surfer Kelly Slater all declined. I could see how super-focused they were. Nothing got in the way of their training and preparation ... not even a prestigious after-party in the United Arab Emirates.

Although I was pretty nervous attending the awards, being there ended up really inspiring and motivating me. Taking on 2011 was a step into the unknown for me, and I was going to need all the help I could get.

Once word got out that I was no longer doing the UTMB, the trolls back home once again stuck their heads outside their caves. There were mutterings that the reason I'd pulled out was because I was scared: the UTMB was the most competitive race in the world and the field was too strong for me. Plus, my Salomon teammate Kílian Jornet had entered and I was scared of him. Yes, Kílian would no doubt have beaten me at the UTMB – I was under no illusions that this was his territory and not mine – but they all seemed to ignore the fact that he was also running The North Face 100 in Australia, the same race I had now entered.

This Aussie 100-kilometre race was a totally new experience – from the obvious fact that it was going to be my first big one-day race, to travelling with an entire squad in the shape of the Salomon team, and having to engage in a series of media activities in the weeks leading up to the race. As you'd know by now, my usual pre-race routine is to hang out on my own and just kind of zone out into my own head space, but here I was attending a whole bunch of movie screenings and media interviews. It was pretty intense and I was like, geez, I wish I could just get off my feet now and chill. I never felt like I actually had the space to focus on the race. I think the team has got a lot better at handling this attention and also saying no to a lot of media requests, but back then it felt like one rad adventure for a bunch of overexcited young athletes. Though I had been there for a school rugby tour back in 1999, for a few of the guys it was the first time they'd been to Sydney, and with everything that was going on it was easy to forget the reason you were actually there.

I was rooming with Kílian too, which, on the one hand, was cool because we were both new to all this media stuff and trying to figure out how to deal with it together. But, on the other hand, there was a slightly weird dynamic because, although we were teammates, we were also competitors.

We did a couple of recce runs in the lead-up to the race – nothing too long, about 20 kilometres each. We'd head out into the Blue Mountains beyond the town of Katoomba, which is where the race starts. It was during one of these that I first witnessed one of Kílian's little pre-race psych-outs. We were running down this one really technical descent – not slowly either, I might add – and suddenly he grabbed his phone out of his pocket and bolted down ahead of us. I had never seen someone hit a descent like that before, and my wide-eyed expression let him know that his tactic had worked.

He was taking these really small footsteps, ignoring the switch-backs, and just flying straight down with what looked like no effort, focus or concentration. I mean, the guy was jumping over rocks and bushes before suddenly grabbing onto a tree to swing himself over a big boulder, while simultaneously unlocking his phone with his other hand.

He did it because he wanted to Tweet a pic of Team Salomon out on a training run, but the clear subtext was to give the rest of us a glimpse of what he could *really* do. It neatly places the thought in the back of your mind that if he wanted to put a minute on you on a descent, he could do it in his sleep.

Kílian actually started his career doing ski mountaineering, where you have to get up the mountain as quickly as you can carrying the skis and then ski down. I think he's so used to going 20 times faster on the skis that when it comes to trail races, running down probably feels like slo-mo.

Later that year, after running Leadville, I went home via the UTMB to not only crew for the Salomon athletes but also to watch the race up close. Kílian employed the same tactic – he would run ahead, wait for the guys, and then show them a flower. He did the same thing when he came to South Africa to run the Crazy Store Table Mountain Challenge in 2011. He was entered into the solo category, and on the first leg he bolted ahead and then started taking pictures of the sunrise over Cape Town. Obviously, for the rest of the field who don't even want to stop at a water point because it wastes time, this is a mind-blower. Here's someone who appears so confident in his abilities that he's prepared to give up a minute to take a photograph. And, yes, he did win the men's solo category – pretty easily.

The thing with Kílian, though, is that he's not really about show-ing off. He's super-talented – almost freakishly so when it comes to running in the mountains – but there's no big ego. The mountains are his playground, and I think he's just having fun. He's quite a spiritual individual too, and you know he's stopping to show you a flower or to take a pic of the sunrise because he genuinely wants to share his experiences with the world. Still, he's a fierce competitor and I think there's a small bit of him that knows he's psyching out the rest of us. I've got to say, I quite admire him for that.

On race day I was feeling pretty good. As it was my first 100-kay race, I was more of a dark horse than an actual favourite, which suited me fine. Katoomba is about a two-hour drive from Sydney, and at around 1 °C or 2 °C, it was bloody freezing when the gun went off at 7 a.m. One of the Australian runners went flying off the front – Stu Gibson, who had won it the year before. You know how competitive the Aussies are – especially on their own turf – and he was determined to show us international athletes that we couldn't just rock up and steal the prize.

Kílian took off after him and basically just played with him for the first 20 kays. The initial part of the race was quite an undulating, technical route that involved going up a few long flights of stairs and along a ridge before dropping down into the canyon. I wasn't far back, and when the trail opened up a little, I could see them 500 metres up ahead – my cue to pin back my ears and push a little. I joined Kílian and the two of us dropped Stu and ran together for the next 15 kilometres, then suddenly my wheels came off. Out of nowhere, I started cramping and had absolutely nothing in my legs. Maybe it was the cold or maybe I just got my nutrition wrong, but I had nothing.

I could feel it at the 36-kilometre checkpoint and then, about three kays later, just as Salomon teammate François D'Haene also joined us, I got shipped out the back. It was a proper psychological slap upside the head. One minute everything's pretty cool and I'm running with Kílian, feeling on top of the world, setting the pace, and the next minute this handbrake arrives out of nowhere. It literally felt like in a matter of 100 metres ... boom! That was it. Me done.

My mate Dean Leslie from The African Attachment was there filming for Salomon, and François caught us just as we popped up onto this road where Dean was waiting with his camera. As part of the ongoing documentary we'd been making, Dean had been with me at quite a few races and would normally follow me, but now, working for Salomon on this gig, he had to go with the front-runners. Dean knows me very well, and he could obviously see by the look on my face that I was in trouble. I can remember him looking concerned and saying, 'Hang in there, dude!' before having to drive off after Kílian and François.

My two teammates took off and I was left behind, cramping and feeling a bit like I had tried to play with the big boys, but had been left with a bloodied nose. Questions of whether or not I'm actually good enough for this whole scene started to bounce around in my head. This was a big international marketing push for Salomon, and although it was my first 100 kay, they had had enough faith to include me in the first proper team they were sending to a race outside of their home turf of Europe. And here I was, letting them down.

For the next 30 kays I forged on, feeling pretty shitty and constantly looking over my shoulder, expecting to see the bunch of determined Australians wearing 'I told you so, mate' grins on my heels. I reckon if they had appeared and I'd dropped three or four places, I might well have chucked in the towel – but, miraculously, there was no sign of them and, even more miraculously, I gradually began to feel better.

I finished the race in third place in 9:54:57, a whole 36 minutes behind Kílian, who won it, and François, who came second. I felt some sense of pride that I'd toughed it out and was able to give Salomon a 1-2-3 podium, and the team was obviously very chuffed too. Deep down, though, I was flippin' disappointed with my performance. Sure, Salomon had dominated an event put on by outdoor brand rival The North Face – box ticked – but I wasn't in the best head space. I can't say I totally enjoyed either the build-up to the event or the race itself – I spent far too much time outside my comfort zone – but I knew this was both a wake-up call and an education into the world of professional trail running.

I'm still not exactly sure what went wrong that day. It could've been a nutrition issue – I'd lost one of my little bottles of Perpetuem during the hustle and bustle of the start, but only noticed it was missing 500 metres further on, so I wasn't going to turn around and go look for it, especially after the way Stu took off and Kílian followed. Or perhaps I didn't eat enough during the race. To be honest, though, I think I just pushed too much to catch the two up front and paid the price in the middle of the race. Chalk up one to experience gained.

Interestingly, I got quite a lot of positive press back home. I left Australia thinking I'd come home to a general sentiment of 'third place – I told you he wasn't good enough', but, surprisingly, the media seemed to be impressed with my efforts, and those who had previously clucked their tongues in my general direction were now slapping me on the back. My gritted-teeth performance kind of gave me more credibility, and showed everyone back home that I didn't simply win everything I entered. It took the pressure off a little too. Not everything I do had to turn into gold, and that was cool, especially after the disaster my next international race would turn out to be.

Fortunately, before I had to swallow that bitter pill, I had a few sips of champagne, courtesy of a win on home soil. On my return, I entered the Old Fisherman's Trail Challenge, a local race from Hout Bay to Fish Hoek, in which I managed to set a new record. It's only 20 kilometres long, which wasn't really my thing, but a win is a win. For the first time, I felt as if I had the respect of the South African trail-running community.

Next up was the inaugural Salomon Zugspitz Ultratrail in Germany – and another dose of reality. It was part of my ongoing Mountain Running 101 course intended to shift my career path away from the stage races, and it would be a good lead-up to the Leadville 100, which was shaping up to be the real focus of my year.

Held at the end of June, it starts and ends in the town of Grainau at the foot of the Zugspitze, which, at just over 2 900 metres, is part of the Wetterstein Mountains and the highest peak in Germany. The route was around 100 kilometres and included a sizeable 5 400 metres of climbing along some pretty spectacular alpine trails across the north-west face of the Zugspitze, and other imposing peaks with names as tough to pronounce as they were to traverse: the Gatterl, Scharnitzjoch, Ferchensee and the Osternfeldern.

We didn't have the full Salomon team there, but with Spanish runners Miguel Heras and Iker Karrera, German Matthias Dippacher and me, the brand was well represented. I got there a week before the race, and Miguel, Iker and I did a few training runs together. I also got to spend a little more time on my own than I had done in Australia, which was a relief. It really is a beautiful part of the world and my solo runs allowed me to explore the lakes and mountain trails. The weather conditions were a little extreme – really warm down in the valley, but within five kays you could be 1 500 metres up the mountain and running in snow and mist. Like the race in Australia, for Zugspitz it was also mandatory to carry a small backpack, which was just as well, as a jacket, and even gloves, were definitely needed.

The race was a proper intro to mountain running, and the climbs would be a lot tougher than anything I'd experienced before. Certainly tougher than anything I'd done back home, and even steeper than what Linda and I had been up during the Trans-Alpine Run the year before. For the first two kays the route was flat, but then it basically went up 1 500 metres for the next 12 kilometres.

For me, though, the race went downhill from the start.

As soon as we hit the first big climb, I started to battle. Whereas all the European guys kept running, I stopped and started power hiking, and then on the descent they flew down and left me even further behind. This was not supposed to be happening. Before the race I'd even backed myself to surprise everyone and win it, but here I was, looking like an amateur against these European mountain goats. Once again, the Self-Doubt Express pulled up to the station and gave me a seat in first class. Within 10 kays, my head was out of the race, and I started to fall further and further back. Here I was, running through this beautiful scenery with awesome ridge lines and quaint little mountain villages – basically epic trails that runners would do anything to experience – and instead of revelling in it, I was being a mopey idiot because I found myself in ninth or tenth place. It made me even more bleak.

I even started thinking of excuses to pull out of the race. 'Geez, actually, you know, my quads are not feeling great ... and then of course I've got Leadville coming up in eight weeks ... maybe I should just pull out and save myself for that.' At one point I thought of deliberately running off-course so I could withdraw, claiming I had got completely lost. I just didn't want to be there.

At about the 45-kay mark I was running down a descent, basically just going through the motions, when I tripped and hit the deck super-hard. I grazed my hands and arms, and really thwacked my head. I just lay there for a while. Part of me hoped that I'd done some proper damage, which would give me a legit way out – but no: apart from missing a little skin, turns out I was okay.

This was also a turning point for me in the race. As I lay there, it dawned on me just how much I was losing the plot here. Before the Sahara Race, when my hamstrings were a bit twitchy in the days before the start, it never crossed my mind to pull out. It was never an option. I would have started the race on one leg and still backed myself to win.

Time to pull myself together – there was only one person who could dig me out of this little mental hole, and that was me. I knew that if I pulled out now, just because I wasn't going to do well, I would be digging myself in even deeper. I didn't want to let myself down to that degree. Plus, this wasn't a door I wanted to open. Quit once without a legit reason, and it gets easier and easier.

To be fair, this whole dropping out of a race is a tricky one for professional endurance athletes. The reality is that if you want to be competitive, there are only so many ultra-distance events you can do in a year. There's only so much training you can do and events you can race in before it takes a toll on your body. Medical opinion is even beginning to identify a condition called overtraining syndrome, which is causing a big performance drop-off in top endurance athletes.

On the one hand, I think if you pull out you're disrespecting the race and the people trying to gut it out to the finish, but, on the other hand, this is your career and could be the smart thing to do. For me, the deciding factor is that either I've injured myself, or if I'm feeling so physically bad that pushing to the finish is going to punish my system so much that it will compromise the rest of my year.

Anyway, back to Zugspitz. Maybe it was the blow to the head, but I saw the light and my attitude started to readjust. Yes, I was definitely having an off-day and, yes, I wasn't going to win the race, but I was in good enough shape to finish, so let's get it done. Make peace with the fact that you're going to end up in the top 10. Yes, it may not meet your own high standards, but, hey, there are a lot of runners who would be very happy with that result.

From then on – around the 60-kilometre mark – the race started to come back to me and I even started passing a few runners, slowly working my way back up the leaderboard. For the last 10 kays, I even had a close battle with Matthias, who was in third place. He was a better technical descender than I was and we had a good backwards and forwards tussle, until the final descent, when he managed to pull away. He beat me by four minutes. Miguel won by some 23 minutes in 10:55:19, with Iker second, Matthias third and me fourth. Another podium lock-down for Team Salomon. But another disappointment for me. Fourth. I hate fourth even more than I hate second place. Those are my worst positions – second is the first loser and fourth is off the podium.

Being able to regroup and compete over the last 10 kays in the mountains was some consolation, but I was not a happy trail runner. Were my expectations too high? Probably. Was I putting way too much pressure on myself? Yes. But, then again, that was also an integral part of what powered my hunger to win. My easy-going 'I'm just out there to enjoy the trails' vibe isn't always a true reflection of my personality. Yes, that is part of why I run, but I also like winning. A lot. I had run two races as part of the Salomon team and, among the guys, I had come last in both. Not exactly a confidence booster. Still, this wasn't the low point. That would come the next day ...

I woke up feeling really depressed – almost like I was hungover. I just wanted to pull the duvet over my head and spend the day hiding. But I couldn't ... I had a training run to do. My coach, Ian Waddell, wanted me to do a three- or four-hour, really slow run the day after the race – the theory being that running on tired legs would help my body get used to that feeling, as it's definitely part of what running a race like Leadville is all about.

I ran around the incredibly pretty lake at the foot of the Zugspitze, but its natural beauty was lost on me as I struggled to complete what felt like nothing more than a chore. Real doubt set in. I stopped running and sat down on one of the many benches around the lake. Why was I doing this? I wasn't enjoying it at all. Why do something you don't enjoy? Isn't that exactly why you stopped working at Faircape? That guy out there on the lake with his stand-up paddle board – he's enjoying himself. This moisture-wicking-apparel-clad, trail-shoe-wearing misery sitting on the bench certainly wasn't. Was I even good enough at this level? These last two races certainly didn't indicate that. Maybe I should go back to more adventure-style stage races. I am good at those. And I was a lot happier doing them, too.

Then I had to attend the prize-giving that afternoon. That was hard. At least I had been on the podium in Australia, but here I didn't even get a mention. It brought me right back to that little boy at the kid's party, who didn't win a 'pass the parcel' prize. I didn't like it. I needed to win a parcel and I needed to do it soon. Like, at my next race.

The only problem was that I couldn't have picked a tougher event to slay this increasingly bigger monkey on my back. Next up was the Leadville Trail 100 Run in the USA. That '100' referred to miles this time, not kilometres ... and it was at seriously high altitude.

STUFF I'VE LEARNT

Don't panic ... it's a long race

I'm going to start off assuming you've put in the pre-race training required for the realistic result you're after. If you're having a bad day because you've either undertrained or physically hurt yourself, then that's another issue altogether. Feel free to panic. In these instances, I'd recommend you pull out of the race rather than risk further harm. It's just a race, after all, and there will be others. However, if you have put in the requisite hard yards but you're still having a shocker, then read on.

A lot can change during the course of an endurance event. If, at some point in the race, your energy levels have red-lined, or you're feeling physically ill, don't panic. You can bounce back. No doubt your brain will be flooded with 10 kinds of negative thoughts – panic, disappointment, frustration – but the trick is to just relax a little, take the pressure off and maybe throttle back. Forget about the goal you had set for the race and just kind of go with the flow for a while. I know that sounds a bit 'hey shoo wow', but I'm not talking about weaving a wild-flower headband and flashing peace signs to the rest of the field. Rather just disengage your mind from the race and take it easy for a bit.

Nutrition is key here too, so make sure you're eating and drinking enough – sometimes spending a few extra minutes at a water or food point refuelling your body can make all the difference.

I've been in this situation a couple of times – at the 2010 Zugspitz race that I described in this chapter, and during the 2014 Trans-GranCanaria event in the Canary Islands. Here I started off the race well enough, but then I began to have stomach issues and twice had to dart into the bushes. Then my legs weren't feeling great ... I was not in the best frame of mind. But having been through the same thing at Zugspitz, I knew now to have a little internal pow-wow that goes something like this: 'Okay, cool, so we're not having a great day, are we? No. Right, let's just switch off from race mode for a bit, ease off the pace and enjoy the beautiful trail you are running along. Make peace with the fact that you're not going to win this one.'

What tends to happen then is that gradually everything starts to settle down ... and slowly your body begins to remember it's actually in top working order, and it can recall the 'Subject: Time to panic' email sent out earlier.

Next thing, you're starting to overtake people, and that's always a great psychological trip switch. Now it's game on again and you can get back to race mode.

Race strategy: lead from the front or come from behind?

Whether you're vying for podium or just looking to finish, you're going to need some kind of strategy for the race you've entered. There are many approaches, ranging from going out fast and hanging on until the end, to running the first half conservatively and then finishing strong, and taking stock of what's going on around you and then adjusting your pace accordingly.

Each has its advantages. Go out fast, for example, and you can deliver an early psychological blow to your competitors, who might start to think the race is already all but over for them. That, however, has rarely been me. It's a risky strategy and you really have to be confident that you'll be in good enough shape during the latter part of the race to maintain the gap.

My personal strategy

Generally, I have been the run-from-behind guy. It takes a certain amount of discipline to be able to let the front-runners disappear into the distance when the gun goes off. You always panic a bit, but you've also got to back yourself to reel them in. That, in itself, is something of an art. Judging when to start increasing your own pace is something that experience will gradually develop. I've run a couple of shorter, 50-mile races, where I've let guys get too far ahead, and even though I've come on strong in the last third, I left myself with too much to do and couldn't catch them. The legendary Bruce

Fordyce, nine-times winner of the Comrades, used the run-from-behind tactic to perfection.

Ideally, what you want to do is let them go ahead, let the egos play out and let them battle each other, but keep them in sight. And by that I don't necessarily mean you have to physically keep an eye on them, but keep an eye on what the timing splits are.

This, of course, is tough to do if you don't have anyone crewing for you, but if you do, make sure you're always getting a split on how far ahead the front guys are. It goes without saying that you have done your homework as far as knowing the route. And then, depending on whether the remainder of the race is flat, undulating or uphill, and how strong you are feeling, you can judge when to make your move.

If you're at the sharp end of the field, you can always ask people at the checkpoints. Often the rules state that they are not allowed to give you splits but, generally, if you ask them, they kind of give it to you anyway. If you're running in first position, you never know how far the guys are behind you, but when you're running second or third, you can always get those splits.

I have run from the front, though

The downside of the conservative approach is that you don't get to really push the boundaries of what you can do. Yes, bolting out into the unknown means you risk blowing, but it could also mean surprising yourself.

I have run from the front in a couple of races – I did it successfully at The North Face Australia 100 in 2012. I was feeling comfortable and definitely went out a little bit harder than I normally do. It's a risky strategy that happened to work out for me that day. Most of the time, though, I'm going to stick with my trusted come-from-behind approach, but where I need to, I will take the risk.

The Western States 100 in California is one race where I might try that. I've had some bad luck there with illness and injury, and I've come second once. The next time, if I run it again, I'll probably go a little bit harder from the front. I don't want to come second again. I'd rather throw it all in and come either first or tenth. A lot of the European races see the front guys start off really quickly, and some of them have the calibre to stick to that, so I might have to go with them in those events.

For the weekend warriors out there

My advice would be to start conservatively and finish strong – especially in ultra-endurance events. It's a great confidence builder when you smash the last half of a race. If you finish feeling broken, you never have good memories of the event and the experience. Finish strong, though, and you'll go into your next event with a far more positive frame of mind ... and endurance sport is such a mental game.

9

THE 100-MILE-LONG VIRGIN

Before Leadville, though, I had some crewing duties to do. My Salomon teammate Julien Chorier was running the Hardrock 100, which starts and ends in the town of Silverton in southern Colorado's San Juan Mountains. It's a seriously tough event and part of the so-called Rocky Mountain Slam, which includes the Leadville Trail 100 Run, the Bear 100 Mile Endurance Run, the Bighorn Trail 100 and the Wasatch Front 100 Mile Endurance Run. The Hardrock route is a big loop that entails around 10 000 metres of ascent through mountain passes in the 3 700-metre altitude range.

My job was to be part of a team of runners who would pace him – something many of the American 100-mile races allow – and I had the leg from 56 to 81 miles. This was exactly what I needed. All the focus was on Julien, which took the pressure off me and, with Silverton situated at 2 800 metres above sea level, it would help a lot with my acclimatisation and prep for Leadville.

Running with Julien lifted my spirits and, ironically, probably helped me more than it did him. It allowed me to see how he approached the latter half of a 100-miler, and it was a bit of an eye-opener. He was super-relaxed and kept on talking to me about nature, pointing out various birds and the odd mountain goat as we ran along. He was really taking the whole experience in and enjoying it ... it wasn't head down and go, go, go. The guy was genuinely loving his run and it rubbed off on me, reminding me exactly why I do this trail-running thing for a living. Julien was in it to win it – no doubt about that – but he was also able to detach himself from that mindset for large parts of the race and enjoy his surroundings. Of course, it was a planned strategy and it helped him maintain a positive mindset during the race, which was crucial for a winning performance. And that's exactly what this was. Julien won the Hardrock 100 in 25:17 – one hour and 53 minutes ahead of the guy in second place.

Great for him, great for Team Salomon, but not all that great for me. Kílian had won the Western States 100 two months earlier and Julien had now annexed the Hardrock, which meant the pressure on me to win at Leadville went up a couple of notches. The monkey on my back gained a few more kilograms. Salomon's plans to push the brand in the US were unfolding perfectly. All I had to do was nail the final event, and they would have all three major American 100-milers in a single year.

At least my body was now fully prepped to perform at altitude. By going from Zugspitz at 1 800 metres to Hardrock at 2 400 metres, by the time I got to the town of Leadville at 3 100 metres, my body was well acclimatised. I also got there five weeks before the race, which gave me time to do a lot of long training runs that would take me up as high as 4 000 metres. But even with the ideal acclimatisation, the adjustment was still tough, and it took a good three weeks living in Leadville before I felt comfortable.

I settled into a good daily routine and, never having run a 100-mile race before, focused on putting in a lot of mileage and familiarising myself with the terrain. My day would involve having something light for breakfast – yoghurt and cereal or a muffin and some coffee – and then out into the mountains to hit the trails for anything between two and 10 hours. If it was a long one, then that was the day done, but if my programme only called for a shorter morning run, I'd do something in the afternoon as well – either another short run or maybe a hike. Vanessa was with me, so I had company, and later my good mates Ryan Scott and Dean Leslie joined us – Ryan was there to cover the race for *Runner's World* magazine and Dean was again filming for our planned documentary.

We spent quite a bit of time exploring the local rivers and lakes together. It was exactly what I needed. It was food for my soul; I could feel my mindset shift from the post-Zugspitz negativity to a head space where I was feeling increasingly re-energised. Not that the pressure dissipated – it was always there. I knew what I needed to achieve and what I wanted to achieve, but just being there for five weeks without anything else to focus on but the race really helped.

It also helped that the US media were paying very little attention to me. They didn't think I had much of a chance, and I'd read a couple of the US blogs that reckoned I was a multiday specialist and wouldn't be able to race for 100 miles. As they tend to do, the Americans were so focused on themselves that I could come and go without much attention. To be fair, though, they've pretty much always had this race to themselves, as the top European guys don't often enter. Leadville might take place at high altitude, but the route is pretty flat relative to the races in Europe, and the Europeans are far better technical mountain runners, whereas the Americans are stronger on the flatter stuff. The big European trail race – the Ultra-Trail du Mont-Blanc – is at around the same time, which basically means the Americans do Leadville and the Europeans do the UTMB. As I said, this was all A-okay with me, though, and it gave me time to slowly zone in on an ideal, relaxed but focused head space.

The backstory to the Leadville 100 is quite an interesting one. It was a mining town that suffered from several boom-and-bust economy cycles. Eventually, former miner Ken Chlouber decided to try to establish a more sustainable form of income for the town. He decided to have this 100-mile foot race. Which was pretty nuts when you think about it, and most of the townsfolk held this opinion too. 'People,' he was told, 'would die trying to run that far at this altitude.'

It didn't stop Ken, though. The first race was held in 1983, and today the Leadville Race Series hosts several trail and mountain-biking events. Ken sold it to the Life Time Fitness group in 2012, but he's still the face of the series and it's pretty cool to see Ken and his wife, Merilee, at the events. He gives the pre-race briefing every year, and every year he gets all emotional up on stage – he's quite a character and has definitely given the race a lot of hype.

Leadville has consequently become a real mecca for the ultra-distance trail-running community, and I got to meet legends like runner Micah True, aka 'Caballo Blanco', who'd featured prominently in Christopher McDougall's best-selling book, *Born to Run*. Tragically, Micah would pass away the following year, having suffered what seems to have been a heart attack while out running the trails near his house in Gila Hot Springs, New Mexico. He and I had a beer at one of the local bars a few times, when he shared some of his stories with me. One thing about Americans is that they're super-friendly. I would bump into someone I kind of knew, and before the day was out we'd be having dinner together. I quite enjoyed that openness – it's very different from back home in South Africa.

Our rand wasn't as weak against the dollar then as it is now, and Leadville is relatively cheap compared with the rest of the US, so we would often eat out in the evenings and then just chill out watching entire series on DVD. I really enjoy Mexican food, and there were some great Mexican restaurants in town. Despite that, I should add that I probably dropped more weight for the Leadville race than for any other race. I probably weighed about 66 kilograms on race day.

Losing an extra kilo or two was never something I thought about or planned, but I think it speaks to how chilled I was there. I seemed to be able to switch off from the rest of the world and focus on two things – running and relaxing. Having the freedom to switch off from the usual demands of my daily life seemed to really help with my recovery between training sessions. I felt at ease. Relaxed. Ready.

The distance was certainly a big unknown for me, but that didn't bother me much. I wouldn't say I was confident ... more like at peace with myself. I knew that if the race went pear-shaped, I'd done every-thing in my power to give myself the best chance of doing well. I might get into a win-at-all-costs mindset later on in the race if I was in a position to go for the victory, but at the start I wasn't entertaining those thoughts at all. I'd beaten myself up at Zugspitz and had not enjoyed the experience. I didn't want a repeat of that emotional low.

The Leadville race starts at 4 a.m., so it's still pitch-black outside. You run with headlamps. It's an 'out and back' route that starts and finishes in the town and, right from the gun, US runner Mike 'The Fruitarian' Arnstein – he's a big advocate of a fruit-only diet – went straight into the lead and headed off into the distance. He's an interesting character and actively promotes himself as 'The Fruitarian Runner'. He arrived at the first checkpoint like a racing driver, shouting and screaming at his crew because they weren't in the right position or something. He looked completely panicked. Carry on like that for 100 miles, I thought, and your chances of spontaneous combustion are high.

I was employing my usual strategy of running conservatively for the first half and, hopefully, with something still left in the tank, I could make my move later in the race. Initially things didn't go to plan, and 30 kilometres into the race my quads were really feeling tired and a little burny. Still, I was in a good, positive head space. I remember seeing Dean Leslie as the trail opened out onto a forest road and telling him and his camera about my painful quads with a big smile on my face. It was weird.

I came down the steep Power Lines hill – this was around 20 miles into the race – in sixth or seventh position. Because of my quads, I slowed down quite a bit on the descents and some of the Americans came flying past me. I didn't mind much ... I figured their own quads would pay the price later. I stayed in the top 10 for the next couple of aid stations. Vanessa would be waiting at each one with a towel laid out with food options from which I could choose. I'd grab some water bottles and whatever I felt like eating.

Slowly I reeled in some of the downhill cowboys and, by the time we'd dropped into Twin Lakes, which was another 20 miles on, I was in fourth place. But I was still not feeling 100 per cent. I was starting to overheat and felt nauseous, but this is common when you're pushing your body at altitude, so I wasn't panicking. Next was the Lake Creek river crossing before a big climb up Hope Pass. I managed to catch a few more guys, and by the time we crested the pass, I was in second position. I could see Fruitarian Mike in front of me – in fact, I'm pretty sure I even saw him sucking on a gel, which frankly seemed very un-Fruitarian of the guy.

Suddenly the adrenalin kicked in. My entire mood and energy

levels picked up, and at the checkpoint I heard Mike was only a couple of minutes ahead of me. It was like being back at that Gobi race, when I was told that there was only one guy in front of me on the first day. I had the same surge of belief again ... I could actually win this thing!

I'd run the descent plenty of times in training and it was a long one – around five miles or so. I put the hammer down and caught Mike about a mile before it flattened out. Mike had his earphones on and didn't quite hear me coming up behind him. I couldn't just blast past the guy because the trail had become quite narrow and technical, but he must've heard something because suddenly he whipped around, quite startled. I jumped alongside and accelerated past one very surprised fruit-eater.

Behind me I heard a shout: 'Are you in the race? What's your name?' I confirmed my credentials and carried on going. A few choice expletives were faintly audible as I left him behind – quite an intense guy.

From there it was only about three miles to the turnaround point, and by now I was super-pumped. At this halfway mark, I picked up my first pacer – Salomon teammate Anna Frost. You're allowed four pacers on the inbound leg of the race, and Frosty was the perfect person to have with me at this point – this super-competitive Kiwi is one of the world's top female trail runners and she knows what needs to be done.

We also passed Mike again as he was making his way to the halfway mark, which only hammered home just how much distance I'd put on him. It was clear that he was not all that happy with life at this point. Frosty ran the next 15 miles back to Twin Lakes with me, which included having to once again go up and over Hope Pass. From that side, though, the ascent is brutal. She made sure I ate and drank enough, and every time I even thought of wanting to stop running and start power-hiking up, she'd urge me to keep going. Frosty kept an eagle eye on our pace and urged me on; she pushed me really hard. I needed it, too. I was beginning to suffer ... badly. Looking back at this race now, it was this section that made all the difference and it's definitely thanks to Anna Frost that I got up that climb and down the other side at the required pace.

Just before Twin Lakes, we went back through Lake Creek, which means you end up with these fine river stones in your shoes. My feet were starting to feel pretty sore as it was. At the checkpoint, I grabbed a fresh pair of running shoes, which always makes a big difference for me. Psychologically, it almost feels like a fresh pair of legs. At least, it does for a few 100 metres. Then your legs remember they've just run 80 kilometres and have another 80 to go.

Out of Twin Lakes there's a little bit of a climb, and you can hear cheering back at the checkpoint when the next person comes in. From the noise coming from down below, I figured I probably had an eight- or nine-minute lead over whoever had just run in.

Phil Villeneuve was my next pacer. A former pro skier and a very decent trail runner, Phil does sales and marketing for Salomon in Canada, and I'd spent a lot of time with him during the Advanced Training Weeks. He would pace me again the following year at Western States.

There's always one thing that comes to mind when I think of Phil: pizza. 'One slice of pizza at a time, Ryan, one slice of pizza at a time' was his mantra to help me mentally break down the race into manageable parts. Cheesy, flat Italian pies aside, Phil would also remind me to keep my running form – 'relax your upper body and breathe!' Even though I wasn't in any state to process that advice at the time, it's a tip I've remembered for future races and it definitely makes for a more efficient and relaxed running style.

By the time we got to the National Fish Hatchery checkpoint – the 76-mile mark – my quads were really starting to feel sore and I was battling nausea. This was at the limits of what I'd ever run before, and I was close to being done. I was a worried runner. Not only did I still have another 38 kays to go, but up ahead was Power Lines ... and guys always get caught going up Power Lines. As you may have guessed, Power Lines gets its name from the fact that this is where Leadville's supply of electricity is routed into the town. These big lines crackle above your head in harmony with the general crackle coming from your pain-wracked body.

I left the checkpoint as quickly as possible, picking up my new pacer, Adam Chase, in the process, and headed out. Seeing how bad I was looking, Adam kept up a steady stream of conversation, wanting to keep my mind off the physical and psychological demons beginning to occupy my body. I wasn't hearing much, though. The only way I could carry on was to try to disconnect from everything and focus on one step at a time. Each step brought me closer to the finish line, and the finish line was where this world of pain would end. The only thing to do was to move forward.

I had zero power in my legs going up that climb, but at least I was moving. I was also starting to have weird energy spikes. Granted, most of them I experienced as lows, where I felt like I was completely and utterly done, but then out of the blue I'd pick it straight up again. Of course, I could just have been hallucinating.

What makes Power Lines especially tough is the four false summits, and these just fry you mentally. Knowing this, in training I'd been up and down here a couple of times, trying to make peace with this piece of topography by visualising what it would be like running up here in the race. If you have the opportunity, you should definitely do this in the lead-up to your race – it will be to your benefit when it appears during the race. You need to accept it for what it is. You can't fight a mountain. It's always going to be bigger than you.

Not that I was contemplating all these zen thoughts at that moment in time. Getting to the top of the pass, all I could think was 'Please let this faaaking race finish …' I might have familiarised myself with the terrain, but this mental hell was new territory for me. On the one hand, I was close to winning an iconic race I so badly wanted, but I was also deeper in the pain cave then I had ever been before. Waaay deeper.

Anxiety set in as well. Could I actually pull this off? I kept looking over my shoulder to see if anyone was catching me. I was moving really slowly now – even on the descents – and you know things are not looking good when that happens. At May Queen, the final checkpoint, 13.5 miles from the finish, I picked up Josh Korn, my final pacer.

This last bit takes you around Turquoise Lake, and we were about two kays down the road when I could hear from the cheers that the next runner had arrived at the May Queen checkpoint. If I just kept moving, I'd actually win this thing! At this point my mind started to amuse itself by playing a few tricks, and I kept hearing voices behind me. I'd look behind me and ask Josh if anyone was coming, paranoid that I was being caught. I felt like a hunted animal.

Poor guy, Josh really had his work cut out keeping me going; that last stretch was absolute hell. It took me to a place inside my head I hadn't been to before. It was weird. My body felt completely finished, but my mind was kind of detached from the whole experience, even a little curious to see what was going to happen. How far could I mentally push myself before my body simply stopped working? My years of running have underlined how important the mental aspect of endurance sport is – as soon as your mind gives up, so does your body. It's what happens near the end of a race, when you get passed by another runner. Your head drops and so do your energy levels. You slow down even more. Pass someone, on the other hand, and it gives you this surge of energy. If your mind is still sending through positive signals, you'll carry on way past what you ever thought you're capable of. It sounds hokey, but you have to embrace the pain and suffering – don't be afraid of it; try to see it as a positive.

Having said all this inspirational stuff, I'd now like to say that I came cruising in over the last stretch, but that would be a lie. I walked some of it. I was just completely and utterly out of it. Done. I started to cramp up and, even though I could see there was no one behind me, all I wanted to do was win the race. If I was running and felt anything tweak, I'd just stop and walk. And then start running again. It was pure survival mode to get to the finish line.

Finally, we hit the town road. It was straight and about 300 metres long, which meant I'd be able to clearly see anyone coming up behind me. Because I was moving so slowly – seriously, just shuffling along – I was still worried I'd get ambushed. I'd made up my mind that if I did see another runner, I would just put my head down, grit my teeth and run.

But there was no one … only the finish line. I made it across.

I had won. I had flippin' won Leadville! Vanessa, Ryan and Dean were all there, and one of them handed me a South African flag. Immediately, the tears came. Relief and euphoria flooded through me. Mostly relief, though.

That was enough running for one day. I headed straight for the medical tent to get a drip, but that turned into something of a drama as well. The doctor couldn't find a vein – probably because I was so knackered – and spent a few minutes jabbing away until she located one. I lay there with a drip in one arm and a beer in the other hand. Exhausted, but happy.

I had finished in 16:46:54, some 32 minutes ahead of the guy in second place (who was not the Fruitarian, by the way – Mike finished an hour and 10 minutes back, in fourth), so my paranoia proved unfounded. Clearly, everyone else had also blown up over the last 20 kilometres. My winning time was the third fastest ever, and although it was still about an hour short of altitude specialist Matt Carpenter's incredible 15:42:59 record set back in 2005, that didn't bother me at all.

A blissed-out night of sleep would've been great, but that never happens after a race like this – there's so much adrenalin in your body and you're feeling so sore that you just toss and turn. It was even worse the next morning. I remember waking up and not being able to walk. The top floor in our house was the only place that had internet connectivity, and I had to crawl up the stairs on all fours to get there.

By mid-morning I could just about walk and we went down to watch the cut-off at the finish. Every few steps, though, my quads would cave in, so I had to brace myself against a wall or lamp post to stop from ending up on my ass. Geez, it's hectic to watch the cut-off, though. It happens at the 30-hour mark, and one guy was just 200 metres short of the line when the signal went. Imagine running for 30 hours, and then missing out by a couple of hundred metres on the coveted silver belt-buckle that each finisher gets.

My legs were still shattered at the prize-giving that evening, which made getting the trophy a little tricky. It's a miniature mining cart on a wooden plinth that must weigh about 10 kilograms. Walking down the stairs from the stage trying to carry that prize was probably the toughest piece of terrain I had had to negotiate during my entire five weeks out there.

It took a couple of days to process the significance of not only winning Leadville, but the whole experience of it. Professionally, it was a huge pressure-release valve. It was the biggest win of my career so far, and it proved those who had doubted my abilities wrong. The next day, my social-media feeds were flooded with messages of congratulations and statements from the media along the lines of 'Ryan Sandes has now proved that he is a world-class athlete', etcetera. I felt totally vindicated. I had won Leadville. It was like winning Wimbledon or the Masters ... it didn't matter what races I would go on to win or lose: I would always be a winner of the Leadville 100.

Looking back now, I feel a bit stupid about how important all of that was to me, but I guess it was a learning curve that I had to go through. These days, I'm a lot more focused on myself and worried about how *I* feel. I'm not here to make other people happy. It was different back then, though, and within the Salomon team I now also had a big 100-mile win under my belt, which, for me, felt like I'd finally earned my place in the inner circle. The year 2011 was the first time Salomon had planned and sent a team to races around the world, and we'd all done really well. I think that helped professionalise the sport to a degree. Greg Vollet's vision had paid off. Here was a guy who had gone to his bosses and said he wanted to put a sizeable chunk of his marketing budget into sending athletes to a series of international races, and obviously he needed to get the results. I had repaid his faith in me, and that felt very good.

It was only once I'd come back home that I realised how much I'd improved as an athlete. The training during the month leading up to Leadville – and the race itself – had been a pivotal time for me as an athlete. I had so badly wanted to do well, and had been incredibly focused on doing everything that I possibly could to prepare for it.

Leadville had also ramped up my training to another level. I remember doing these 500-metre repeats on a slight decline, just so I could build up my speed. At altitude it is harder to go fast and, at the end of those, I'd be on my hands and knees gasping, wanting to throw up. The long training runs at this altitude also pushed me way out of my comfort zone, but my recovery time was also ideal. In between training, with Vanessa around, I was super-relaxed, which makes a big difference as well.

It was also a pivotal time in my relationship with Vanessa. We grew a lot closer spending time together in Leadville. I started feeling a lot more comfortable around her and opened up to her a lot more. I think Vanessa also got to see what really drives me. She was there through that pretty dark pre-Leadville patch, and there to witness my quest for redemption.

It was also cool to have guys like Ryan and Dean around. And Anna Frost, too. I'd shared a lot with her, and we've become close friends since then – I've subsequently also seen her go through some pretty dark moments with injuries and come out the other side. That's the thing about endurance sport – it definitely peels you like an onion. It strips off all those artificial layers and removes the personas you like to present to the world. When you're out there, deep into a race, completely shattered, all pretence has long since thumbed a lift on the sweeper bus.

So, yes, for me, sharing a race like that with Anna is just as much her victory as it is mine.

STUFF I'VE LEARNT

Disconnect to recover

In my experience, your post-race or post-training recovery is a lot better when you're in a good head space. If you are stressed, unhappy or caught up in this 1 000 km/h modern life we lead, then your recovery is proportionately slower. In today's information age, with social media and the like, you spend so much time in front of a laptop or mobile-phone screen that your mind never switches off.

It's something I have to constantly remind myself about. As a professional athlete, my sponsors want to see my profile grow not only on traditional media platforms, like print, Web and TV, but also on social media. Brands like Salomon, Red Bull and Oakley don't want generic, clichéd posts like 'Wow, thanks, Oakley, for my cool new shades' – they're after something a lot more authentic that will resonate with the public. They'd be way more interested if you posted a rad pic or video of you wearing the new eyewear, but that means you have to head out to the trails and spend a day shooting with a GoPro camera.

It's something I really enjoy doing and my mind is always on the go, but I also have to make sure I'm in the best condition I can be in to compete. That is, after all, what I'm paid to do. I have to consciously make an effort to disconnect from it all.

I guess it's about finding the balance that works for you.

Keep eating!

There will be times in any endurance race when you're feeling nauseous, and the thought of food will just make it worse. I'm afraid you're just going to have to bite the bullet and shovel some food down your throat. If you don't, you risk blowing your whole race.

Don't wait until you're hungry

Whatever endurance sport you're doing, as a basic rule of thumb, keep eating and drinking regularly so that you never feel hungry or thirsty. Don't stuff yourself, obviously, but just keep up a regular intake. Some folk say you should only eat or drink when you feel the pangs, but I completely disagree with that. By then, it's often too late.

On a recent training run, I started to feel a little hungry and my energy levels began to drop. I'd just finished a tempo run and had an easy 20-minute run back home, with a small climb at the end. I figured I'd hang on and have a recovery shake when I got back. Bad idea. Halfway through that easy run home, I was over the edge. It happens so quickly. If I'd eaten something when I had first started to feel hunger pangs, it would probably have taken 10 minutes to get into my system, and I would've been okay.

Some guys I know like their watch alarm to go off, say, every 30 minutes to remind them to take a gel or whatever nutrition plan they're on, but you don't have to be that hardcore. Just make sure you are routinely taking in something. And, as always, listen to your body.

Phil Villeneuve, my pacer at Leadville, was very good at making sure I was eating. Every 10 minutes towards the end of the race, he'd be going, 'Eat, eat, eat!' I didn't want to. In truth, all I wanted to do was lie down and sleep. I was a bit grumpy at that point, and I'd be like, 'Geez, dude! I just had some Perpetuem like 15 minutes ago. I can't have any more ...' But Phil was adamant and I just had to get it down me.

Fortunately, I've got a pretty strong constitution, so I get just about anything down. In any endurance sport, if you lose your stomach late in the race, it doesn't matter how good or fit you are, that can be your race done. Part of being an endurance athlete is having a strong constitution as well.

10

OF RACING CARS
AND KARMA
AND LITTLE OLD LADIES

It took me a good three weeks before I could actually run again. The cheesy irony was that Leadville had, in fact, left me with legs that felt like lead. My muscles were so damaged by the race that for the next 10 days I just hobbled around. Running was out of the question.

En route home, I flew back via Europe to have a look at the UTMB race, which starts and finishes in Chamonix, France. As mentioned in the previous chapter, this is the premier European 100-miler; it follows a mountainous route through France, Switzerland and Italy. It was definitely on my radar to run it at some point, and helping to crew for some of the Salomon runners meant I could get a first-hand look at what running this famous race would entail. And when I say 'crew', I certainly don't mean 'pace'. Just walking to the aid stations was hard and, besides, they don't allow pacers at the UTMB.

It was an entirely different beast from something like Leadville, that's for sure – it's as long, but there are way more wicked ascents and tricky descents. It didn't have the altitude factor that makes Leadville so hard, but this race was definitely one for the mountain goats. My abilities as a technical mountain runner were improving, but I wasn't quite there yet. One for the future ...

Back in Cape Town, I had a few days' rest before I had to get back into my race gear. It was an easy one, though – as part of a local Salomon team, I would be running one leg of the Crazy Store Table Mountain Challenge. A few of the athletes from the Salomon international team had come to South Africa for a series of running clinics, and they had entered the race as well. It was this race where Kílian, who had entered the 37-kilometre solo category, stopped to take pics of the sunrise. Anna Frost was also there and she won the women's solo, and along with Greg Goodall and Nicholas Bupanga, we won the team category pretty easily too.

By now my legs weren't feeling too bad – good enough to have a bash at the Otter African Trail Run in early September. I touched briefly on this race in Chapter 7, but to recap, it's a 42-kilometre run along the Garden Route. One year they run it from the Storms River mouth to the Groot River estuary in Nature's Valley, and the following year, calling it the Retto ('Otter' spelled backwards), it's run the other way around.

I'd started running again only about 10 days before the Otter and I wasn't even sure I was going to do it until the very last moment, so I kept it super low-key. Fortunately, by race day the last of the Leadville-induced lactic acid had seeped out of my quads and I had a good race.

It was pretty tactical in the beginning. Andre Gie had won the race the year before, passing Iain Don-Wauchope right at the end, and everyone had thought he'd run the perfect race. I was in the front group, and everyone's game plan seemed to be one of 'let's all follow Andre'. There was a bit of needle going on as well, and after about 10 kilometres the route took us up some stairs, which Andre proceeded to power-hike. The stairs were narrow, making it difficult to pass, and Bruce Arnett, another top South African trail runner, piped up with a somewhat sarcastic comment, asking if this wasn't supposed to be a running race.

Andre is generally a pretty chilled dude, but I could see he was pissed off. He eventually turned around and invited Bruce to have a go at running it, using a few choice words I can't repeat here. No one made a move. A little later he turned around and again issued his invitation. This time, Bruce took up the offer and started running ahead. I kept power-hiking up the stairs for about two or three minutes, cruising along, but then realised I didn't want to let Bruce get too far ahead, because I knew he was on a mission to beat me. I pushed on a bit, caught him, and a while later passed him.

The toughest part was getting across the Bloukrans River. I was the first athlete to arrive at the crossing, and there was a rope strung across the river where the race crew had to guide the runners across. I could see a line slightly higher up the river I wanted to climb, to get back up the other side of this steep river gorge, but the guys kept telling me to follow them. So I did. And just about got swept out to sea for my troubles. It took me about three or four minutes to get back, and I was pretty frantic by the time I grabbed the rope and pulled myself onto a rock on the opposite bank. Despite that little setback, I still managed to come home ahead of the field, in the process beating the record by around seven minutes in 4:40:15.

I would return in 2014 to take part in the race again, running the Retto with ex-cricketer Mark Boucher and two of his mates, Sean Weldon and Brad Cameron, to help raise awareness for his anti-rhino-poaching campaign. Having been a huge Proteas fan all my life, I had the rad opportunity to run with South Africa's greatest ever wicketkeeper. Rather than racing it, my job was to make sure Team Boucher got their finishers' medals ahead of the eight-hour cut-off time. We did it, but it was a helluva close thing. All the splits we were given at the aid stations were like, 'don't worry, you guys are way under', but just after the halfway mark, it dawned on me that they were talking about the nine-hour cut-off time and not the eight-hour one. You're still classified as a finisher under nine hours, but only get a medal if you duck in under eight. We wanted that medal, which meant I had to crack the whip a bit and speed things up.

But poor Bouch was pretty broken, and just after halfway he hit a really low patch. I was still pushing him hard, and fully expected him to turn around and tell me to piss off and leave him alone, but he never did. The fact that we ran the second half of the race faster than the first is testament to Bouch's famous fighting spirit, especially because the reverse route is easier upfront and gets pretty technical towards the end. For me, it really hammered home the mental drive and discipline it takes to not only be an international cricketer, but to achieve what Bouch did in his career. We finished in 7:51:34 – giving me the interesting record of being the person who posted the largest gap between two times at the Otter!

Running at the back of the field gave me more insight into what the rest of the runners goes through in a race. You're suffering at the front of the race when you push for a certain time or try to win, but the runners at the back are pushing themselves just as hard, but for almost twice as long. It was pretty inspiring to see.

I love the Otter. As a race, the distance is a little short for me, but it's one of my favourite trails in the world. Yes, the American Rockies and European Alps are spectacular to run through, but if you told me I had to run the same trail every day, it would definitely be the Otter. I think the mountains intrigue me, but my soul will always yearn for the ocean. Running along the coastline, with its forests and ravines, and then the ocean below, is always something special.

Besides, there's some incentive for me to go back and give it another full go. In 2013, UK runner Ricky Lightfoot blitzed the race to win in a time of 4:15:27, and South African runner Iain Don-Wauchope now holds the Retto record of 4:23:24. Maybe it's time I made another appearance …

Towards the end off my year, I had one more adventure planned, and rather a special one at that – Nepal 2011. It was one of the 4 Deserts 'roving races', and although my career ambitions were now focused on single-day, ultra-distance trail races, this event was taking place in a region that was high up on my bucket list to visit. Besides, the 4 Deserts Series had been so influential in my career that I guess I'll always have an affinity for it.

Turns out Nepal wasn't quite the tranquil land of Buddhist monks and high mountain retreats you might think it is. Or, at least, it wasn't for me. Maybe it was karma having a chuckle. But the whole thing was a bit of a battle, which began with the journey to the race start in Pokhara.

I flew into Kathmandu via Dubai, and stayed there for about three days before planning to catch a connecting flight to Pokhara. The city – the second largest in Nepal – is about 200 kilometres west of Kathmandu. Being close to Annapurna, the city is often affected by big weather systems. Which is exactly what happened on the day I was supposed to fly in – bad weather closed in around Pokhara and all flights were cancelled. That was a problem. We had to be at the race briefing the following evening, leaving me only one option – a 200-kilometre taxi ride through the night.

Fortunately, there were a few other competitors in the same boat, so we clubbed together and organised a couple of taxis. For one of the Americans, though, this wasn't going to cut it, and he started talking big about chartering himself a helicopter. That was way outside my league, so I jumped into a little yellow taxi, which looked like it came off the production line sometime in the 1950s, with two guys I'd never met before. As the taxi started driving off down the road, we spotted Mr Loudmouth American sprinting after us. Turns out none of the local chopper pilots were willing to risk the weather, despite the fistful of dollar bills he was waving around. We stopped and let him in. He was, at the end of the day, a fellow trail runner, trying to make his way in an unfamiliar country.

It didn't take long for our newest passenger to regret his decision. And he was not alone. Nepalese taxi drivers might possibly be the worst drivers in the world – which, as a South African, is saying something, given the reputation of our own taxi drivers. Apparently, it's accepted practice to gently bump into the car in front of you if it's not making the kind of forward progress that meets with your satisfaction. They also have a habit of driving into oncoming traffic and hooting until it gets out the way. Still, that wasn't the worst of it. What really made the trip a total nightmare were the roads on which we had to drive. The one from Kathmandu to Pokhara is literally the scariest piece of public asphalt I have ever been on.

We're talking high mountain passes that are so narrow, there's just enough space for two cars side by side, with no shoulder to move onto if anyone behind you wants to pass. If we came up behind a truck, our driver would simply hoot, hoping perhaps that this was enough warning for other road users, and swing out into the oncoming lane to overtake. A couple of times, I could practically see the writing on the headlights' bulbs of the cars coming towards us before our driver swung back into his own lane. It was proper scary.

Mr Loudmouth American – unluckily for him – was in the front passenger seat and he was freaking out, literally close to tears a couple of times. When we stopped for food and water, he got out and was like, 'I'm done!' We bought him a few beers, which seemed to calm him down a bit. It didn't last long, though.

Having made it to our hotel alive, we all checked in – except Mr Loudmouth. He was told they had no booking under his name. The guy broke down right then and there, bawling his eyes out. Shame! Luckily, the manager took pity and somehow made a plan to accommodate him.

We had survived the journey, but an army of local stomach bugs awaited us at the race village. A whole bunch of runners were sick the day before the race, and by the third stage half the field had pulled out. It's always a hazard at any endurance-sport race village, and once one person gets it, it just spreads.

I had taken my usual precautions (see the section at the end of the chapter on 'Stuff I've learnt' for more details) and managed to dodge the bullet, but sadly a couple of other South Africans – Hout Bay mates of mine, Robert Graham and Andrew Espin – had to drop out after Day 1 because of it. One guy thought he might get through it if he took a sleeping pill, but the poor dude woke up the next morning to find he'd soiled his sleeping bag. He pulled straight out of the race, binned his sleeping bag and headed back to Kathmandu.

The race was the usual 4 Deserts format – seven days, six stages, 250 kilometres – and, as you'd expect from a race in Nepal, altitude was once again a factor. The course would reach a maximum altitude of 3 200 metres, and the total elevation gain across the week was around 9 000 metres. As prep, I had spent 10 days about 3 000 metres up in the AfriSki ski resort in Lesotho's Maluti Mountains, where I did a few training runs, but mostly I just did a lot of hiking. Although I didn't spend as much time there as I would've liked, after spending all those weeks in Leadville, I figured my body would adapt a little quicker than normal.

And it did, but it turns out it wasn't my lungs I had to worry about … it was my ankle.

Day 1 was 40 kilometres with a few climbs, including a major one right at the beginning of the stage, which obviously suited me, and I seemed to pull away really easily. I won the stage by just over 50 minutes. With a lead like that, I could basically just sit back and take it easy for the rest of the race. It was the same for Day 2 – another 40 kilometres and another easy win, this time by 20-odd minutes. And it was basically heading the same way on Day 3 as well … until a gang of old ladies showed up.

During the race, every time the route would take us past a temple, these women would run out with red paint powder and try to dab it on you. No doubt it means good luck or something similarly well intentioned, but near this one temple an entire village of old ladies ambushed me.

Everyone was very excited because I was the first runner to come through, and they were all throwing this red stuff at me. Because of the high altitude, I was already breathing heavily, but then suddenly I'm also breathing in all this red powder, and there's paint everywhere over the race kit I have to wear for the next three days. I'm trying to look all happy and grateful while trying to swat them away at the same time … and this might've been where karma took offence because, a little further on, with some paint still in my eyes, I jumped over a rock and landed awkwardly, going over on my right ankle. It happened so quickly … one second I'm bounding down the mountain, jumping off rocks and generally feeling like I'm in a very happy, if not redder, place, when suddenly there's a popping sound and pain shooting up my leg.

It wasn't the first time this had happened, either. Back in 2009, while training for the 4 Deserts Namibia race, I had been running along the Constantia Green Belt in Cape Town when this dog suddenly went for me. It came out of nowhere, and I wasn't really concentrating. I jumped off the trail, into the grass, and went into a hole. It was a severe sprain, and ever since then my right ankle has always been dodgy.

I stopped and was almost immediately overtaken by nausea. There was still about 20 kilometres to go. Nothing I could do but grit my teeth and hobble on. At least nothing was torn or broken, but, from what I could tell, I'd hyperextended the ligaments. Surprisingly, no one overtook me and I won the stage by a few minutes, although savouring the victory wasn't high up on my list of priorities. I plunged my throbbing ankle into an ice-cold stream, threw back a few Myprodol painkillers – they're also anti-inflammatory – and had the ankle strapped up nice and tight.

I now know that the strapping part wasn't the best thing to do. It restricts the movement in that part of your body, which means you start compensating – and therefore stressing – other joints, ligaments and muscles in your body. But I'll discuss this in more detail later on, because injured ankles would become something of an issue for me. Back then, though, it was the only way I knew how to get through the rest of a race.

The next day the ankle was really sore and properly swollen, but I'd strapped the living hell out of it, and with a whole bunch of those magical little red and green capsules in my pack, I was standing at the starting line. I wasn't going to be running very fast, but at least I was still in the race. For a few horrible moments there, I'd thought that was me done. On Days 2 and 3 my stomach hadn't been feeling too great either (the high altitude often does this to your system), and every time I ate something, I would feel nauseous. As a result, my calorie intake wasn't quite what it should've been. As I was not running on a full tank, I was getting a lot of energy lows throughout the race.

For the first 10 kays on Day 4, my ankle was pretty sore, but I hobbled along, and eventually it warmed up and there was a little more movement. It bugged me for the rest of the race, but I managed to win that 43-kilometre stage by 20 minutes, and then Day 5's 75-kilometre stage by 30 minutes. With a 2.5-hour lead, the race was obviously in the bag, and the final 15-kilometre stage was just a formality. Another 4 Deserts win to add to my CV.

The fact that I had won by a big margin, despite running on a dodgy ankle for half the race, clearly indicated two things: yes, the field wasn't all that competitive, but it was proof of just how much I had improved as an athlete. It was a clear indication of how my time at Leadville had bumped me up to a level where my mountain-running skills and ability to get up big climbs quickly had improved dramatically.

Leaving Nepal – just like my journey there and basically my entire race – was another challenging experience. Thankfully, there was no problem with my flight from Pokhara to Kathmandu, but once back in Nepal's biggest city, I discovered that my flight to Dubai had been cancelled. The ticket office at the airport was like, 'Sorry, you have to go back into town and sort it out at the Emirates airline office.' This was Saturday night, which meant the office was only going to open on Monday morning, and there was no flippin' way I was going to risk this Nepalese karma for the rest of the weekend.

That meant I had no choice ... but to call the one person I knew whose over-the-phone, customer-service-demanding persona can make anything happen.

'Hi, Vanessa? Babe? It's Ryan. I'm stuck at Kathmandu Airport, my ankle is sore, I haven't eaten much in days, and now they've cancelled my flight home ...'

Next thing, I was on standby for the last flight out, which I managed to get on. I think I made up my mind to marry her right there and then.

Vanessa may not have shared the same thought, though: I was back for only a few days before I had to pack my bags for a little adventure race in Tasmania. At that point, she was probably feeling more like my travel agent than the love of my life and future wife.

The adventure race was the Mark Webber Tasmania Challenge – an event hosted by the Aussie ex-Formula One and now sports-car driver, who's always been a keen endurance-sport athlete as well. Back then,

Mark was still part of Red Bull Racing and, as a Red Bull athlete too, I was lucky enough to have an invite sent my way. Actually, the invite had come just as I was about to fly to Nepal for the 4 Deserts race. Tristan Werner, South Africa's marketing manager for Red Bull, called me while I was sitting in the airport lounge ... it sounded like a cool trip and a fun way to end the year.

Held over five days in the wilds of the Australian island state of Tasmania, it was a multidisciplinary race in which you had to mountain-bike, kayak, trek and run for 350 kilometres, from the Freycinet Peninsula to the finish back in the state capital of Hobart. You do it in pairs, and you and your partner have to solve a few clues along the way as well. I was teamed up with another racing driver, Rick Kelly, a Red Bull athlete who drove for Team Jack Daniel's Racing in the Australian V8 supercar series.

Rick was a lot of fun and super-competitive – in the way that racing drivers are. Obviously, in his line of work, milliseconds make all the difference, and right at the starting gun he was elbowing other competitors out of the way to get to the front. Being a little more experienced at this stuff, I had to be like, 'Rick ... hey ... whoa! You're going to have to take your foot off the gas there a little. We are not going to make 10 kays at this pace, let alone 350.'

There were other challenges too. Like paddling.

Having spent a fair amount of my misspent youth bodyboarding, watersports were not unfamiliar to me, but I'd never been kayaking before. Rick had kayaked quite a bit, thank goodness, because having to negotiate rapids in a two-man kayak – even relatively small rapids – was a big ask for me. Especially when you only have one paddle, which is what happened to us. We got sucked into a small rapid that flipped our boat, trapping me underneath, because I hadn't taken the time beforehand to figure out how to unclip my feet – a shocking rookie error, given the possible implications. Fortunately, they were pretty minor, but in my frantic thrashing about to prevent myself from drowning – which, frankly, would've been a very disappointing end to what was looking like a promising career – I lost my paddle.

And that meant we had to negotiate the rest of the leg sharing a single paddle. As a result, navigating our way through further rapids had less to do with actual navigation than blind luck.

At least my mountain-bike skills were okay – Vanessa's love of mountain biking meant I would sometimes tag along on her rides – and Rick's were pretty decent too. It seems motorsport skills translate well into mountain biking. Mark Webber is very good on a mountain bike, and so is my Red Bull colleague, Dakar winner Giniel de Villiers. Trying to keep up with any of these guys on the descents is impossible – the lines they take and their abilities to judge corner speeds are a direct result of their motor-racing skills.

As I mentioned, Rick was a little on the competitive side, and on one of the bike legs we had slowed a little so that one of the film crews could get some footage they wanted. Next thing, this French duo came straight through the middle of us and basically knocked Rick off his bike. Ironically, they were sponsored by Garmin ... navigation should not have been a problem. Of course, bumping a racing driver is right up there with waving a very big red rag in front of a very pissed-off Spanish fighting bull. The Bull saw Red (see what I did there?), and Rick took off after these now rather worried-looking Frenchmen, and harassed them all the way down the 15-kilometre descent. Rick could've overtaken them at any time, and he let them know it. I, on the other hand, was as wide-eyed as those Monsieur Garmins, trying all I could to hang onto Rick's back wheel.

Rick and I ended up coming seventh in the event – not a bad result, given our lack of experience in adventure racing – and we've stayed in touch ever since. After spending some time in my world of endurance sport, I also got to spend time in his world, sitting in the passenger seat of his race car for a few laps. Those V8 supercars are brutes, and the acceleration and G-forces they pull through the corners are staggering. Not being used to it, it felt like something was simultaneously sitting on my chest and trying to pull my head off my shoulders. I couldn't speak. Rick unfortunately took my lack of screaming as a sign that he wasn't quite pushing the envelope far enough, and started going faster and faster.

That little bout of nausea aside, the whole event was a rad way to end a big year for me. It was great to do a race in a part of the world I'd never been to before, and to do it without feeling any pressure whatsoever. Perhaps I'll do more of these when I reach my sell-by date as an ultra-distance trail runner. I'm never going to stop running, but I know I will always have that competitive edge, and there's no way I'm going to enjoy being passed by a bunch of youngsters with a 'woohoo, we're passing Ryan Sandes!' grin on their faces.

So, yes, I think I'm definitely going to prefer just running on my own in the mountains, and maybe doing the odd adventure or mountain-bike race where I'm not really expected to perform.

STUFF I'VE LEARNT

Dodging the race-village stomach bugs

I've yet to succumb to the dreaded race-village trots and I do have a pretty cast-iron constitution, but there are still some basic rules that I've followed to prevent those constant runs to the portaloos.

Drink only bottled water

For anyone travelling outside their own country, this one is a no-brainer. Whether you're in Delhi or New York, I'd recommend sticking solely to the bottled stuff. Locals in those countries will all have digestive systems immune to whatever nasties are doing the backstroke in the tap water. Your system won't know what's hit it.

Use bottled water to clean your teeth too

An obvious point, but oddly, many people forget this.

And don't use ice

There's little point in fastidiously drinking bottled water and then plonking a couple of ice cubes into your glass. It's very, very unlikely those ice blocks have also been made with bottled water.

Food is trickier ... but keep it simple

Sometimes, when you are doing a local stage race, you can often skip the race-village food tent and eat out in the local town. But many races are held in remote regions and, of course, if you're competing overseas, then you have to head for the tent. Try to keep it simple, though, and don't eat anything too exotic. During a race, I'll eat boringly bland stuff. Think 'basic fuel' and not 'tastebud explosion'.

It goes without saying that if your race is in an exotic and particularly foreign place, don't eat at any local restaurants before or during the race. Stick to the race-village food tent and save your adventurous eating for the days after the race.

Smuggle stuff

When travelling, I'll usually take as many home favourites with me as possible. There's always some biltong and nuts hidden away in my bags somewhere. (Didn't find that, did you, Mr Pakistani Customs Official?)

Always pack hand sanitiser and use it often

The bugs are inevitably transmitted via hand contact. Clean your hands a lot – especially before you enter the food tent and definitely after you leave.

And anti-bacterial wet wipes too

They're not only good for wiping your hands, but use them to wipe other places too. No further explanation needed here ... right?

Don't shake anyone's hand. Not even fellow competitors'. Use the old fist pump.

Running shoes ... minimalist or maximalist?

Four or five years ago, minimalist shoes were the 'next big thing'. The theory was that the human body is designed to run barefoot, and running shoes with their cushioned heels have not only weakened the tendons and muscles in our feet and legs, but also caused us to run incorrectly, striking the ground with our heels and not the forefoot.

Suddenly, a whole bunch of performance shoe brands were coming out with shoes that had minimal cushioning and were supposed to mimic the natural motion of the foot. New Balance and their brand ambassador, ultra-distance trail runner Anton Krupicka, lead the way.

I agree with that approach ... mostly. Yes, running barefoot or with minimal cushioning does all those things its supporters claim, but the key is to slowly adapt to it. You can't just chuck out your traditional running shoes, lace up a cushionless pair and hit the road or trail. You are absolutely going to get injured – either a repetitive strain injury or bruise your foot (or worse) on a sharp rock that you haven't seen. If you've injured your foot like this, you'll know just how long it takes for this kind of niggling injury to heal well enough for you to be able to run unhindered again. Rather start off by running in them once a week for three or four months, and don't go longer than a few kilometres at a time to start off with.

I've gone a lot more minimalistic over the past few years, and I do think it's better. I'm incorporating more barefoot running into my training, but I still see it as more of a training exercise to strengthen my body. And I've introduced it slowly over time. I really wouldn't recommend running an ultra-distance race in them. Anton, it would seem, paid the price and he's been suffering from shin splints for a couple of years now. I believe he's now running in a shoe with more cushioning.

In fact, brands like Hoka have now come out with so-called maximalist shoes that offer extra cushioning. So now it's gone from one extreme to the other. They're not going to injure you, and if you're an average runner in an ultra-distance race, spending the better part of a day out there running, they might be the answer if you battle with your knees. But I don't think this extra height is to everyone's taste either. For me, I prefer to feel the trail underneath me, and I like shoes that have adequate cushioning and are light and flexible enough to bend and mould to the natural movement of my foot.

My recommendation

If you want to try minimalist shoes, incorporate them into your training programme, but do it slowly. And when it comes to maxi-malist shoes, give them a try, but remember that they are just another option out there. The downside is that because there is so much cushioning, it can weaken the muscles and tendons in your foot.

11

THE BEST 100-MILER I'VE EVER RUN, EVEN THOUGH I ONLY CAME SECOND

After the breakout year in 2011, the following one brought with it its own pressures. There's an old adage in sport – winning a major title is one thing, but repeating that success is something else altogether. I needed to back up those wins in 2011 with a few more first places in one-day ultras. And first up to prove the previous year wasn't a bit of a fluke was the Vibram Hong Kong 100.

Unlike the European guys, who basically have an enforced off-season, thanks to the chilly winter weather over December and January, Cape Town's Mediterranean-like summer over that time meant I was still able to enjoy the spectacular trails of what surely must be the world's most beautiful city.

Despite the Kathmandu dramas, I was always up for travelling to new and interesting places, and having done a little homework on Hong Kong, it seemed like a pretty cool place to visit. For one thing, the race route kind of reminded me of Cape Town. Obviously, Hong Kong's a lot bigger than Cape Town, but the topography seemed very similar – a big coastal city surrounded by these epic mountains. You can be running through the mountains – like it's this jungle wilderness – and then suddenly you pop out and right there below you is this teeming city.

The RacingThePlanet organisation have their headquarters in Hong Kong, and Salomon sent over a couple of their athletes too, so I knew a fair number of people. That's always a double-edged sword for me – on the one hand, it's great to be among friends, but it can also be a little distracting.

I arrived in the city in mid-February, a week before the race, to get a feel for the place and do a couple of recce runs of the route, but pretty much got sucked into a lot of promotional and press activities. As I said, I enjoy doing them, but you have to be careful not to let it have a negative impact on the real reason you are there. Every day, sometimes twice a day, we would have stuff happening – either a group run, testing gear, or a talk in one of the outdoor stores.

I didn't get a lot of time to switch off, but I was getting better at managing my time and respectfully declined some of the invites. It allowed me to escape into the mountains on my own for some easy training runs, and to mentally start focusing on what I had to do. Vanessa arrived a few days before the race and, rather than being a distraction, she helped me get my game face on. By now, her mountain-biking abilities had got to the point where she had entered the Western Cape's famous Cape Epic race – an eight-stage, 800-kilo-metre race over some of the toughest climbs you can do on a bicycle – and she fully understood what I needed to do to prepare for a race. Vanessa would go on to get her 2012 Cape Epic finisher's medal and complete the feat again in 2013. I'm super-proud of her for that!

The Hong Kong race was in its second year as an event, and had attracted a pretty competitive field. A fellow Salomon athlete, New Zealand's Grant Cruise, was there, along with Nepalese mountain runners Aite Tamang, Bed Sunuwar and Sudip Kulung, China's top ultra-trail runner Yun Yan Qiao, and local Hong Kong runners William Davies and Jeremy Ritcey, who'd come first and second the previous year.

Looking at the route profile, it definitely looked like a race of two halves. The first half was pretty flat with a lot of the trails having been concreted over, which was pretty sad. I guess they wanted to encourage walkers and hikers to use it, but still, it seemed a pity. The second half of the race was a different story altogether – a series of spikes that increased in altitude up to Hong Kong's highest peak,

Tai Mo Shan, at 957 metres. There was a total elevation gain of 4500 metres and the last 25 kilometres looked pretty brutal. You definitely needed to save a little gas in the tank for that.

At the starting gun, I went off fairly quickly for me. I was feeling good and pushed the pace a little. For a second, I thought I was just going to pull away from everyone, but quickly the guys I mentioned earlier caught up, and then went flying down the descents as I dropped off the back. There was a time when that would've psyched me out, but now I was feeling pretty chilled and comfortable running in sixth place, knowing that there was still a long way to go – not to mention that little sting in the tail at the end. Forgive the smugness, but experience is a wonderful thing. Whereas previously at races like Zugspitz, I would be fighting myself and dropping my head, here I was taking it cool, biding my time, and essentially backing myself to catch them later on.

The first part of the route took us along the eastern coastline past these white sand beaches, reminiscent of Thailand, and small Chinese fishing villages, and then turned inland through bamboo forests and over big ridge lines. Slowly I started picking my way back to the front. I was lying in third place when I came into a checkpoint at around the 40-kay mark, to find the runners in first and second – the two Nepalese guys, Aite Tamang and Bed Sunuwar – making themselves a pot of two-minute noodles.

Clearly needing some urgent refuelling, it appeared they hadn't paced themselves too well. And looking at the small backpacks they were running with, given the hot and humid conditions, they obviously weren't carrying enough water or food. Seeing me arrive seemed to re-energise them pretty quickly, though, and they slurped down their noodles and bolted from the checkpoint. I took after them.

I ran with Bed for a while, with Aite again taking off in front of us. Bed was looking like he needed what his name suggested – the guy looked finished – but this 'go big or go home' strategy the Nepalese seemed to adopt kicked in once more, and he hammered down a descent into the next checkpoint, at around the 55-kilometre mark.

I was happy to let them go again. I'd scoped out the course enough to know that this middle section through the hills, overlooking the famous Hong Kong metropolis, was the easy bit. The climbs that lay ahead were where this race would be won or lost.

I didn't dawdle at the checkpoint, but made sure I ate and drank properly. I was feeling pretty good, and I wanted to make sure I got my hydration spot on. I caught Bed on the next big climb, and then at 60 kays I caught Aite near the top of another. That was his cue to take off again, trying to open up another gap on the descent, but I hung in there, shadowing the Nepalese for the next 10 kays.

At the top of Beacon Hill – about 30 kays from the finish – I pulled alongside and, while I definitely felt a bit tired, I could see from Aite's body language that he wasn't in his happy place. I ran with him for a few minutes to get a feel for things, and on a small descent he moved out of the way a little and let me by. He was done. With that adrenalin rush that propels you as you pass someone, I hammered home my advantage on a relatively flat section, and pushed hard to get a gap before the long drag up Tai Mo Shan. I could almost hear my switch click over to race mode: 'Okay, enough of this biding my time stuff. Let's do this.'

There were two big climbs to contend with, and I started taking a bit of strain, particularly on the steep set of stairs up Grassy Hill. I had to power-hike, but I kept looking behind me in case Bed or Aite were coming for me. About three-quarters of the way up, I happened to glance back and noticed someone actually running up the stairs. One or two unpublishable words came tumbling out of my mouth. Maybe Aite had got a second wind? Maybe he's had some more noodles or something? I knew the Nepalese guys were very erratic – hammer, blow-up, regroup, hammer, blow-up, etcetera – and maybe they were on the regroup and hammer part of the cycle. I had to dig pretty deep, constantly looking back through the mist and haze, waiting for this guy to catch me.

But he didn't. And 'he' wasn't even part of the race. It turned out the guy behind me wasn't a competitor (the trails were still open to the public), but someone out to see if he could run the stairs, and who also happened to be wearing the black, yellow and blue clothing similar to Aite's.

Relieved, I crested Tai Mo Shan, with the final 10 kays a long descent to the finish. I put the hammer down and a few 100 metres from the finish, one of the guys from Salomon Hong Kong handed me a South African flag. I crossed the line in 9:54, almost two hours faster than the previous year's time and 25 minutes ahead of Aite Tamang, who was, in turn, nine minutes in front of compatriot Bed Sunuwar.

I was stoked to have snuck in under 10 hours – there was a lot of talk before the race saying it wasn't possible – but even happier to get the year going with a win. I felt like a real pro. I'd been involved in a lot of promotional activities in the build-up to the race, and then gone ahead and won it. My sponsors were wearing broad smiles.

Personally, it was a real confidence builder too. It reinforced my Leadville win and was proof that I was definitely now up there with the world's elite ultra-trail runners.

Which, of course, meant it was time to conquer the world of triathlon.

I arrived back home on the Wednesday and, that weekend, having dusted the cobwebs off my mountain bike and fished my Speedo out the back of my cupboard, I lined up for the start of the XTERRA off-road triathlon outside the Western Cape town of Grabouw.

It was cool to do a race – a 1.5-kilometre swim, a 28-kilometre mountain-bike section and a 12.5-kilometre trail run – just for fun without the pressure of expectation. I'd obviously had a little practice on the bike during the Mark Webber Tasmania Challenge, but my swimming was very rusty. It didn't help that my prep was a little sketchy too. The swim was the first leg and, because I'd grabbed the first pair of goggles I found in my kit bag – I think they may have been my water-polo ones from high school – they filled up with water as soon as I started swimming.

The swim wasn't exactly my finest moment as a sportsman, and I had to move wide of the bunch just to actually see where I was going.

This meant that for the bike leg I was well down the field, in the thick of the action. The bike leg is well known for being super-technical, and has one particular rock garden that will chuck you over the handle-bars if you don't get your line right. I'd ridden it successfully during a Saturday practice run, but during the race on Sunday it was a logjam of riders gingerly trying to pick their way through. I eventually just shouldered my bike and ran it.

I ended up running it faster than most were riding it, so I made up a bit of time, although I still managed to fall down hard a couple of times during the leg. That's the thing about mountain biking: sure, it's easier on your legs than running, but fall off and the impact on your body is hectic. Come off and you spend a long time kind of trying to fix problems. I saw my chiro – and now coach – Lawrence van Lingen the next Monday, and he was like, 'Geez, why is your body so out?'

Fortunately, I survived, and was actually feeling really strong on the run, where I was able to make up a lot of places and ended up with a top-25 place. Not too bad considering my inexperience in the first two legs. I reckon if I had come out of the swim a bit better and got into more of a rhythm on the bike, I might've even cracked the top 20, which would have been cool. Still, I really enjoyed the event and it was great to just go out there and have some fun.

After that, I had a couple of months off from big races to give my legs a break. Obviously I was still training, but it was focused around my next target – The North Face 100 in Australia. I had a score or two to settle with that particular event, after having finished third there in what was a very tough race in 2011.

Having learnt my lesson the previous year, I was determined not to get sucked into a media circus before the race. The North Face 100 is Australia's biggest trail event and by now the trail scene had really taken off there, but I kept it more low-key this time around. Vanessa and I landed in Australia and went straight up to the Blue Mountains, where the race is held. We stayed there for about 12 days so that I could re-familiarise myself with the route – specifically a long stretch of jeep track called Megalong Road, where I'd really suffered in 2011. I needed to make peace with that road. We drove back to Sydney on the Sunday for a few selected interviews set up by Red Bull and a group run for Salomon, and then headed back to the Blue Mountains on the Tuesday.

If it sounds like I'm pegging my third-place 2011 result on too much pre-race PR activity, I'm not. I'm trying to show how much I'd wised up from that experience and was getting to grips with what does and doesn't work for me.

Like with the Hong Kong race, my plan was to use Australia as build-up for the Western States 100-miler in Squaw Valley, California, later that June, which was always my main goal after Leadville. Knowing my strength was still not of the super-technical European sort, and that I was more attuned to the heat and long, more gradual climbs of the US races, Western States – like Leadville – was more up my street.

After Hong Kong, I had also got it into my head that I wanted to try to win an ultra-distance race on every continent. Australia and Europe would be the final ticks on my list. But it's not like I was going to specifically travel back to either of those places time after time to try to win a race. To complete my collection, I needed to give this Aussie race a full go. In the week leading up to the race, I got into race mode quite early.

As Vanessa will testify, I can get super-grumpy four or five days before a race. I know it's selfish, but it really does become all about me. I just want to be left alone. She handles it unbelievably well, though. It's difficult for her too. There is a national park next to the Blue Mountains that has a cable car up to the top of one of the peaks, and she wanted us to take a day trip there, but I was like, 'No. Sorry, babe, I'm getting into the zone. I just need to chill.'

So I can get a bit weird in the days before a race. I can feel myself starting to change. My competitive nature starts to take over. I can't help it. Even driving on the roads, I almost want to start racing other cars; I don't like it when someone overtakes me. It's then that I know I'm starting to get my game on.

The Hong Kong and Australia races were also nicely spaced ahead of

Western States, so I was in good racing shape by the time I lined up at the start in Katoomba. I was being touted as one of the favourites for the race. I was the only representative from the Salomon international team. Mick Donges, a Salomon Australia athlete, was there – a really good up-and-coming trail runner; we'd done a few recce runs together.

One of them was that big climb at about the 80-kay mark. Called Kedumba Pass, it's this 10-kilometre gravel road that had messed with my mind the year before. This time around, Mick and I really gave it horns up there, and I could see I was a little stronger than him and made a point of driving the fact home – a little something I had learnt from Kílian when he had left us in the dust on those descents. A couple of times, I would surge ahead and then wait for him, trying hard to disguise my heavy breathing.

On race day, somewhat unusually for me, I went balls to the wall from the starting gun. In the early stages, I pushed a lot harder than I had done for other races. One of the Aussie athletes – Andrew Lee – had shot off the front, and I went after him quite hard. I wasn't going to let anyone get away from me. After eight kays, I caught him and, seeing he was looking a little breathless from the effort, I put my head down and kept going.

At about 23 kilometres, there is a big climb up some stairs, and again I pushed hard to the top, where I saw Vanessa waiting for me. From the clapping I could hear for the next runner arriving at the checkpoint behind me, I probably had a five-minute lead over who-ever was in second. Same thing at the 40-kay mark, where you do this loop around Aboriginal burial grounds. After going past the check-point, I could hear that my lead was now closer to 10 minutes.

It was all going well through the next couple of checkpoints, but I had a moment at the 65-kay mark when my legs started to feel a little crampy just before a steep climb. Trying to keep the panic under con-trol, I chanced the odd look behind me to see if anyone was catching up. Fortunately there was no one in sight, and by the next checkpoint I started to feel a lot better.

All I needed to deal with now was the Japanese tourists.

The checkpoint was situated at a big viewing platform at the top of some metal stairs, and to get down to the bottom the athletes had to use them, as did the tourists. The stairs were pretty narrow, and my descent coincided with a busload of Japanese folk wearing floppy hats and expensive cameras glued to their foreheads.

I have no idea why they don't close the course for the race, and it seemed like my timing seriously sucked. I ran down as fast as I could, screaming for people to get out of the way. It was chaos. They obviously had no idea there was a race on, and were somewhat surprised to see this sweaty trail runner half slipping and sliding down the stairs and pushing them out of the way.

Luckily, I managed to get to the bottom intact. And, weirdly, by taking my mind off the race for a while, it helped me mentally too. It was something so completely different and unexpected that I realised I was actually now feeling fairly fresh. At the 89-kilometre checkpoint, I was told I had a 20-minute lead, which meant, bar any disaster, the race win was in the bag. Great … except it also presented me with something of a dilemma. Turns out I was also ahead of the course record time. A record time that Kílian had set the year before.

What to do? There was a pretty steep climb to the finish. Should I go for it? Or, with Western States – my ultimate goal for the year – coming up in just six weeks, should I rather finish the run conservatively? Obviously, I went for it.

Initially, the trail was fairly flat and I started to push hard, but then it got a little more technical, and trying to jump over this rock, I clipped my foot and fell.

Flying through the air, I could feel my calves, quads – basically everything – just cramp up. Gingerly picking myself up off the ground, I spent a few minutes having to massage the cramps out of my legs. I was like, 'No, dude. Don't be stupid. Take your time. Jog to the finish. Don't try to be a hero now.'

So I backed off a bit over the last few kays, and finished what I'd started. I ended up winning in 9:22:45, about 30 minutes ahead of Vajin Armstrong in second, and three minutes outside Kílian's record time.

I've always had a somewhat conflicted attitude towards records. Obviously, they're cool to break, and there's always a large degree of personal satisfaction in knowing you're the guy who has run that particular course faster than anyone else, but I've never set out to break a record in any race. Naturally, those personal FKT (fastest known time) projects are different – the whole purpose being to set the quickest time over a particular route or between two set points. Besides, even though Kílian's record was broken by a jubilant Brendan Davies in 2013, running it in 9:16:12 (and then again by Dylan Bowman in 2015, in a time of 8:50:13 – but that was a new route), I know Kílian was taking it easy when he won.

I was very stoked with my win, and that was cool enough for me. I had achieved my goal of crossing the finish line first, and it felt like I was building some great momentum. I'd gone there, achieved what I wanted to do, and I had enjoyed doing it.

Getting back home after spending a couple of days in Sydney, I didn't have too much time to recover before it was off to California for my focus race of 2012 – the Western States 100-Mile Endurance Run. Three weeks before the race start, Vanessa and I packed our bags and travelled to our rented house in Incline Village, which was near the race start in Squaw Valley. Having done my long runs back home, my plan was to stay there, do some recce runs and then, a week before the race, travel down to Auburn, where the race ends, and acclimatise more there.

The thing with Western States is that the first half of the race is mountainous and at an altitude of 2 300 metres – Squaw Valley hosted the Winter Olympics back in 1960 – and then gradually descends through these canyons to Auburn at about 200 metres, where it's flippin' hot and dry. We're talking mid-40s °C. My plan was to spend some time training at altitude, and then spend the final week in the heat to get my body used to that. It seems to take the pores in my skin about a week to get used to extreme heat.

Unlike Leadville, where the route is pretty much signposted most of the way, finding the trails out of Squaw Valley was way trickier.

I wanted to scout the route a little and get in a couple of long runs, but managed to get properly lost on the first one. Fortunately, I bumped into a couple of fellow trail runners, Bill Rose and Tony LaPlante, who were able to give me a good idea of the lay of the land. Bill has subsequently become a good friend of ours, and Vanessa and I always stay at Bill and his wife, Theresa's, house whenever we're in his neck of the woods, so to speak. They've kind of become our American family.

As Americans generally are, Bill is the outgoing type and wasted no time in firing a hundred questions in my direction. What was my name? What was I doing here? Why had I come all the way from South Africa? Had I run any ultra-trail races before? I mentioned that I'd done Leadville the year before and that it went quite well.

Turns out, as I later discovered, Bill had finished a number of Western States 100s, he helped maintain the course, rebuilding bridges and cutting down trees, and is a legend and well-respected person among the trail-running community. They had obviously never heard of me, and I wasn't going to boast about my achievements, but it did make me smile at how locally focused Americans can be. For the Auburn trail-running community, it's all about Western States – they even call Auburn the 'Endurance Capital of the World'. That's literally its official title. They kind of know about Leadville, but don't pay it too much attention.

My prep in those weeks leading up to the start went really well, and after Australia and Hong Kong, I was in a confident mood. Then, about 10 days before the start, I sprained my right ankle really badly during a recce of the course. For about three or four days afterwards, it was feeling so sore I couldn't even run on it, but after having some rehab and a couple of runs with it tightly strapped, I decided I'd come all the way here, so I might as well give it a full go.

So I did. There I was at the starting line with virtually no movement in my ankle, thanks to the swelling and strapping. It didn't help that the weather was also horrendous – bizarrely cold on the day of the race, especially for that time of year. I was totally unprepared. I had a jacket with me, but only a lightweight one, and my hands got so cold that I couldn't get the jacket out of my pocket.

Despite everything, though, I was feeling good and ran in the leading pack that did the big initial climb from Squaw Valley up to the escarpment. In those first 10 kays, you climb around 1 000 metres, but the pace wasn't too hectic and I was feeling pretty comfortable. A few guys then broke away – Timmy Olson, Ian Sharman, Nick Clark and Dave Mackey – but I wasn't too concerned and continued to run at my own pace at about three minutes back, keeping an eye on Mike Wolfe, who I was using to judge my own pace. My main concern was the cold – there was even hail and some snow up at the escarpment – and with my hands basically frozen, I couldn't get the gels out my pocket either. At the first crew point, though, Vanessa was there to help me and I got some sustenance down.

Gradually, I started reeling everyone in, and I still felt pretty chilled – I knew that with Western States the race really only starts at the town of Foresthill, which is about 60 miles in. I caught the lead group just before the canyons, and ran with them for a bit. Running up Devil's Thumb, the big climb out of the canyons, I was with Mike Wolfe, and Timmy was about a minute up ahead in the lead. I dropped Mike just before Foresthill, picked up my pacer, Phil Villeneuve, and we caught Timmy in the run towards River Crossing. For the next 10 kays or so, Timmy and I swapped the lead a few times, and at one of the aid stations along the river, I had a good look at Timmy. He looked shattered. Done. I was like, cool, time to put down the hammer, and off I went.

Except he wasn't. There was a short, sharp little climb a few miles on that I power-hiked. Next thing, I hear a sound behind me and it's Timmy. Running. He had this weird, super-intense look in his eyes – like he was in berserk mode or something – and he blew right past me all the way to the top. Talk about a mental blow.

I still thought I might reel him in. From the top of that climb, it's pretty flat to the finish – very runnable – and I backed myself to catch him. But every time I got to an aid station, I'd hear that his lead over me had increased. Eventually I thought, okay, nothing I can do. It was Timmy's day and, as good as I was feeling – because I was still feeling pretty fresh – I was going to have to settle for second. Timmy won in

The start of the first stage of the 4 Deserts Gobi race. I hadn't felt this nervous about a sporting event since my first-team rugby debut. My legs were like jelly and my heart was in my throat

About 12 kilometres into the first stage of the 4 Deserts Sahara race. The temperatures were still relatively cool and I was feeling fresh. The scenery was amazing and I was super stoked to be leading by such a big margin. About an hour later, the Sahara Desert gods switched on the oven and things got properly hot

Day 4 of the 4 Deserts Sahara race: I was nearing the third checkpoint (±31 kilometres), which you can see in the distance. It was hot, but I had my yellow leader's jersey on, so life was good. It got lonely out there and it was nice to see the race volunteers at the checkpoints and have a chat

I had just won the 4 Deserts Atacama race in under 24 hours. I was stoked but also relieved to have another victory under my belt. A few days earlier, due to the devastating earthquake, I didn't know if I would even make it to the race. The race finished in the town of San Pedro. Pizza and beer had never tasted so good

Some of the gear I used during the 4 Deserts Antarctica race. To this day that yellow base layer still keeps me warm (and no, I don't have a tail – it's a shadow!). Most of the gear were prototypes made specifically by Salomon for the race (and yes, that is biltong that I smuggled into Antarctica)

Leadville 100: Returning back over Hope Pass with my pacer, Frosty (Anna Frost), just ahead of me. It was my first 100-miler, we were nearing 3 600 metres above sea level and I had run over 55 miles at this point. Most importantly, though, I was leading the race. I had never felt so tired and sore, yet so alive, in a race before. You can see from the photo that I'm in a very big pain cave

With the legendary Micah True (aka Caballo Blanco from the book *Born to Run*) at a local coffee shop in Leadville. We got to hang out a bit, and Micah's free-spirited lifestyle was a huge inspiration to me

© Emma Garrard

Western States, 2012: at Duncan Canyon aid station, which was the first time I got to see my race crew. Vanessa and Patrick helped me refuel, and that's Dean Leslie in the background shooting a video for Salomon. Patrick is from Salomon HQ (SLAB shoe design). It's cool how involved Salomon are with their athletes – it's a big deal for us

Finishing the 2012 Western States 100-miler. I might've come second, but in my opinion it is the best 100-miler I have ever run. You can't beat the feeling of running the final few hundred metres of a race with the South African flag in your hands. I love my country

Hong Kong, 2012, with Grant Guise (New Zealand), Jen Segger (Canada) and Vanessa. We did some sightseeing before the race and here we are in front of a local temple. I avoided eating any of the local food, though. Running a hundred kilometres was adventurous enough for me

Pre-Leadville 100-miler 2013, training run with Scott Jurek. Scott lives in Boulder, Colorado, so he knows the area quite well, and he took me on a 40-kilometre loop in the back country just outside of Leadville. I had just arrived from Cape Town, at sea level, so it was tough going for me. But it was great to run and hang out with Scott, who had won the Western States a record seven times in a row

© Jenny Jurek

© TransGrancanaria

Winning the 2014 TransGranCanaria, especially after a rough 2013, was a very sweet victory for me. I just felt stronger and stronger as the race went on. The atmosphere during the race was electric, as the Spanish are super passionate about any endurance sports

What the faaak have I got myself into? This was my first experience of the Drakensberg. I had not slept much that night due to the cold and we had woken up to snow. I suddenly got very nervous about our upcoming Drakensberg Grand Traverse

One of the rare occasions I ran ahead of Ryno during the 2014 Drakensberg Grand Traverse. He was in charge of navigation, so I just tagged along behind him most of the time. If I had been in charge of navigation, we would still be out there

After 41 hours and more than 210 kilometres of running and scrambling, we reached Bushman's Nek border post, the finish of the Drakenberg Traverse. After running on such rough terrain for that distance, my feet felt like they were going to explode. I even contemplated becoming a road runner. Ha! That only lasted for about a day

Dousing my head with water to cool down during the Racing the Planet Madagascar 250-kilometre stage race. I had just missed a checkpoint, so I was feeling a little hot and thirsty. A nice little reminder of just how tough a multiday, self-supported race is

14:46:44, shattering the existing record. I was 17 minutes back (and with the second fastest time ever), and Nick Clark came third, another 41 minutes behind me.

I wasn't super-bummed about it. I'd felt really good throughout the race, despite my ankle – in fact, it's still the best I've ever felt in a 100-miler. Even though I came second. My master plan was always to have three goes at the races I really wanted to win – Western States and the Ultra-Trail du Mont-Blanc – and for a first crack at Western States, I was happy with my result.

Besides, all the training I had put in also set me up for the rest of the year, especially for a personal project I had been planning for a good six months. It was one that has some very special memories, and something that would also go a long way to settling another old score.

STUFF I'VE LEARNT

Anger can help you focus

It's not always easy to keep your focus when you've built up a lead. An endurance sport is as much a mental game as it is a physical one, and any negative thoughts are going to affect your physical performance. As good as I was feeling in the first half of The North Face 100, as soon as we got near Megalong Road, I could feel my energy dropping and thoughts of my tough time there in 2011 started to creep into my head.

The route exits a cool piece of single track that flows onto a horrible stretch of gravel road, with cars driving past you, meandering upwards for what seems like forever. It's just flippin' miserable. My legs were feeling heavy, and suddenly I was feeling a little nauseous.

Fortunately, I also began to get pissed off. I didn't come all this way, built up a lead like this, only to lose it because my head was harping on about the miserable time I had had there six months previous. I needed to snap out of this negative head space, and the anger definitely helped.

Why you should try to recce a race route

This, I guess, will somewhat contradict an earlier section on 'Stuff I've learnt', where I talked about the advantages of ignorance. There are advantages to be had in ignoring tales of how difficult a particular route may be, and rather tackling it for the first time with fresh-faced positivity.

However, in a long trail race – where the route is often not all that well marked – it definitely helps to know where you should be running. Studying the route map is a given – especially if you are looking at doing well within your age group, or even winning the whole thing – but doing a recce of the course beforehand is crucial.

Obviously, this is entirely dependent on whether you have the time (not a luxury most amateur athletes have, given that you are inevitably holding down a day job as well) and whether the race organisers permit scoping out their race route.

The North Face 100 in 2012 was a great example of how running parts of the course the week before helped me considerably. The route took us through an ancient Aboriginal burial ground – something the race organisers had obviously got permission to do – but on race day some of the locals moved the route markers. Some of the guys missed a crucial turn-off. But when I came through – because I was familiar with the route – I had no such problem.

A pre-race recce also allows you to visualise the route. If there's a really steep climb, for example, you can have a look at it, work out where to conserve your energies and where to push it. You can picture the mindset you're going to have in that particular place, and make peace with it.

Keep a training log

Here's a small, but very valuable piece of advice: keep a training log or journal. I only started doing this from 2014 and, trust me, I really wish I had done it sooner. You can go the whole hog and keep track of what you are eating, how you are feeling and your goals, but that's a little too OCD for me. These days I keep a written record of the physical training I am doing – the workouts and the kilometres covered.

It documents what's worked ... and what hasn't

Instead of having to wrack my brain to recall exactly what I did in the lead-up to winning Leadville in 2011, having logged it would have been way easier for me to then replicate it.

You don't always have access to your coach

Travelling to remote parts of the world often means you're without internet, mobile or landline connectivity. If you need some advice, the best thing is often to refer back to your journal. After two, three or four cycles of training for races, you will begin to find a rhythm of training that works for you.

> ### It's a motivator
> As your journal grows with accumulated miles, the actual physical evidence of the hours of effort will be a source of pride and motivation to keep going.

12

UP A BIT, DOWN A LOT ...
AND THEN UP A BIT

Posting an FKT – fastest known time – for the Fish River Canyon trail was not only the kind of personal project that was beginning to appeal more and more, but it would also help exorcise some of those demons that had been irking me ever since I came second to Salvador Calvo Redondo in that 4 Deserts Namibia race back in 2009. It was, you'll recall, where my race fell apart on the very first day running up that steep climb out of the canyon. Coming second hurt like hell.

This certainly was one place that completely pulled me out of my comfort zone and really stretched me. There was something really humbling and magical about the area ... something that drew me back there. Have a look at the documentary that The African Attachment guys made called *The Beauty of the Irrational* on Vimeo. If I was really rational about my decision-making then, I wouldn't run it – there were far more reasons not to run it than there were to do it. For one thing, I'd had a big year and getting some well-earned rest was the smarter decision. Then again, I've always craved adventure and need to do something different than just race all the time. This time it would be just me and the canyon ... and a mission to break the FKT for the 76-kilometre traverse that starts 13 kilometres west of Hobas and ends at the Ai-Ais Hot Springs Resort.

I'd actually been back there in March 2011 to recce the route. I hooked up with two Namibian guys, Tinus Hansen and Russell Paschke, who know the Fish River area very well and, through their African Extreme Promotions events company, run the Fish River

Canyon Ultra Marathon. In fact, Russell was one of three guys who ran together to set the current FKT of 10:54.

The recce, unfortunately, turned into something of a disaster. The canyon is actually closed in March and opens only at the end of April due to the heat and variable conditions. Flash floods are a genuine danger. Doing a recce then was risky, but Tinus and Russell thought it was possible. Vanessa and I, along with Dean and Greg from The African Attachment, Ryan Scott from *Runner's World* and Trevor McLean-Anderson from Velocity, all trekked up to Namibia.

The recce started too late – around 9 a.m. – and soon we were running and power-hiking in the blazing heat. Russell dropped off the back and Tinus had to go back and find him, which took around 45 minutes. Eventually, by around 6 p.m., we got to the rendezvous point at the bottom of an emergency exit out of the canyon, where we'd arranged to hook up with Dean, Greg and Vanessa. As luck would have it, it had rained up-country and the various sluice gates along the Orange River were opened (no one tells you this) and the canyon began to flood. It also began to rain, which only added to the considerable nightly temperature drop, and we were all sleeping out in the open on the river bank. Trevor – a tough guy who's done several Iron Man events and the Cape Epic mountain-bike race – must have slept on a spider's nest or something because he had the crap bitten out of him as well. It was a hideous night.

By morning, it was obvious the water levels had risen significantly, but there was a wide section of the river where the water was relatively docile. During the route you cross the river several times, and if it was looking sketchy here, there would be no way we could cross it further downstream, where the canyon narrowed and the water really picked up speed. We made the call to pull the plug on the recce and the FKT attempt. It was a good decision. We barely managed to get across, floating the very expensive camera equipment on the small air mattress Vanessa had slept on. Then it was a steep hike out of the emergency exit. By the end of it, I was properly over the whole thing.

One thing I did learn from that ill-conceived expedition was that if anything went wrong during the record attempt, it would take a long time for anyone to find me. The only contact I'd have with any-one would be at the start, then three-quarters of the way, where there's a place you can actually drive into the canyon, and then at the end.

Which is why, when I returned at the end of July 2012, I brought along a helicopter that would both track me and ferry the film crew documenting my run from the air.

By this time, I was also a different runner. After winning Leadville, Hong Kong, The North Face 100 in Australia, and coming second at Western States, my self-belief and confidence had grown consider-ably. In 2012, I returned to the canyon with a completely different mindset. I was far better prepared for what might happen, but also more at peace with the place. A 'me versus the canyon' approach was clearly not going to work – this place could kick my butt if it wanted to, and there was nothing I could do about it. This time around, my attitude was to focus on enjoying myself and this spectacular place, and just kind of go with the flow a bit more. Whatever happened, nature would always be greater than me and anything can happen out there. I had to come to terms with that. Besides ... I had a helicopter.

I was in a good head space, and having Dean there filming also had a calming effect. I'd grown up with the guy, and I think we've built quite a close relationship. He'd seen me at my most vulnerable, and I felt like I could open up to him a lot. The interviews we did – some of which are in the *The Beauty of the Irrational* documentary I mentioned earlier – also helped me to really focus on what I wanted out of the attempt.

On record-attempt day, the weather was perfect. I wanted to start just after sunrise, so I had enough light to see during the descent into the canyon, and hopefully finish around 2 p.m., so I wouldn't have to spend too much time in the blazing heat. I started off a little too quickly. With the support helicopter hovering above and the send-off from my crew, I got a little too excited and, pumped with adrenalin, I hurtled down into the canyon. By the time I hit the sandy river bank below, my legs were like jelly and I thought I had overcooked it a bit.

But, apart from a little energy dip around the halfway point, the run was pretty much perfect – almost dreamlike. I felt completely at one with the canyon. I felt like I knew, understood and respected it. And, in return, it was allowing me to have a brilliant experience. It felt like I was gliding along … everything was just flowing. I was jumping rocks, taking some chances, not always seeing where my feet were going, but relaxed enough to just kind of go with it. Every now and then I'd pass a couple of hikers – some of whom knew I was going for the record – and I'd get some cheers.

The recce had obviously helped a lot, but there's not always a definite trail to follow – in fact, in many places there are several different trail options to take. You've just got to relax and realise that you're not always going to get it right. I had a little map book with me, but if you're constantly looking at it you're going to waste time. Inevitably I put my trust in my instincts, picked the line I thought was best, and went for it.

I must've crossed the river about 12 or 13 times and, although a couple of crossings were fairly big, where I actually had to swim, the river wasn't flowing too quickly, so there were no worries there. Once or twice I got a little bit lost and had a mild panic – you don't want to have to backtrack too much – but apart from that I got into a really good groove.

Feeling so at one with the whole experience, I wasn't even looking at my watch, and it was only with about 12 kays to go that I realised I could actually make it in under seven hours. Cue the Ryan Sandes push for glory. Only not. As if the canyon was slapping me on the back of the head for dropping the connection we had, I was hit by a sudden and massive energy drop. I actually had to walk for about 100 metres while quickly shoving some sustenance down my throat. Then I got lost. Panic set in: I wasn't going to break seven hours.

I quickly made my peace with this fact, switched off race mode and started to go with the flow once more. With five kays to go, I was back in the groove and once more feeling the canyon's love. I arrived at the finish in Ai-Ais, touched the rock we'd agreed on, and looked at my watch … 6:57.

There were quite a few people at the finish – my crew, obviously, but also folk from the local hotel. It was a good feeling. I kind of figured, bar any disaster, I'd crack the existing record, but the real buzz came from the experience of being in that canyon and feeling so connected to it. I guess it's like the 'stoke' surfers talk about when riding a wave. In the canyon, I had the stoke. Sure, I lost it for a while there, but, luckily, the canyon quietly reminded me of why we were all there in the first place.

My last big race of 2012 was a local one – the Salomon SkyRun. This is a 100-kilometre, self-navigation race between Lady Grey and Balloch in the Eastern Cape and, given the race's name, I was keen to be part of the event. As it takes place so late in the year, the timing didn't always fit in with my international schedule, and it's a pretty tough race as well. So far, 2012 was the only year I have competed.

The race starts in Lady Grey, and you climb for the first nine kilometres. Once you're on top of the Witteberg mountain range, you head along the ridge line towards Balloch Farm. From there, you crest a really steep climb, drop down the other side through long clumps of tough grass, making the run down the super-steep mountain a chaotic affair, do a big loop and come back to the finish at the Wartrail Country Club.

It's easy to injure yourself, and in training my foot went into a hole, smacking my knee on the ground and straining my quad – and that was on a part of the route about 95 kilometres into the race. That year I was the only guy who finished while it was still light, so this is something the rest of the field is doing by the light of the moon – if there is one – and a head torch to guide them. It's pretty gnarly.

Because the route is unmarked, I went there beforehand and did my homework. As I mentioned before, when I line up at a race I need to know where I'm going. I don't want to end up getting lost with a hundred and one excuses. I spent a weekend there with a mate of mine and also one of the race organisers, Adrian Saffy, and we hiked the route through the night from the start to Balloch. In the weeks leading up to the race, I also ran it twice. From Balloch it is quite easy to do the last 40 kilometres, so I recced a few bits of that route as well.

The race started in the dark at 4 a.m., and I was seen as the favourite. Unfortunately, the record holder, Iain Don-Wauchope, wasn't there – he'd called Adrian the day before and said he wasn't feeling up to it – but the defending champ, Bruce Arnett, was at the start, as was my mate Ryno Griesel. The first part of the race is one long nine-kilometre climb, and initially I got slightly lost and was separated from the bunch. I managed to catch them soon enough, though. Once up at the microwave tower, with the sun beginning to rise, I was feeling pretty good and decided to push really hard on my own until the next checkpoint.

At 30 kilometres, though, I hit a bit of a wall. All of a sudden, running from the Snowden to Avoca checkpoints (the highest section of the race), I started feeling super-low in energy and my stomach wasn't feeling great. Mentally, this section is also quite draining – everything looks the same running along the ridge. The weather also turned particularly nasty, and for the rest of the race we were dogged by rain, hail, wind, thunder and strong winds. At one point, I was even thinking of lying down and having a bit of a power nap. In hindsight, it was probably the altitude and I might have pushed too hard early on. A few weeks after the race, I found that I had giardiasis, a parasite infection in the stomach, which may explain the nausea.

At the Balloch checkpoint, I managed to eat and drink loads, which seemed to help. I started feeling a lot better. There was also a Red Bull aid station at the turnaround point and I filled my bottles with half Red Bull and half water, which also perked me up nicely for the rest of the race.

After that came the infamous 'Wall' – this really steep grass embankment that goes up for about 500 metres. Basically, it's a straight line up with the occasional little zigzag to ease the pain. I remember getting to the top, which usually takes about 35 to 40 minutes, and hearing the noise down below at Balloch, which sounded like the next guy had just come through. With a lead like that, I could basically switch off race mode and cruise into the finish. I ended up winning in 12:36, and in the process beat Iain's record by more than two hours. I was happy with that, given the weather and it being my first-ever Salomon SkyRun.

In 2014, Iain went crazy hard and finished really strong to smash it in 12:08, which was flippin' impressive and will be tough to beat. The race organisers have also upped the ante with a sizeable $10 000 for anyone who goes sub-12.

They were also talking about rolling it over and making it $20 000, which is one helluva tempting carrot, but I also need to think about the longevity of my career. It's a lot of cash, especially in trail-running terms, but I never started doing this sport for money. And I would soon learn the dangers of doing too many ultra-distance races.

At the end of 2014, I came down with glandular fever. It made me realise just how much I was putting my body through every year. My favourite time to run is in the summer sun, and the problem with living in South Africa is that it means running in November, December, January or February – a time when I should be resting a little. I've tried to change that over the past few years, but I still don't think I take enough time for a proper off-season. That's not to say I want to stop running over that time, but it means stepping away from the endurance side and working on strength and things like that. Mentally, it is also really refreshing – it's good to change the routine with lots of shorter high-intensity training. I love running for hours in the mountains, but after doing it for seven months or so, you kind of need to step away for a reboot.

Thinking long term, once I stop competing I still want to enjoy running. I definitely don't want to walk away hobbling on stuffed ankles, wearing a knee brace and breaking out in a cold sweat every time I look at a pair of running shoes. I'd rather end my competitive career when I'm still motivated to run, instead of running myself to death and being completely over it. I still want to be amped.

That said, the SkyRun is a very special race for me. I have wonderful memories of the place – from the night hikes with Adrian, to time spent there with Vanessa and our much-loved dog, Thandi. In the week leading up to the race, the renowned action-sport photographer, and a good mate of ours, Craig Kolesky, stayed with us and he'd brought a ton of biltong with him (that's strips of dried meat for all you non–South Africans reading this). Thandi, who can sniff out a sliver of biltong at a thousand paces, must have thought she'd died and gone to heaven. Needless to say, she got into Craig's room and polished it all off. The poor guy was devastated. Thandi didn't move for two hours. I was actually quite worried. And a little sorry for Craig, who was left eating tuna and two-minute noodles for the rest of the week.

The year ended on a personal high for me – not with a race I won, but with one I had created. The year 2012 saw the inaugural Red Bull Lionheart, a short, lung-bleeder of a run up Lion's Head in Cape Town. The qualifiers were on the Saturday, followed by a series of knockout heats on the Sunday. It was basically a steep sprint straight up one of Cape Town's iconic mountains, and then a blast back down, praying you don't catch your foot on a piece of granite. The winning time is around 25 minutes, which shows how hard you have to push it. You're red-lining all the way. Doing that several times a day, as you progress through the heats, makes for a uniquely tough event.

I had dreamt up the idea, pitched it to Red Bull, and being the kind of company that loves putting on innovative events, they jumped all over it. I never really thought South African National Parks would ever grant permission, but kudos to them for doing so.

Red Bull Lionheart has been going for four years now, and has become a very successful event. I'm starting to think it's time to shake things up, though – maybe change the format to something different, or a downhill race, perhaps down Devil's Peak. It could even be something like an endurance mountain-bike race, where everyone still has to make the climbs but you only time the downhill sections.

Ironically, I've never won my own event but, then again, I guess the short, sharp stuff has never been my forte. The longer, the better for me …

In terms of racing, 2012 was a pretty stellar year for me. I won a couple of significant single-day races and placed second at the prestigious Western States. Just as well … because 2013 was a bit of a shocker.

Western States was again my focus and, after coming second, I was amped to claim the winner's bronzed-cougar trophy. Some of my mates wondered why I wanted one if I already had my own bronzed cougar, but Vanessa didn't think that joke was all that funny. (She's four years older than me.)

The year actually started off rather well with The North Face TransGranCanaria, a race across the Canary Islands. There's an 83-kilometre and a 125-kilometre event. I chose the shorter distance, given my planned assault on Western States later in the year, but this still involved some serious climbing – around 4 500 metres.

I got there a week before, and the organisers put me up in a really basic mountain hut – no electricity, cold-water showers and boarding-school-style meals. I didn't mind it too much – there being some cool trails to run – but my accommodation took a turn for the better when my fellow Salomon athlete, Germany's Philipp Reiter, turned up.

Philipp's a cool guy. He likes his luxuries, though, and was, shall we say, typically German in voicing his displeasure about our accommodation. He's fairly young and the organisers talked him into doing the race, even though he was busy with his studies at the time. Clearly they didn't mention the mountain huts in those initial discussions. The next day, they moved us down to this five-star resort on the beach. I wasn't complaining. Nothing wrong with a little chilling out on a pool lounger. Nice one, Phil.

The race route has a bit of everything – really mountainous in the beginning, and cold too. It's a very early-morning start and the higher you go up through the forests and volcanic mountains, the colder it gets. The latter part of the race heads back down to the coast and then it can get to 35 °C.

The initial 11 kays is basically straight up – something like 1 600 metres of climbing, which is proper tough for such a short distance. Philipp was also my main challenger in the race, and for the first half I kept my eye on him. I was in the top five for the early part, but once it flattened out I seemed much quicker than the other guys, so I made my break. It wasn't really a strategy. I was just kind of running and seeing how it went. I remember feeling very well the whole race, really enjoying it, and I ended up winning in 8:11:27, around 16 minutes ahead of Philipp, who finished second. Technically, the win also meant I'd won an ultra marathon on every continent: the Canary Islands are part of Spain, which is part of Europe ... I'm claiming it!

I was still on a high when Vanessa and I went off to Australia, once again for The North Face 100. It was in May, only a few months after the TransGranCanaria, and while that's a fair gap between ultra races, it's starting to cut it a little fine. For an athlete, though, it's often difficult to be disciplined in this regard. You race, do well, and then you kind of get into that mental attitude where you just want to keep going. You feel really good about yourself, and you want to keep racing. I've seen a lot of top guys make that mistake and, I'm sad to say, I've done it too.

Bounce from one race to the next and then, suddenly, in one event, you don't quite get the results you want. You think you've just got to train more, and then you just keep overtraining, and so the fatigue sets in ... and the downward spiral begins.

Having won the year before, I was seen as the favourite and the press were saying things like, 'The only way Ryan Sandes is going to lose is if something unfortunate happens to him in the race.' And they were right. Only the bad thing happened before the race even started.

After spending about three or four hours on my feet at the race registration, doing interviews the day before the race – a rookie mistake on its own – I finally got a chance to sit down and decided to have a hot chocolate. It tasted good, but straight afterwards I started feeling a little odd. Like it wasn't sitting too well in my stomach.

I woke feeling kind of okay the next morning and was fine the first 10 kays ... until I had some Perpetuem. That made me nauseous. My energy levels dropped and I could feel my body temperature increase, even though the ambient temperature couldn't have been more than 7 or 8 °C. I tried some gels, hoping those would get me going, but they went straight through me and I had to duck off into the bushes. It was all happening ... top and bottom ... not pleasant!

I tried pressing on, but by the time I got to the aid station at

34 kilometres, I was properly done and pulled out. I remember sitting on the toilet for, like, 30 minutes – by then easily 40 or 50 minutes behind the leader – and thinking: What do I have to gain trying to run half-dehydrated just to finish the race? It would completely sap everything I've got for Western States, which was just six weeks later.

Still, it was a hard decision to make. I'd never bailed in a major race before, and for me it always felt like you were being disrespectful to the event and the other runners. There were athletes out there who would literally give everything and crawl across the finish line to get their finishers' medals, and here I was pulling the plug with less than half the race done. Obviously, in terms of the year ahead and my career as a whole, it was the smart choice, but emotionally it was flippin' tough.

I got a lift to the next checkpoint, where Vanessa was waiting for me. She was obviously surprised and concerned to see me. She gave me a hug, and the Australian Salomon brand manager Naima Madani, who was also there, tried to console me, but I was feeling bleak. I got into our car and kind of broke down in tears.

Things were about to get bleaker, though.

After a couple of days my stomach began to feel better, and within a week I was training again. Harder than ever. Really pushing myself. Punishing myself, if truth be told. I kept on thinking back to Australia. Wasn't I focused enough? Was I undercooked? I was angry with myself – and because of that, I think I just lost my connection with my body.

I would push super-hard during my training sessions, and even though I could feel my legs were tired – because I can be mentally focused (or perhaps 'stubborn' is a better word) – I overruled what my body was trying to tell me. And that, I think, is a large part of the reason I was to suffer the worst injury of my career so far ...

It was a rainy afternoon, and I was doing what should've been nothing more than a routine recovery run through the Constantia Green Belt with our dog. Except, in the first 20 minutes, I almost went over on my ankles three or four times. Obviously, something wasn't quite right; my legs were too tired. I was pushing it way too hard. But, me being me, I carried on.

Then, running a fairly easy piece of single track above Constantia Nek, I went over on my right ankle. I heard it pop and felt this excruciating pain shoot up my leg. I stopped running immediately. I knew I'd done some real damage. I couldn't put any weight on my right foot at all. I knew straight away that Western States was no longer going to happen for me and, to be honest, I thought that could even be my career finished, right there and then. It was *that* sore. Vanessa had to come and get me, and I had a full scan done first thing the next morning.

Luckily, the diagnosis was way better than the one my imagination had dreamt up. I hadn't broken any bones, snapped any tendons or ligaments, but I had hyperextended the ankle, severely stretching the ligaments, which caused small tears on both the inside and outside of those ligaments. I had also suffered some internal bleeding on the inside of the ankle. No major drama, but not ideal either. And there was no way I would recover in time to do Western States ...

It would mean two weeks without any running, followed by four weeks of virtual running in a swimming pool, where your feet don't touch the ground, though you're still putting your legs through the range of motion that running demands. You are basically treading water for an hour. Mind-numbing stuff. After the pool, I did a couple of sessions on Velocity Sports Lab's zero-gravity machine, a treadmill with a harness suspended above it that will take up to 80 per cent of your body weight. I started off running with half my weight suspended in the harness and, over a two-week period, gradually reduced it to 95 per cent, and then 100 per cent of my weight. I'd then do about 40 minutes on the zero-gravity treadmill, and then do a slow 15- or 20-minute run on the road.

And then I shifted my attention to Leadville.

After winning it in 2011, I'd skipped the legendary high-altitude ultra in 2012 for my Western States quest, but, now, if I pushed my recovery, I fancied my chances to not only be at the Leadville starting line in six weeks' time, but also to be competitive.

I know! What was I thinking?

I was actually in pretty good shape by the time I got to the US for the race. With loads of miles already in my legs, I quite quickly regained fitness. My plan, once in Leadville, was not to overdo it in the week leading up to the race. Then I fell again ...

It must've been my fourth or fifth run there when I tripped and took a bit of a tumble. I kicked a root and, not wanting to land on this rock in front of me, I kind of twisted out the way and landed awkwardly. I felt something tweak a bit in my lower back, but jumped straight up and kept going. I didn't think much of the incident until two days later on my next run, when my breathing was oddly laboured and the left side of my back was weirdly tight. Initially, I reckoned it was the altitude, but then I started to feel actual pain.

Thinking that maybe I'd slipped a disc or something, I paid a visit to a local Leadville chiropractor, who told me my lower back muscles were in spasm and basically acting to compress my spine. Despite a couple of sessions, he couldn't get the muscles to release. After chatting to my then chiro, Lawrence van Lingen (he would become my coach in 2014), back in South Africa, he sent me some videos on breathing drills and stretches that would release my back. They actually eased the pain considerably, and by race day I was feeling good. In fact, for the first 30 miles of the 100-miler I didn't even think about my back, until my hip flexors suddenly started to tighten up. My back was obviously pulling everything out.

This was just before Twin Lakes and I was lying third at that point, but I could feel something wasn't right. Near the top of Hope Pass, the pain was starting to get worse and I was half running, half walking, and then eventually just hobbling up to the top. I was nowhere ... it was just too sore to even run. I tried to stretch it out with the exercises Lawrence had given me, and then thought maybe running down the other side of Hope Pass would help, but sadly not. I stumbled down the last few kilometres to the dirt road, realising that that was my race done. I took my number off and hitched a ride to the next checkpoint at Winfield, where I knew Vanessa would be waiting for me.

It was an easier decision to make to pull the plug on this race than it had been in Australia, but, emotionally, I felt worse this time. It took me a long time to get over Leadville 2013. I felt very bad because I had more crew with me than usual, and I thought I had let them down badly. Apart from Vanessa, Ryan Scott was with me again, this time doing some interviews for Red Bull and Salomon, plus I had pacers – other athletes there specifically to help me in the race.

I remember doing a video with Ryan afterwards, apologising to everyone for letting people down back home. I just felt like a complete failure – like I had let myself down, and Vanessa, my family, my sponsors, and all the people supporting me back home.

I wasn't in a good head space.

Back home, it took my mate Dean Leslie to pull me aside and offer the advice I needed. He basically told me to get the hell out of Cape Town, spend time on my own, and just disconnect from all the pressure for a while. Dean knows me, and he was spot on.

I booked a little chalet in the Matroosberg mountains, a couple of hours outside Cape Town, and for two weeks I just chilled and ran. But only if I felt like it. For the first time in years, I didn't follow any specific training programme; I'd wake up in the morning and run only if the mood took me. Often I would just hike to the top of the mountain and literally just sit up there for an hour or two on my own, mulling over my life. Vanessa and my mate Ryan Scott joined me for a few days, but most of the time I was on my own. I needed to press the reset button.

It worked. I got back to Cape Town on the Saturday, decided on the Wednesday to enter the Crazy Store Table Mountain Challenge, and the following Saturday ran it, won it, and then flew to Patagonia.

Though let me qualify that: when I say 'flew to Patagonia', it involved about 10 connecting flights, including the scariest plane trip I've ever been on. It was a late-night flight on one of the domestic South American airlines, and we hit the gnarliest turbulence I've ever experienced. All the lights went off, the staff were shouting in Spanish, and most of the passengers were holding rosary beads and praying. At one point, I thought that was it ... From that day on, I've been super-nervous about flying.

Anyway, the reason I was there was to take part in the 64-kilometre Patagonian International Marathon held in the Torres del Paine National Park in Chilean Patagonia. They had invited me and paid for my flights and accommodation. I was always up for an adventure and it was exactly what I needed. The field wasn't too strong, and I won the race fairly comfortably, but that wasn't what made me feel better. It was the place. Patagonia is one of the most beautiful parts of this wonderful planet of ours that I have ever had the privilege to visit. The epic mountains, glaciers and massive lakes would be the healing I needed. I had flown in five days before the race, rented a car and explored the national park on my own. No group runs, no media commitments, nothing.

It was the perfect end to what had been a pretty flippin' miserable year.

STUFF I'VE LEARNT

How to run technical descents

Through trial, error and observation, it took me a while to be able to run quickly down a trail – especially the steep, technical descents. These are the fundamentals I have learnt.

Don't micro-manage the trail

It depends on your speed but, as a rule of thumb, always keep your eyes looking at the trail about five metres ahead. You don't want to be looking directly down and micro-managing every footfall. Trust your brain. Your eyes have already scanned the terrain ahead, and you'll almost instinctually know where to place your feet.

Take small steps

The more technical the descent, the smaller your strides should be. This means you can make quicker adjustments, and you'll be able to react if the terrain is really loose or slippery. If you look at someone like Spaniard Kílian Jornet, it's almost as if he dances down the mountain.

Don't be too upright ... and lean back a little

You want to lower your centre of gravity to give you more stability. You also don't want to be leaning too far forward because, if you trip, it's going to be messy. If you do lose your footing, you rather want to fall backwards so you can use your hands to break your fall.

Use your momentum and don't apply the brakes

The key is to remain relaxed – get a rhythm and sense of flow going. Using your quads as brakes is going to mean a jarring descent that will be hard on your knees. You want to keep those feet dancing. Relax, but keep your concentration levels up.

Take it slow at first

Don't take what I've said and go balls to the wall down the next trail. It will take practice and probably a couple of falls. Be patient, get the technique right, and rather build up your speed and confidence.

My typical training week

Because I've built up a big base in my legs over the years, my training is very specific. Training programmes depend on where you are in your career as an athlete. What you'll read below is what I would do in the three months leading up to a 100-miler, like Western States.

I start every session with 15 or 20 minutes of mobility exercises that trainer Michael 'Gunshow' Watson has been teaching me. Depending on what my day is like, I normally try to get out at 9 a.m. If it's a double session, then I'll try to start a little bit earlier. My coach, Lawrence van Lingen, has tried to make me put more emphasis on sleep and recovery.

Monday

This is a rest day after a long run on Sunday, though I would do an easy strength and mobility session with Michael.

Tuesday

Depending on what race I'm focusing on, I'll do an easy three-hour hike and run. Often I'll try to get as much elevation going as possible in a run to build up strength. I'll also try to switch off a little bit. I'll stop my watch for half an hour, and just sit there and check out the view.

Wednesday

In the morning, I would do 45 minutes on the self-powered True-Form treadmill. Because it's self-powered, your running form and technique have to be really good to generate the drive that keeps the treadmill rollers turning. You've got to really lift your foot up and drive it back to get that good extension. It helps to fire up my back line – my glutes and hamstrings – and open up my hips. It's hard work – 20 or 30 minutes on there, and you really feel it.

After that little warm-up, I'll go for a quick 10-minute run on the road, as the TrueForm switches on a lot of muscles. Then back to the TrueForm for some fast 10-second bursts with a standing rest of 10 to 20 seconds in between. I do about six to eight repeats of this with a 10-minute easy run on the road, and then repeat this eight to 12 times.

In the afternoon, I'll do some hill repeats after a 20-minute warm-up. I'd find a steep hill on the trail and do repeats of 15, 30 and 45 seconds for about 50 minutes. You can't go too hard at the beginning, so rather keep it controlled. If I feel, after 35 minutes, that I've done too much, I'll back off. No use in frying myself. After that I'll do a 50-minute run to cool down.

Thursday

I'll do another hike or run, as I'm mimicking what the route will be like in a specific race. So, for Western States, for example, I know there are some climbs where I will need to power-hike. You drop down into the canyons and then you've got big climbs out. So I'll do an easy run for 30 minutes, then 20 minutes on a flat section at a heart rate of 145 beats per minute (I would repeat this two or three times), and then hike for two hours, but run all the downhills.

When I ran Western States in 2014, I felt I was too slow and sluggish on the flat sections. I wasn't recovering after some of the climbs. I need to teach my body to be more efficient on the climbs – yet still maintain my climbing speed – and then recover quicker, so when I'm on a flat section I can get into the rhythm and get straight into that speed.

After that session, I'll do a 10- to 40-minute run at a heart rate of 145 beats per minute, and then finally an easy 10-minute walk to cool down.

Friday

This is a rest day, though occasionally I'll do a session with Michael. It will be an easy one – more about getting movement back and making sure my hips are moving properly.

Saturday

I do an hour and 30 minutes with a tyre. I will generally go down to the field at the False Bay Rugby Club and tie a second-hand tyre to my waist with a long rope and one of those straps weight-lifters use. I warm up without the tyre for 30 minutes, and then do six to eight tyre pulls where I run, while pulling the tyre for two to five minutes, with a rest of 30 seconds to one minute in between. Then I'd do a 20-minute session to cool down.

Sunday

This would be a long one. I'd do a 30-minute warm-up, then 3 x 20-minute repeats, where I'd run 20 minutes of flat trail at tempo pace, and then five minutes in between at easy pace. After that, it's an easy two- to three-hour run, with the last 20 minutes at tempo, followed by 10 minutes to cool down.

13

IT WAS THE BEST OF TIMES, IT WAS THE WORST OF TIMES

Before I get slapped on the back of the head, I need to mention one thing that did go particularly well for me in 2013. I asked Vanessa to marry me. And she said yes! It was while I was still recovering from my ankle injury, and we'd gone to Knysna for the Oyster Festival. I ran the Knysna Marathon and Featherbed trail races for some training, and did some fundraising with Magnetic South (the Featherbed's organisers) for a young boy who needed a kidney transplant.

Vanessa and I had been together for around three years by then, and the pressure was on. My mom was in on it too, sending me pictures of engagement rings and eventually even helping me get all the quotes and wangling a good price. My mom knew a wedding was one step closer to having a grandchild – something she was longing for – and she even tried half-seriously talking us into having a baby out of wedlock. I think she may have even offered to pay for the ring.

I was a little concerned about the timing of the whole thing. On the one hand, you don't want your sponsors to think, 'Hang on ... he's having the worst year of his career, and now he's planning a wedding! Maybe he's losing focus?' Then again, I've always had a very open relationship with all my sponsors, and they know me well enough to understand that losing focus was never an issue. Plus, of course, this was the love of my life.

I bought the ring and gave it to my mom for safekeeping, as I had originally wanted to propose at a later stage, but the ring was figuratively burning a hole in my pocket. When I asked my mom for the ring back, she obviously knew something was up, but I didn't want to tell her too much. My mother has many wonderful qualities, but keeping a secret she's excited about isn't one of them. My sister's fiancé at the time, Brad, made the mistake of telling my mom his plans ahead of their proposal, and my mom was already popping champagne the day before he proposed.

I kept the whole proposal pretty impromptu. I wanted the timing to be right, and I wanted to be in a good head space. Vanessa had witnessed the rough time I'd been through over the preceding few months, and she'd been amazingly supportive. She had been very committed to me throughout my career, and I felt it was the right time and a very natural step for us.

There was a gap of two days where we didn't have anything specific planned, and my idea was to propose on the beach. We had met in Knysna and it was the three-year anniversary of that day. The timing was perfect. I wanted to go down to the beach with some champagne and pop the big question with the sun setting over the sea on a wild and beautiful Knysna beach. Ryan 'Romantic' Sandes, they call me.

Unfortunately, the weather that day was shocking, and Vanessa hates the cold. She wanted to stay indoors and chill, but I managed to drag her out and, miraculously, the clouds dissipated for a few hours – long enough for me to pluck up the courage. But, just as I was about to propose, she decided to go to the bathroom. I had to wait for her to come back, and finally did the whole drop-down-on-one-knee thing.

At the beginning of our relationship, I was pretty clear about the fact that my running career comes first, and we needed to take things slowly. But Vanessa seemed to understand me better than anyone and, a year into our relationship, I knew she was the one. We're not exactly similar people, but we complement each other really well and share the same interests. Basically, we just get along really well. She brings out the good qualities in me and vice versa – which I think is quite rare.

Always, and often to her detriment, she puts other people ahead of herself. She'll spend a lot of time taking care of other people, going out of her way for them. I love her sense of humour when things are bad, and Vanessa's definitely got an adventurous spirit too – I could see that in the way she took to trail running. Along with her mountain-biking prowess, she'd also improved a lot as a trail runner, especially after being with me at Leadville 2011, where she did plenty of running while I was doing my thing.

Just after that, we both ran the Otter back in South Africa, and she came in way quicker than I had expected. Having already finished, I went and had a shower and was doing a couple of interviews when I heard over the loudspeakers that Vanessa Haywood had just crossed the finish line. I had to get my stuff together and sprint over there to welcome her.

Her passion and drive for all the things she does inspires me, and it was one of the factors that helped me get myself together in 2014. Vanessa helped me realise that a major motivation, which would normally drive me, had been missing in 2013. There were no personal projects – no personal quests like that Fish River Canyon FKT. I needed to do something that satisfied my sense of adventure, but didn't involve the pressures of a big race.

It was time for another epic FKT ... this time across the Drakensberg. The prospect of the Drakensberg Grand Traverse got me amped, as I think a lot of my success can be related to the adventure and excite-ment of trail running. Adventure pulled me into the sport, and some of the racing I had subsequently done – although it was all my choice and necessary for my career – was a lot less about adventure and more about calculated and specific racing. Having those adventure projects is something that still inspires me, and I needed a project like that to keep me motivated. And, as adventures went, this would be a big one. The quoted length for the traverse is 210 kilometres – easily the longest single distance I would've attempted – but in reality, with the rugged up-and-down terrain, it feels more like running 300 kilometres.

Ryno Griesel had first floated the idea a couple of years earlier, when I met him at the 2012 SkyRun. An experienced and competitive trail runner (Ryno came third at SkyRun that year), he had plenty of experience running in the Drakensberg. He mentioned that if I ever wanted to have a crack at the FKT from Sentinel Peak to the Bushman's Nek border post with Lesotho, he'd be willing to help. The route starts at the Sentinel Peak car park, goes through checkpoints at Mont-aux-Sources, Cleft Peak, Champagne Castle, Mafadi, Giant's Castle, Thabana Ntlenyana, and finally finishes at Bushman's Nek.

Initial planning for the attempt first started back in October 2013, when I did a recce with Ryno, his mate Cobus van Zyl, and photographer and quality trail runner Kelvin Trautman. And like my initial Fish River recce, this, too, was something of a disaster. Looking back now, I'm a little embarrassed at how naive I was in my approach – I'd had some experience of the Drakensberg doing the SkyRun, but that wasn't the real deal. I was totally unprepared for the conditions, taking only the lightest gear. Even the jackets I took were borderline water-proof. They could get you through a race, but were totally unsuited for what this traverse required.

The recce plan was to do a fast, three-day hike over the full traverse. It was October, which is quite a stable time for weather, meaning there shouldn't be too much rain, and while it might get a little nippy, it shouldn't be too bad. Except ... we nearly froze to death on the first night. We camped just past the chain ladders above the Sentinel Peak car park to get a feel for the conditions.

I spent most of it awake and shivering – and then awoke to find everything had turned white. It had obviously snowed during the night. Not that any of this bothered Cobus. There I was walking around with two jackets, a beanie and gloves – basically every piece of clothing I had with me – and he was cruising around in shorts and a T-shirt. He's a seriously tough guy, a super dude, who really helped us out. Cobus was an ace with maps and navigation, and sat down for hours to help us plan the proper routes and GPS co-ordinates. I think, at times, he was more excited than us about breaking the record.

Cobus also carried a gun, which took me a while to get my head around, but even in this remote part of the world, you have to keep your eyes open. In the past they'd had problems with locals – minor issues like stuff being stolen from their camps at night, but some tourists had also been mugged up there, so you do have to be a little vigilant. There's also a bit of drug smuggling that goes on in these mountains, and Ryno and I once saw eight guys marching with these big white sacks on their shoulders. It was right next to Giant's Castle at one of the trail exit points and near some major roads. They were clearly smuggling weed off the mountain, and you definitely want to avoid them.

That said, both Ryno and Cobus knew the Berg backwards. As a student, Ryno used to rock-climb, and for many of the peaks in the area you've got to hike quite a long way. That's actually how he got into trail running. Scary drug smugglers and snow or not, we had to get the recce done. Red Bull South Africa had pitched it to their international head office, and a fair amount of euros had been released to support the logistics and filming of the project.

The next day, we went back down to the Witsieshoek Hotel to prep and get our gear ready, and then early that morning drove to the Sentinel car park to start the traverse route proper. Even though we were only power-hiking over four days and three nights, it was tough going. They were long days out on the route, sometimes stopping for Kelvin to film, with minimal sleep each night thanks to the cold weather. On Day 3, we were also hammered by a biblical thunderstorm. Ryno and Cobus had been in these situations before, and were more used to it than Kelvin and me. The two of us were properly out of our comfort zones. At one point this massive lightning strike hit the ground near us – the static was so strong it actually shocked Ryno and Cobus up ahead. Next thing, they're bolting back down the trail towards us shouting, 'Turn around, turn around!' I shat myself. Luckily, there was a little cave further down, and we regrouped there.

The weather eventually caused us to cut the recce short, and we didn't finish the traverse route, but at least I got to see first-hand what the Berg was capable of. I would return for two more recces in early 2014 to pay my respects. In January, Ryno and I hiked from the start at the Sentinel Peak car park to Giant's Castle, and then the following month we started at Giant's Castle and ran to the finish at the Bushman's Nek border post. On this final run the altitude really got to me, and at one point I basically collapsed and had to sleep for an hour. That didn't exactly bode well for the record attempt, but at least it equipped me with a much better sense of what I was in for. This was going to be one seriously daunting undertaking...

A week in the Canary Islands helped me take my mind off it for a while. Not that it was a holiday – I was there to run the 125-kilometre version of the 85-kilometre TransGranCanaria event I had won the year before. And, to be honest, I was pretty nervous. There was a serious amount of climbing – 8 500 metres of the race distance – and it would be the most I'd ever done in a race. Ryno and I had also announced our Drakensberg Grand Traverse project on the back of the TransGranCanaria, so I wanted the race to go well.

   I didn't help that my legs were feeling pretty knackered. During the last Drakensberg recce, we'd used a helicopter to film the run for the Red Bull documentary called *Travailen*. It involved me running up and down quite a few peaks in order to get the perfect shot. And ahead of the TransGranCanaria, I could feel it in my legs. Vanessa and I were staying in the middle of the island – it's the high point of the race at about 85 kilometres – and that gave me the opportunity to do some route recces. While my legs felt fatigued, they still had some spring in them, though, which was encouraging. It's when your legs feel okay but have little or no power that you have to worry.

   TransGranCanaria was now also part of the inaugural Ultra-Trail World Tour, made up of existing races around the globe – among others, the Western States 100, Ultra-Trail du Mont-Blanc, Mount Fuji 100, Hong Kong 100 and the renamed The North Face 100 (Ultra-Trail Australia) were all part of it. The idea is that you could accumulate points at each of the 10 races with your best three events counting towards the title for the Ultra-Trail World Tour. It seemed like an interesting concept, though I was a little sceptical of running too many big races in one year... and even three was pushing it. More and more of my fellow competitors were picking up injuries and suffering from various ailments, which pointed to the fact that their bodies were simply fatigued. As mentioned, the medical fraternity was even starting to talk about overtraining syndrome being an actual medical condition. On the other hand, I was doing Western States anyway – perhaps I could have a shot at the overall title?

The event started at midnight – not something I was generally used to in a race at all. The Berg recces, however, had us hiking and running many nights, so I was a bit more confident than I would've been six months earlier. It was a competitive field as well. Western States winner Timmy Olson was there, as well as Sébastien Chaigneau, Miguel Heras, Julien Chorier, Dylan Bowman, Jason Schlarb, Mike Wolfe and quite a few of the other top European guys.

The route kicks off with a 15-kilometre climb from the town of Agaete, straight up the mountain, and initially I was with the lead pack, but dropped back quite a bit thanks to a series of mishaps. First I had stomach issues. I was using Perpetuem – the final time I would do so – and it just wasn't sitting well in my stomach. I'm not dissing Perpetuem here, but I reckon I'd been using it for so long that my system had basically had enough. I ended up having to take a few toilet detours. I then had a big fall on one of the descents and, again for good measure, had to go to the toilet one more time.

Dylan Bowman and I then got a little lost going through one of the towns, and by the time we got to the next aid station, we were 13 minutes off the lead group with about 60 kilometres already completed.

The next 30 kilometres were pretty much uphill, and from eighth position I slowly started reeling the guys in. I remember thinking about my dad quite a bit on the climbs – how he'd managed to get his life back together after having a rough time following my folks' divorce. It took him a while but, digging deep, slowly he'd turned his life around. It seemed like a good strategy for Sandes junior to adopt in this situation, too. I dropped Dylan, then caught Julien, then Timmy and a couple of other local guys. Timmy looked okay, but the other two guys looked like they had pushed way too hard.

Timmy and I chatted for a few minutes. He is a genuine guy and there are not a lot of competitors with whom I could run during a race and shoot the breeze, but I feel super-comfortable around Timmy. If there was one competitor I wouldn't mind being beaten by, it would be him. Perhaps that's not entirely true ... if there were one person who wouldn't entirely bum me out if he beat me, it would be Timmy.

I remember him saying that he was feeling a bit tired, but you never know with Timmy. He looked utterly done at Western States in 2012, but then proceeded to roar off into the distance. What to do then? Put down the hammer even though it was still quite early in the race? Or do I hold back a bit and run with him?

Down slammed the hammer.

On a gradual descent I upped the pace and, seeing he wasn't following me, accelerated a bit more. And there I was ... leading one of the most competitive fields in which I'd ever run. The buzz was tempered somewhat when I ran out of water and food about four kays from the next checkpoint. I was stoked to be leading, but a bit delirious from a sugar low. I vaguely remember arriving at the aid station and grabbing some Red Bull energy shots from a worried-looking Vanessa. Now in proper animal mode, I frantically grabbed a whole lot of stuff and set off.

I didn't want any of my competitors to see me walking, so I ran the first 500 metres, then walked for the next 100, stuffing my face. I literally downed a packet of GU Chomps, a type of energy chew, and some peanut butter M&Ms in a little ziplock bag. Twenty minutes later I was good to go, and I felt fine for the rest of the race. I was still worried Timmy would do a Timmy, and kept looking back over my shoulder to see if I could spot him among the myriad green-vested marathon runners (there's also a 42-kilometre TransGranCanaria event that starts later, and we had caught them by now). Fortunately, this day was my day and I would win in 14:27:42, nine minutes ahead of Julien Chorier, who had also passed Timmy near the end.

Then the shit hit the fan. I got disqualified.

Shortly after I had crossed the finish line, some official came up to me to check my gear – standard practice, as there are certain mandatory items each runner has to carry. He's speaking Spanish so I don't completely get what he's saying, but he's pointing at my backpack:

'Cover?'

'What?'

'Cover ...'

'You mean like rain jacket?'

'No ...'

Then I got pulled away to do a TV interview and he was, like, don't worry about it ... or at least that's what his non-committal shrug seemed to imply. He certainly wasn't acting like this was an even vaguely serious situation. I thought nothing of it.

The next morning I was on my way to the prize-giving when I saw a Tweet saying Ryan Sandes has been disqualified. You can imagine my surprise. The reason given was that I wasn't carrying an emergency space blanket. Except I was. That was the 'cover' the guy was asking me about. If he had said 'emergency blanket' or opened my pack, he would've seen it.

Apparently the race referee – part of a separate Spanish Mountain Federation to the TransGranCanaria race organisers – said they had tried to contact me the day before to get my side of the story, but that simply wasn't true.

I'm not sure if it was the language barrier ... I don't know. It was weird. Dylan Bowman was also disqualified, and he also didn't know about it. He finished ninth, and he found out about his disqualification only when he was back in the States and realised his name was missing from the published results. The reason given was that he didn't finish with his race number fully visible. He was like, 'Hold on, I just ran across some hectic terrain and a part of it got ripped – that's the nature of trail running!' It took a while, but eventually he got reinstated.

Initially, I felt like all the wind had been taken out of my sails, but Vanessa was having none of it. She had a proper go at the race officials – a very heated discussion that involved plenty of hand gestures. It was a real roller coaster of emotions for me. I was speechless when I first heard, then I flew into a rage, then realised there was nothing I could do, and then finally had to calm Vanessa down before a disqualification became the least of our problems.

Eventually it was agreed that I could write an appeal, and within

10 minutes they came back and said, cool, you're reinstated as the winner. It had been, they said, a language issue. I think they also realised that it was their first year as part of the Ultra-Trail World Tour, and the publicity fallout from this would have been pretty detrimental to their future. It was a learning curve for me, but also a learning curve for the sport.

Looking back at my race wins, the TransGranCanaria to me was one of my biggest. It was a super-competitive field and many of the big names ended up dropping out at later stages of the race. Scott Jurek had run it that year and he's done the Hardrock 100 in Silverton, Colorado. He reckoned the TransGranCanaria was, kilometre for kilometre, the hardest race he had ever done.

I needed to put that all behind me pretty quickly, though – Ryno and I were doing the Drakensberg Grand Traverse in two and a half weeks. We flew back to South Africa and almost immediately packed our bags for the Drakensberg. I spent about a week chilling, catching up on admin and doing some light training. My legs were obviously knackered after the TransGranCanaria, but I kept in touch with Lawrence, and under his advice I kept my training limited to short, intense stuff to get my body to shrug off the previous week's intense effort in readiness for the 210-kilometre traverse. I also bought a heavy kettle bell and started doing some strength exercises. Lawrence's thinking was that strength exercises would help my body shrug off the endurance mode it was in and switch to an anabolic mode, which would help speed up my recovery.

And geez, did it help. I bounced back from the TransGranCanaria really quickly. It genuinely surprised me.

To what I had committed myself only really began to sink in a few days before the start. Dean and his film crew were there, and they wanted to get some footage beforehand. It was a careful balancing act for me. We needed to get as much back-up footage as possible, but Ryno and I also needed to save our legs for the epic challenge that lay ahead.

Good weather was crucial for the whole thing, and I remember counting down the hours and obsessively checking the weather websites. We were scheduled to start at 1 a.m., which meant an early night for both of us. I couldn't sleep, though – I was way too anxious – and nodded off at about 9 p.m., only to wake up again at 10.30 p.m. We had a 30-minute drive up to the car park at Sentinel Peak, where we'd kick it all off, and during that drive it *really* sank in. This was flippin' daunting. It's one thing lining up at the start of a big race with all the hype, media and support staff. Standing in a car park in the dark, with hardly anyone around, is a whole other ball game.

The plan was to complete the traverse in somewhere between 45 and 50 hours. It was definitely doable, but we seriously needed things to go our way. The weather had to play ball, and neither of us could get injured. Given my dodgy ankles and the terrain we'd be running on – more than half of it would be straight-out bundu-bashing – that was one very big ask.

We were also taking a sizeable, but calculated, risk with regard to our equipment. We were travelling light. I took the bare minimum. I was wearing running shorts, shirt, socks and shoes, and had as extras just two waterproof jackets and a pair of waterproof pants. The gear was probably too light, but the weather was looking really good and the risk seemed worth taking. We did have a back-up team and a helicopter that was going to track and film us, but the chopper could fly only during daylight.

For the first 10 hours, I was the one holding us back and telling Ryno to slow down, mainly because I'd rolled my ankle again. And cut my hand. Just before the first peak, I slipped on some rocks and went down hard. It was pitch-black, but I could feel the blood on my hand, and we had to stop and bandage it up. One little slip-up – it was now crystal clear – could quickly put an end to the whole attempt. Then, later, while marvelling at the wonderful sunrise unfolding before us, I went over on my right ankle. I was running along, with the helicopter, backlit by the rising sun, swooping down to get the shot ... this perfect cinematic moment I enhanced by jumping over a piece of grass and landing awkwardly enough to roll over on my ankle. 'Crap ... here we go again,' was my first thought. We had to stop again to strap it up and, for the next 15 hours, I was in survival mode. Then, just as that ankle started to recover, I rolled the left one as well, though not as badly. The terrain is just so technical and you're constantly running through high grass that covers boulders and holes.

For the rest of that first day, we tagged one peak after the next. It got really hot. Ryno went a bit quiet in the afternoon; he doesn't like the heat. Put him in a blizzard and he is right at home, but not the blazing sun. He was battling to get food down, but the guy is so mentally strong that he just kept going. Eventually, I had to stop him and get him to eat. Nutrition is so crucial in any endurance undertaking, and especially so for this, but because Ryno was also taking on the navigation duties for both of us, he had a lot to deal with. He had to navigate, keep the pace up, and still think about eating and drinking properly. All I had to do was follow him and make sure my food and water intake was consistent. The pressure was definitely more on Ryno, so I had to make sure he kept eating.

Along with the PVM meal replacement powder that Ryno carried (he'd mix it with water), he also brought a whole lot of those little red mini cheeses. I forced him to eat two or three of those, which helped, and we carried on through the afternoon and into the night.

And it's not just a case of making sure you get in three good meals, three times a day. You have to continually eat to fuel the effort. Every 25 to 45 minutes, I'd be eating and drinking something. My usual race fair would be gels, Perpetuem, GU Chomps and Red Bull mixed with water, but for this I wanted more solid food. The slower pace at which we were travelling also allowed my body to digest the food easily. I had a special batch of Llama bars that confectioner Lexi Bird had cooked up for me. She had added extra fat and raw chocolate to her usual recipe, as well as sachets of nut butter, nuts and biltong, and protein powder that we'd mix with water along the way. There are plenty of water sources in the Berg, so that was never an issue. I also had the usual gels and GU Chomps too, but didn't end up using much of them.

Around 1 a.m. – 24 hours in – we tried a little 30-minute power nap, but as tired as I was, as soon as I lay down, I couldn't sleep. Even with the great weather, it was still cold at night and I'd wake up shivering every five minutes. Frustrated, we eventually decided to get up and keep running just to stay warm. We stopped again later on for a quick 10-minute nap, but otherwise we just kept going for the rest of the night. I needed a little shut-eye badly, though. I was so tired, my headlight was starting to give me tunnel vision, and I'd drift 100 to 200 metres behind Ryno. He kept having to look back to see what was up. I begged him to please just let me sleep for 10 minutes. Wearing my waterproof pants and jacket, I dropped straight to the ground, not even bothering to take my pack off, and literally passed out.

I was also starting to hear phantom helicopters. We did have a support chopper, but it was tracking us only during the day. During that night I kept looking around, telling Ryno I could hear it. Obviously there was nothing there. I can just imagine him rolling his eyes and shaking his head at this rank amateur with him. Coming from an adventure-racing background, trekking for hundreds of kays over unfamiliar territory with no sleep, was something Ryno was used to. Me, I'm more of the 'nice bright flags marking the route and a good night's sleep' kind of a guy.

When the sun did eventually come up, it was one of those sights you slot into your memory's Personal Highlights showreel. The sun rose just as we were summiting Thabana Ntlenyana, the highest peak on the traverse. The whole sky lit up in streaks of orange-and-purple hues. It was pretty epic witnessing that, let me tell you, running along the top of the Drakensberg mountain range.

It was weird, too. As soon as the sun started to rise, I could feel my spirits lift and I began to feel more alert. I was like, 'Okay, cool. Let's finish this thing.' The temperature started picking up again and, even though Ryno was battling a bit, we kept each other going. I tried to push the pace, but Ryno wisely kept me in check. After that last peak, there would still be another 11 hours of rolling hills to negotiate.

The final few hours were really tough for us. I could see the big Red Bull arch at the Bushman's Nek border post below us, but first we had to negotiate this big drop down the mountain. You have to know exactly which exit point to take – not easy when you are as mentally fried as Ryno and I were – and I knew an adventure-racing team had cocked it up a few months earlier and ended up having to spend the night there. Not what we wanted.

Credit to Ryno's navigation skills, though. He got it spot on. Even this close to the finish, we needed our A-game through a super-technical boulder field, and by now my feet were also taking strain big time. They were swollen, my toes felt like they were about to explode, and it felt like I was running with crushed glass in my shoes. It was basically just a case of one foot in front of the other to the finish.

We eventually crossed the line in 41:49, shaving almost 20 hours off the previous record. I was super-stoked to finish, as much because the whole thing was over as because we had broken the record. This traverse was without doubt the toughest thing I had ever done and, with the injuries and sleep deprivation, it felt as if I was running scared most of the time. Relief was probably my strongest emotion at the finish. It was only the next morning over breakfast that the nature of our accomplishment really sank in. Looking back now, the record is pretty irrelevant to me. I am proud of it, make no mistake, but I'll be more proud to tell my grandkids that my good mate and I crossed the mighty Drakensberg on foot.

The traverse also had other benefits for my career. All the recces we did and the run itself helped really develop my mountain-running skills. Afterwards, I was a far stronger runner on this terrain than I had ever been. It also put into perspective what *real* endurance is. Running a hundred miles might be tough, but doing this kind of thing – totally unsupported like Ryno and Cobus had done before – is truly hardcore. They would phone each other on a Wednesday afternoon, set up plans for a traverse that weekend, throw everything into a car, drive up to the Berg on a Thursday afternoon, get there at two in the morning, park the car at Sentinel Peak car park and off they'd go.

Sometimes they'd make it and sometimes they wouldn't – which then meant getting back to a road and flagging down a minibus taxi to take them back. Then it was another eight-hour drive through the night on a Sunday to make it back for work at 8 a.m. on Monday. That, to me, is proper hardcore living.

One big downside of the Drakensberg traverse, however, was how much it took out of me. I reckon it took me six months to physically recover. Which is why flying to Japan three weeks later for another 100-miler was probably not the smartest thing to do.

Then another crack at the Western States 100 was again my focus for the year, and originally I was going to do The North Face 100 as prep, but I was also starting to think more about the Ultra-Trail World Tour title. And the Ultra-Trail Mount Fuji was part of the series. After the traverse I was like, 'Phht ... it's only 100 miles. I'll blaze it.' Besides, Japan was also on my travel destination bucket list.

Vanessa and I got there a week before, but managed to recce only the last 10 to 15 kilometres of the race. I could feel my legs were still fatigued from their exertions in the Berg, but then the day before the race I went for a short eight-kay run and my legs felt amazing. On race day I was really positive. It was an odd starting time too – 4 p.m. – which means you run through the night and finish at lunchtime the following day.

The initial pace was crazy, with guys flying off in front, but, as you know by now, that is not usually my vibe. I hung back a little, knowing that the trail was either super-flat, or steep, muddy mountainside. At times you even have to pull yourself up with ropes. On the descents you can use the ropes or you just slide down – often on your butt – using the trees to brake your momentum. It made for interesting running, and at around 40 kilometres I was in fifth position, with a long, flat section coming up. Usually that's where I would make up places.

Not this time, though. My energy levels were flagging and, judging by the headlamps approaching from behind, I knew I was being caught, and we had a monster 15-kilometre climb ahead of us. I took my time refuelling at the next aid station, and by the time we hit the climb I was starting to feel good again. Maybe it was all that time in the Berg, but I dropped the guys behind me and made up places until I was in second, trailing fellow Salomon athlete François D'Haene.

That's as close as I got to him, though. Knowing he was too far up the road, I backed off, happy to finish second in 20:18:59 – an hour and 10 minutes behind François, who ran an unbelievable race. Even if I had been well rested, I don't know if I could've matched him that day.

My goal going into the race was to get points for the Ultra-Trail World Tour, and second place was okay with me. It shouldn't have been, though. And I don't mean I should never be satisfied with anything other than first, but more that I shouldn't have been thinking about the Ultra-Trail World Tour at all. At the start of the year, my goal was to focus on Western States in June, with the TransGranCanaria as an early race to fill the gap. Australia was going to be the build-up race for Western States, but then the whole Ultra-Trail World Tour got my attention and suddenly there I was, trying to chase two rabbits. It backfired.

In the end I came second in the Ultra-Trail World Tour series, and pretty much fried my legs for Western States. As planned, I went over to the US a month before the race, and once again we stayed at Incline Village – a little removed from everything, where I could escape all the hype and really focus on running. I was feeling pretty confident too … maybe too much so. You almost need to go into Western States with your back against the wall a bit, and at that point I was now leading the Ultra-Trail World Tour. My back did not feel like it was up against anything.

Unfortunately, on race day reality slapped me square on the fore-head. I was nowhere. My legs had zero power, I had stomach issues, and the heat really got to me. I had run in hotter conditions before, but clearly my system was now waving the white flag. I just couldn't get into the next gear … my legs weren't just tired, it was more like there was just nothing there. I ended up finishing fifth and feeling completely spent.

We stayed in the US for another week – Ryno was with us as well – and spent some time in San Francisco, where I went for a couple of short runs, but within five kays I could feel my legs had no spring in them.

Mentally, I was over-running.

Back home, I went straight to the Oakley X-Over event held in Jeffreys Bay over a week in July. It's a fun, multidisciplinary competition with guys like South African rugby legends John Smit, Bob Skinstad and Butch James, cricketer David Miller, mountain bikers Greg Minnaar and Kevin Evans, triathlete Raynard Tissink and surfer Jordy Smith competing. The events included surfing, mountain biking and golf. The whole thing was just what I needed – some fun activities, a few beers and a proper laugh with a great bunch of people. I didn't think about trail running once.

After that we spent a week relaxing at my mom's holiday house in Cape St Francis, where I promptly got the flu. For a week I was man down. I took four weeks off with no running – which, let me tell you, I was entirely happy to do. I had no desire to put on running shoes, and I didn't miss it at all. From October 2013 all the way through to Western States in June 2014, there was always something happening and always something on the go.

By early August I was starting to feel a little better, which was just as well, because I was scheduled to run a multistage RacingThePlanet event in Madagascar in August. I know, I know ... but I'd always wanted to travel to Madagascar, and I hadn't done a RacingThePlanet event since that little adventure in Nepal back in 2011. Besides, Madagascar was also on my bucket list (I have a long bucket list).

My plan was to use the race to get back to my usual fitness levels, and I didn't do more than a week of hiking and three weeks of running as prep. It included four days of back-to-back runs, and I didn't even feel like a runner until the third day.

The race wasn't that competitive and, despite Japanese runner Wataru Iino's great performance and a disputed time penalty that was handed to me, I wasn't pushed too hard. I crossed the finish line of the six-stage, 250-kilometre race in 22:46:42, some 25 minutes ahead of the Japanese runner.

It was a rad experience and I'm glad that I got to see Madagascar, though it did make me realise how much more I am enjoying the one-day events these days. They might not be as competitive, but they're very tough in their own way. Six days of not showering or brushing your teeth remains pretty hardcore!

It would turn out to be something of a false high because, from there on, from a health point of view, my year took a serious dip.

I felt okay partnering with South African cricket legend Mark Boucher during the Otter to raise funds for his Castle Lager Boucher Legacy initiative called 'Rhino in Safe Hands', but, later, during the annual Red Bull Lionheart event in November, I started feeling seriously light-headed and dizzy. It was a blazing hot day and for the first kilometre or two on the ascent I felt great, until I hit the big rock steps where the proper climbing starts. Suddenly my legs went heavy, and I began to feel light-headed. In fact, I felt terrible. I usually back myself in the heat and my ability to make up time on the descents, but I just had nothing in my legs. I was all over the place, and I even fell once or twice when my one leg just buckled. I could feel my heart rate was going through the roof. I pulled the plug and withdrew ... there was no real choice.

Withdrawing from what was essentially my own event wasn't great, but it would get worse. Thinking I merely had a low-level virus, I took a break for 10 days and resumed my training, but continued to feel generally tired and a bit crappy. I just thought it had been a long year. Then, a couple of weeks later, at the beginning of December, I really crashed. By now I wasn't just feeling lethargic on my training runs, but actually struggling to get out of bed. All I wanted to do was sleep.

A trip to my GP, Dr Natalie Clarke, for a battery of blood tests would reveal I had glandular fever. My red and white cell levels were way down, and my body was taking strain. I was scarily weak and tired.

During that December I still had some commitments I was determined to honour – including the Sabrina Love Ocean Challenge in Knysna, which raises money for special-needs kids. We then drove to

Swellendam to celebrate the wedding of some good friends of ours, but by 9 p.m. – even though it was New Year's Eve – I had to bail. Vanessa had to drive us back home ... my body was shutting down. More blood tests would reveal that my white blood count had dropped even further – in fact, by so much that my GP was considering putting me in quarantine. It was the sickest I'd been in years. My body was done.

Looking back, 2014 was one of the best years of my life – Vanessa and I got married, there was adventure and some great races. But I don't think I respected my body enough. It was a tough lesson to learn, as 2015 would show.

STUFF I'VE LEARNT

Listen to Gunshow

Michael 'Gunshow' Watson is my strength coach. He doesn't say much, but when he does, people tend to listen very carefully. Gunshow has not only given me a much better idea of how my body works, but he has also helped me strengthen key muscle groups. I am a better athlete thanks to him.

I asked Gunshow to give me some key take-outs for any reader of this book. This is what he said, so listen up:

1. Develop a good base of movement to prepare yourself for running. Running will not prepare you for good movement.
2. Strength and stability training for improved running performance will act as a buffer against injury.
3. You are your brain. If you are carrying an injury, or some muscle weakness is causing instability, your brain will apply the handbrake to full performance in order to prevent further injury. Remove the key weakness to allow enhanced force production.
4. Recovery is key. Active recovery is a vital, but often neglected, component of training programmes. Relaxed walks outdoors are excellent for resetting the nervous system. Have a way of monitoring fatigue on your nervous system (checking variability of your heart rate is a simple way of doing this).
5. Your oblique muscles tie your hips and shoulders together. Make them strong and balanced to give yourself a good fixed point of stability for your limbs to work from. Pallof presses and chopping patterns (where you hit a tyre with a 10-pound hammer) are some of the best exercises for this.
6. Ankle injuries are a common occurrence during trail running. They will lead to delayed activation of the gluteus maximus on the same leg. Make sure to mobilise the ankle after injury and to include single-leg training to strengthen your feet, ankles and glutes.

The secret to being a good climber

Here are a couple of pointers to conquer those big, intimidating ascents.

Build functional strength

To be a climber, you need strength, and to do that you need to develop your glutes, hamstrings and calves. It's functional strength and good mobility that you want, though, so it's not just about hitting the gym and doing squats and deadlifts, but doing some field sessions as well. Gunshow and I would also do some 60-metre sprints on a grass field, to get all my muscles to properly work the full range of motion. You should put as much emphasis on moving correctly, making sure your hips aren't locked up, and that everything is supple, mobile and moving smoothly. This really is where you can get some big gains.

Run up a lot of mountains

To build natural strength, there's no substitute for actually running up a mountain. Look at the Europeans – they're excellent climbers compared to the Americans. And us. Why? Because they have spent their lives running up some really big mountains. And I don't mean stuff like 650 metres up Table Mountain's Platteklip Gorge, but trails where you climb 2 000 metres over 10 kilometres.

Pace yourself

Initially, you don't want to push too hard and run to the point where you can't run any more. I'd rather run until I'm at 80 per cent and then start power-hiking at a decent speed. You don't want to run to a stop, and then kind of hobble along. If you're familiar with the trail, it helps a lot and you can plan accordingly, but if not and it's a race, try to do your homework as best you can.

Trick your brain

If you're about to tackle a monster climb, don't keep looking up to the summit, because it's only going to psyche you out. It's as if your mind starts comprehending that it's got a long and torturous section to get through and it subconsciously wants to slow you down. Obviously you have to look up every now and then to make sure you're running the right line, but for the most part, try to keep your focus on the trail a metre or two ahead.

Find a happy place

If you're really suffering, take a step or two outside the pain cave and focus instead on the trail you're running on. The great thing about outdoor sport is the outdoors, and you are inevitably surrounded by natural beauty. Find something in your field of view – an epic lake in the distance or majestic trees in a forest – and really try to focus on that. Keep a positive mindset and keep at bay the 'what the hell am I doing here?' demon. Once that thought pattern slips into your head, your whole day is going to get a lot harder.

14

LESSONS LEARNT

There was one event at the end of 2014 that I left out of the last chapter. And purposefully so too. On 25 October 2014, Vanessa and I were married. This is something that feels more appropriate to mention at the end of a book that has chronicled my life so far. This closing chapter is about my future, my plans and where my head is at. And, as she's been for the last five years, Ness is part of that future.

The wedding and reception for 180 people – all organised by Vanessa – took place at the beautiful Nitida Wine Estate, near Durbanville in the Western Cape. I remember waking up in the morning, not really feeling nervous, then I went for a run, had a shower and finally suited up. It was only *then* that the significance of what I was about to do sank in. Luckily, one of my best men, Frank Solomon, had the presence of mind to bring a little hip flask of whisky with him, and a few nips just before the ceremony helped settle my starting-line nerves.

I will admit being a little tense during the ceremony and might have tugged at my collar a bit and maybe exuded a bead or two of sweat, but I survived, said my 'I do', and the two of us then enjoyed what turned out to be a fantastic party – and we were the last to leave. A couple of days later we flew to Mauritius for our honeymoon.

Like most married couples, the subject of kids comes up a lot and I think we're both ready. With the demands of my career and the travelling I do, I know it's going to be harder for Vanessa than me. I want to be as hands-on a dad as possible, but I guess you've got to find a balance. Other ultra-trail runners I know – and mates of mine too – have had kids, and I can see how fatherhood has inspired them. I think it will definitely inspire me too. Hopefully, we can also travel together as a family. Especially, as South Africans down here at the southern tip of our great continent, I reckon it's crucial to get to know other cultures around the world. I'd almost put more emphasis on that than school. Over the last eight years I personally have learnt more than I did at any school. Don't even ask me to remember anything about high-school maths!

So what does the future hold? Well, if it's anything like the last decade, then I'll be happy.

I've had some incredible highs, both personally and professionally, but also some real downers. These last 12 months, for example, have been pretty tough from a trail-running point of view: I've had to pull out of three big races. Intellectually, and from a career point of view, I know I made the right decisions, but emotionally it was hard. Really hard. Ultra-trail running is an endurance sport, and fundamental to that is the ability to endure. Quitting a race because it's the smart thing to do while others are out there trying to finish and sweating blood – and sometimes shedding it – is a flippin' hard thing to make peace with. Emotionally, you feel guilt and remorse, like you have disrespected the sport itself. But my analytical self knows that to have any kind of longevity in the career I have chosen, I need to look after my body.

That's why I first pulled out of Transvulcania. Part of the International Skyrunning Federation's 2015 Skyrunner World Series, this race is held in Las Palmas, in the Canary Islands, and I was using it as a warm-up for what was once again to be my target race for the year ... the elusive win at the Western States 100.

I sent Steve – my co-author – this email the day after I withdrew:

I have been focusing my training purely on WS100 over the past few months because if there were only one race left that I could win, it would be Western States.

After doing a lot of big mountain races last year, plus, of course, the Drakensberg Grand Traverse, I thought I would still have the muscle memory of all that climbing left in my legs for Transvulcania. My main focus over the past few months has been flat running and some very specific WS100 training, and I thought Transvulcania was going to be the ideal prep race for it. Here on Las Palmas it's hot, and the route has more climbing and descending over 73 kilometres than the entire WS100 course. I guess I was wrong…

My legs were not prepared for all the climbing Transvulcania threw at me, and after 20 kilometres I could feel I was losing power in my legs. I backed off the intensity, but at 30 kilometres I knew any chance of a good result was over. I always try and finish whatever I start, and I have been very critical of myself about my previous two dropouts. However, at 33 kilometres I decided my race was over. It's always a tough call to make, but this time it felt a lot easier and made a lot more sense.

I feel a lot more comfortable in my own skin and I don't feel I have anything to prove. I am a professional athlete focusing on the Western States 100-miler. That means to gain race experience and build my body up. If I had continued yesterday I would have just destroyed my legs and, mentally, it would have also taken its toll. At 33 kilometres I was frustrated, my legs were crampy and I gave myself two options. One, suck it up and run for my life to try and get a top 10. This would have left me broken and it would've definitely set me back in my WS100 training. It would have been a stupid decision. Or, two, drop out, swallow my pride and focus on WS100. I seem to do well after having a setback and I can use this disappointment to motivate me.

I decided to drop out at 33 kilometres and took a two-kilometre walk back to the previous aid station to get off the mountain. I was disappointed. Failure is never a nice feeling, but I felt at ease with my decision. If it was a focus race then I would have sucked it up, put myself in the hurt box, and run for my life.

It sucks having to explain myself to everyone, but this time I didn't feel like I was letting everyone down. This setback will add more pressure on me for WS100, but if I channel it correctly it will just be a positive.

I have a bit of loser complex today, but I will get over myself. It's the usual ups and downs I have had after dropping out of a race, but I know I made the right decision. The previous two times I doubted my decision. I can also learn from the experience. Trail running continues to get more competitive and you really need to focus and train in a race-specific way. It probably wasn't the best decision to pick one of the most competitive races in the world to use as a prep race, but it's been a great experience here and I definitely would like to come back. I have not finished with Transvulcania. I will be back to cross that finish line!

That was in May 2015. Western States could still salvage my year, and my training seemed to go pretty well. I was feeling quite positive too. Vanessa and I travelled to Big Bear in California a few weeks ahead of the start on 27 June, but this time I didn't even get to do the race. I caught what seemed to be a stomach virus the day before the start, and had to withdraw. I was gutted – literally and figuratively – but there was no way I could've competed that day, and even a few days later I was still feeling grim.

I emailed Steve again:

Western States was a huge disappointment, especially because I had been specifically focusing on the race for so long. In some ways maybe I put a little too much pressure on myself going into the race, and took the fun element out of the whole experience at times. Has anything changed about how I feel about the race? No, it is still the one race I dream of winning and I will hopefully be back there next year. In the past I have tended to focus too much on the future and what races I am going to run, etc. It is important to have long-term goals and dreams, but you need to live in the moment and enjoy the present. I really want to run WS100 again, but I first want to get through UTMB and Raid of Réunion before focusing/thinking about next year.

Looking at the present, I am really excited to be running the two 100-milers (UTMB and Réunion) this year that are left on my bucket list.

I am less than three weeks away from UTMB and feeling really excited about the new experience and adventure. You can't beat the feeling of putting on your shoes, running out the door and exploring a new mountain. I have no expectations going into UTMB, except to have a great adventure and enjoy the experience. Yes, I would love to win the race and I will run myself into the ground to do that. I am hoping I can push my body and mind further than I have ever done before, but if I do that and it's only good enough for eighth place then I will be happy. I am really hoping to take my training and use what I have learnt over the past couple of years to have a great race. Like I said, I would love to win, but I can't control that and wasting energy on that is stupid. I want to keep my relaxed head space going into the race, enjoy every moment and hopefully take my body and mind to the next level in the race.

You can hear the disappointment and anguish there, but also my determination to push through and not end the year without a prominent race result. Despite not even getting out the starting gate at Western States, my sights immediately swung across the Atlantic to the Ultra-Trail du Mont-Blanc. I'm on it straightaway, being positive, talking about 'adventure' and 'pushing my body and mind', trying to build up this belief that I could do well there.

Vanessa and I flew to France and stayed in a B&B in Chamonix for the three weeks leading up to the race. I appeared to have got over whatever bug I had caught in Colorado, and my training in these beautiful alpine mountains was going well enough. I was even starting to get my game on as my training log notes show:

The rage: She is returning! I am feeling super-pumped now. I started getting a little too excited on my run. During my 15-minute warm-up some dude came running past me. I thought,

fuck that, and ran past him and wanted to tackle him when passing, but that may have not gone down so well. Ha! I am not well.
I had a good think about the race and my year so far. It's time
to get the rage and harden the fuck up. I think it's time to put
WS100 behind me and properly focus on UTMB.

Only not. I had to pull out of this one too ...

While my legs seemed okay during training, they just couldn't
maintain a sustained race-pace effort. By the 20-kay mark they felt
super-heavy, sore and filled with lactic acid. I tried to back off a little
and walk to see if I could somehow recover, but they just got worse.
My heart rate started spiking as well – my heart seemed to be working
extra hard to get the lactic acid out of my legs. By 36 kays my race
was done. Something was not right. The next day my legs felt like
they had done another 200-kilometre Drakensberg Grand Traverse.

Seriously worried about what the hell was going on with me, back
home in Cape Town I had a whole bunch of tests done. Unfortunately, there was no clear answer. It looked like my liver and immune
system hadn't fully recovered from the glandular fever, and the best
thing to do was to have some intravenous vitamin C boosts, get plenty
of rest and lay off running for six weeks.

I also decided not to run the 165-kilometre Grand Raid de la
Réunion, on Réunion Island, as originally planned, and set about trying to get healthy. Which, as we speak, is what I'm doing right now.
Because what I definitely don't want to do is find I'm suffering from
overtraining syndrome.

It's a condition the medical fraternity has identified over the last
couple of years, and it seems to affect mostly ultra-distance trail runners. I have seen so many athletes come onto the scene, get great
results for a couple of years and then implode. American Geoff Roes
has been the one guy courageous enough to talk openly about it. One
of the best ultra-trail runners to participate in the sport, Geoff was
unbeatable before 2011, winning and setting course records at a bunch
of US ultra-distance races and 100-milers. He won Western States in
2010, but in the years that followed began having severe symptoms

affecting nearly all of his body's systems. For an athlete to have your body fail like that – and have no idea what the underlying condition was – must be super-tough to deal with. At one point he even thought he had cancer. I can only imagine how hard that must've been for him.

He's not the only one either. You hear of guys running 300 kilometres per week in training and, because one person is doing it and posting great race results, suddenly everyone else reckons it's what you need to do to win. It's simply not sustainable, though. Suddenly they either get chronically fatigued, or suffer from a series of leg and foot injuries. I've even heard stories of guys whose muscles have basically started to consume themselves.

Ultra runners are so headstrong that they just run themselves into the ground. It's easy to push your body for two years or so, running several 100-milers and getting the results. The wins inspire you to keep pushing and pushing. But, trust me, you pay a mental and physical price.

Looking in from the outside, trail running gets portrayed as a superfun and healthy sport where professional athletes get to travel around the world, spending all day running in the mountains. And that's not far off the mark. It's an awesome lifestyle. But I promise you, it's also flippin' hard, and it can break you.

I have always been very selective with my racing and listened to my body, but in 2014 I think I simply got it wrong. I fell into the trap of over-racing and paid the price by being burnt out for Western States, getting glandular fever, and then still thinking I could push through and do the UTMB.

One thing getting ill has done is to make me stop and take a good look at my training, racing and my future in the sport. I have realised that in order to prolong my career, I needed to back off on my training and not repeat a schedule like the one I undertook in 2014. I have reduced my training by 20 to 25 per cent. 'Less is more' is my new approach, and I've gone back to the amount I was doing in my earlier years, preparing for the multiday races. But it's not easy when you hear of guys putting in massive training blocks. There's me, feeling bleak and frustrated having only gone a little overboard for one year in 2014, yet others are running close to 9 000 kays a year and they seem to be fine. It seemed very unfair.

Initially, I was seriously pissed off at my whole situation, but realised soon enough that I needed to let go of that emotion: it wasn't going to help. Obviously my body was telling me to slow down a bit, and once I listened and accepted that, I immediately started recovering that much quicker. I think your mind is very powerful like that. You've got to be kind to your body. I dug myself into a hole in 2014. I forgot to respect my body and what I do. Lesson learnt.

Back to that question then ... so what does the future hold?

I'm going to be competing, that's for sure – there are some races I want to win. I can feel I'm continuing to improve as an athlete, and I still have my best 100-miler in me. When I first started off running I reckon I was pretty average, but I've been able to keep progressing, working on my weaknesses and improving my strengths. With Lawrence's help, I'm training smarter and getting faster, and with Gunshow's guidance I'm getting functionally stronger. It's all helped me be competitive in a sport where the level of competition is getting higher and higher.

I can't see myself doing another multiday, self-supported race again. I've definitely done that and bought the very smelly T-shirt. They were all phenomenal experiences, the adventure was rad and they launched my career, but I'm over running with a heavy backpack, sleeping on the ground, and not showering or brushing my teeth for days.

Although I'd initially promised myself I'd only give Western States a go three times – which is what I've now done – I didn't even start the last time, so that does feel like some unfinished business for me. It remains a goal, but perhaps not one I'm going to have a crack at in 2016. From now on, there'll be no more running three 100-milers in a space of three months, which is basically what I did in 2014. I want to do one 100-miler race a year – or at least make sure there's at least an eight-month gap between them – and for the next year or two that's going to be the Ultra-Trail du Mont-Blanc. I didn't grow up in the mountains, so that race has always been a little bit foreign to me and quite intimidating. But it's just the kind of challenge I love. My mountain-running skills have steadily improved and are at a point now where I believe I can be competitive.

I definitely want to incorporate free-running projects into my schedule – perhaps not always as tough as my little Drakensberg adventure with Ryno, but that kind of thing continues to fuel my love for running. Also, if I'm cutting down on my races, these projects still keep me amped, strong and provide good balance in my running. I've been looking at some traverses we can do in Africa: perhaps a run across the Rwenzori Mountains, which border Uganda and the DRC – that might be something to tackle.

After all the disappointments of 2015, running through the Drakensberg with Ryno helped me find my mojo again. In early November we headed deep into the Berg, and just ran. We chose a route and, without any goals, simply ran until we felt like turning around. It was my soul food.

I also want to continue travelling, too. I have seen some amazing places on this planet of ours, and in recent years I've been lucky enough to share them with Vanessa. And, who knows, there might be three of us boarding a plane in the coming years. I've always been intrigued by adventure. My idea of a holiday has never been staying in a cushy resort, lying on a pool lounger and ordering drinks with little umbrellas. Wherever I've been, my running shoes have allowed me to experience first-hand interactions with local communities and cultures. Running through the Gobi, Madagascar, Chile, Egypt, Nepal and Hong Kong has just been mind-blowing. It's changed my whole perspective on life, and it's certainly made it crystal clear that material wealth is not the key to happiness. The problem with the world these days is that it's driven by greed and ego. It's such a short-sighted and pointless way to live your life, isn't it? I'm not going to be able to take any money to the grave with me.

I want to be someone who has lived his life to the fullest. I want to lie on my deathbed smiling and thinking, 'Shit, bro ... you've lived a flippin' crazy life.' I want a bunch of epic memories. I want to know I've pushed myself to the max. And, hopefully, in doing that, I've done some good and added to this world rather than taken from it. Trail running has given me so much, and every day – even during those times when injury and illness have made life seem bleak – I continue to be thankful for what the very simple act of putting on a pair of running shoes and running along mountain trails has done for me.

If there's one piece of advice I can leave you with from all the 'stuff I've learnt', it's this – I love what I do, and so should you.

ACHIEVEMENTS LIST

INTERNATIONAL RACES

2008 Gobi March (China) – first
2008 Sahara Race (Egypt) – first
2009 Namibia Desert Race – second
2009 Jungle Marathon – first, new record
2010 Atacama Crossing (Chile) – first, new record
2010 Gore-Tex TransAlps Race – third in mixed pairs
2010 The Last Desert (Antarctica) – first
2010 4 Deserts champion and only competitor to win each of the
4 Deserts races

2011 The North Face 100 Australia – third
2011 The Salomon Zugspitz Ultra – fourth
2011 Leadville 100 Mile Trail Run – first, third-fastest time ever
2011 Racing the Planet Nepal – first

2012 Vibram Hong Kong 100-kilometre Ultra – first, new record
2012 The North Face 100 Australia – first
2012 Western States 100 Miler USA – second, second-fastest time ever
2012 Fish River Canyon trail – 6 h 57 min, sets fastest known time

2013 The North Face TransGranCanaria 83 kilometres – first
2013 The North Face 100 Australia – DNF (stomach virus)
2013 Leadville 100-miler – DNF (back injury)
2013 Patagonian International Marathon 63 kilometres – first
2013 The North Face San Fran 50-miler – ninth

2014 The North Face TransGranCanaria 125 kilometres – first
2014 The Drakensberg Grand Traverse 209 kilometres – 41 h 49 min,
sets fastest known time
2014 The Ultra Trail Mount Fuji – second
2014 Western States 100 Miler USA – fifth
2014 Racing the Planet Madagascar – first
2014 Ultra Trail World Tour – finishes second in overall ranking

SOUTH AFRICAN RACES

2009 Hout Bay Trail Challenge – first, new record
2009 Salomon Night run – first

2010 Salomon Featherbed Trail Challenge – first in morning and
        evening race
2010 Hout Bay Trail Challenge – first in team category, new course
        record
2010 4 Peaks Trail Run – first, new course record
2010 Hi-Tec Puffer Ultra Marathon – first, new course record
2010 Hout Bay Triple Trouble Marathon – first, new course record

2011 Fisherman's Trail Challenge – first, new course record
2011 Table Mountain Trail Challenge – first in team category
2011 Otter Trail Run – first, new course record

2012 Salomon Skyrun – first, new course record
2012 Red Bull Lion Heart – third

2013 Crazy Store Table Mountain Challenge – first
2013 Red Bull Lion Heart – fourth

2015 Table Mountain crossing – FKT 2 h 02 min, fastest known time

Awards won
GoMulti magazine – 2008 Trail Runner of the Year
Runner's World South Africa – Running Hero of 2008
OutThere magazine – 2008 Adventurer of the Year runner-up
Runner's World South Africa – Running Hero of 2009
Runner's World South Africa – Running Hero of 2010
Men's Health magazine – Best Man Competition 2010 Young Guns
    Category Winner
Runner's World South Africa – one of the Running Heroes of 2011
Runner's World South Africa – one of the Running Heroes of 2012
Western Cape Ministerial Commendation Award 2013

ACKNOWLEDGEMENTS

If you had told me as an 18- or 20-year-old that at the age of 33 I would be writing a book about my ultra-running career, I would have laughed and called you crazy. I guess shit happens, though. Life is beautifully unexpected and we never know where our path might take us. The last eight years have been one hell of a journey – not in my wildest dreams did I ever think I would take *this* particular path. I have had some incredible highs and some lows along the way. My running shoes have taken me to all corners of the globe, I have met some awesome people on my travels, and, most importantly, these shoes have allowed me to live my dreams and become the person I am today. This is by no means the end; my cupboard still has many more pairs to take me on loads more adventures.

I am incredibly proud to be South African. We have our problems, but being South African has inspired me to want to achieve, and to showcase our awesome country on the world stage. To everyone who has supported me along the way, your encouragement has kept me moving forward at times when I thought taking another step was not possible. To the people who have doubted me, thank you, too. I appreciate your honesty and you, too, have brought out the best in me.

To my dream givers, you have become my family and there are no words to describe how grateful I am to you for enabling me to live my dreams. Trevor, you are a legend … I don't know how to thank you enough, bru!

In order to run 100 kilometres or more in one go, you need to be fit, healthy and, most importantly, injury free. I am lucky to have an amazing support team. Thank you, Ian, Lawrence, Michael, Sally, Chris, Rob, Benita, Arnaud, Willie, Nicole, Dr Natalie and Dr Phil. Kelly and Katie, thank you for all the hard work you have put in behind the scenes to help me manage my brand.

To my mates: I miss you guys. The biggest sacrifice I've had to make since I started running was to spend less time with you. Regardless of that, you all supported me every step of the way and if it had not been for you guys, I wouldn't have had the balls or stupidity to enter my first ultra, the 4Deserts Gobi Desert race.

The most important thing you have in life is your family. My family is complicated, but I wouldn't want it any other way. Thank you all for playing a role in shaping me into the person I am today. To my mom and dad: saying 'thank you' does not do justice for what you have given me and sacrificed for me. You have both always supported and believed in me no matter what. My parents and my sister Ashleigh's love and confidence in me have allowed me to chase my dreams, no matter how crazy they have been.

Every run with T-dog (Thandi) is filled with stoke and excitement. Her love for fresh air and the freedom of open trails is contagious and it has kept me grounded and reminded me to always love what I do. To my wife Vanessa, being able to share my adventures with you has made the past few years that much more special. Thank you for putting up with my grumpy pre-race moods and for being the most supportive and caring person I know.

Last but not least, Steve: thank you for all the hours of dedication, taking down my ramblings and crafting them into my story. It has been a radical process, and I think Vanessa is slightly jealous that you know more about me now than she does! It's been an honour to have you tell my story: Thank you!

RYAN SANDES
CAPE TOWN, 2016

ACKNOWLEDGEMENTS

I hit his car. Usually – at the very least – this kind of thing ends up in an argument. This time, though, it ended up in a book. How I happened to scrape a white SUV parked on the side of the road is not important (though I can just add that it was a light scrape and it really wasn't my fault), but the serendipitous coincident was that said car belonged to one Ryan Sandes.

Initially it didn't feel very serendipitous at all. 'F***k, it's Ryan Sandes's car.' But after he and I had established that the damage was minor and could be polished out, we returned to a subject we had first discussed a couple of years earlier. Back then I was editor of Red Bull's magazine *The Red Bulletin*, and being a Red Bull athlete, Ryan was the subject of a few features I'd written. Our interviews had gone really well and we discussed the possibility of expanding the partnership into a book at some future point.

Then I left *The Red Bulletin* and we kind of lost touch a little ... until I hit his car. In that time I'd become an increasingly enthusiastic mountain-biker, to a point where I was (I'd like to say 'competing', but that might be overstating things) 'participating' in various multi-stage races around the country, including the ABSA Cape Epic. Apart from shining a bright light on my own limitations, it also gave me an appreciation of and some real insight into what it takes to accomplish what Ryan has.

Not only is Ryan's personal story fascinating and inspirational, but as an amateur endurance-sport athlete, I found his insights and advice enormously beneficial; it translated well into my own sport. If you're a road runner, a cyclist, an adventure racer or a paddler, I'm pretty sure you'll find this equally helpful too.

Ryan, it was a singular privilege to crash into your car and write your book. Thank you for the opportunity.

Of course, this book couldn't happen without the team at Penguin Random House. My thanks to Janet Bartlet, who project-managed *Trail Blazer*, and Laetitia Sullivan, whose editing finesse added the final touches.

As ever, my thanks to my family: my wife Medina and daughter Holly for the support and encouragement during those early mornings and weekends when it was only the tapping of a keyboard that signalled my presence at home.

STEVE SMITH
CAPE TOWN, 2016